Journalism in Crisis

Corporate Media and Financialization

INTERNATIONAL ASSOCIATION FOR MEDIA AND COMMUNICATION RESEARCH

This series consists of books arising from the intellectual work of IAMCR members, sections, working groups, and committees. Books address themes relevant to IAMCR interests; make a major contribution to the theory, research, practice and/or policy literature; are international in scope; and represent a diversity of perspectives. Book proposals are refereed.

IAMCR Publication Committee: Marjan de Bruin, Jamaica
and Claudia Padovani, Italy

IAMCR Book Series Editors: Marjan de Bruin, Jamaica
and Claudia Padovani, Italy

IAMCR Publication Committee Members:

Arnold de Beer (South Africa), Valerio Cruz Brittos (Brazil), Andrew Calabrese (USA), Bart Cammaerts (United Kingdom), Joseph Man Chan (PRC), John Downing (USA), Cees Hamelink (Netherlands), Todd Holden (Japan), Shelton Gunaratne (USA), Rosa Mikael Martey (USA), Guillermo Mastrini (Argentina), Divina Frau Meigs (France), Virginia Nightingale (Australia), Kaarle Nordenstreng (Finland), Hillel Nossek (Israel), Francisco Sierra (Spain), Helena Souza (Portugal), Ruth Teer-Tomaselli (South Africa), Thomas Tufte (Denmark), Janet Wasko (USA), Bob White (Tanzania), Brian Shoesmith (Australia)

Titles

Democracy and Communication in the New Europe
Farrel Corcoran and Paschal Preston, eds., 1995
Globalization, Communication and Transnational Civil Society
Sandra Braman and Annabelle Sreberny, eds., 1996
The Global Journalist: Newspeople Around the World
David Weaver, ed., 1998
Theoretical Approaches to Participatory Communication
Thomas Jacobson and Jan Servaes, eds., 1999
Consuming Audiences? Production and Reception in Media Research
Ingunn Hagen and Janet Wasko, eds., 2000
Global Trends in Media Education: Policies and Practices
Tony Lavendar, Birgitte Tufte and Dafna Lemish, eds., 2003
*Spaces of Intercultural Communication: An Interdisciplinary Introduction
to Communication, Culture, and Globalizing/Localizing Identities*
Rico Lie, 2003
Ideologies of the Internet
Katharine Sarikakis and Daya K. Thussu, eds., 2006
From the Margins to the Cutting Edge: Community Media and Empowerment
Peter M. Lewis and Susan Jones, eds., 2006
Journalism in Crisis: Corporate Media and Financialization
Núria Almiron

Journalism in Crisis

Corporate Media and Financialization

Núria Almiron
Universitat Pompeu Fabra, Barcelona

Translated by
William McGrath

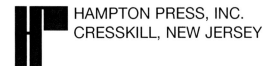
HAMPTON PRESS, INC.
CRESSKILL, NEW JERSEY

Printed in the United States of America

Library of Congress Cataloging-in-Publication Data

Almiron, Núria.
 Journalism in crisis : corporate media and financialization / Núria Almiron; translated by William McGrath.
  p. cm. -- (The IAMCR series)
 Includes bibliographical references and indexes.
 ISBN 978-1-57273-980-2 (hardbound) -- ISBN 978-1-57273-981-9 (paperbound)
  1. American newspapers--Ownership. 2. Journalism--Economic aspects--United States. 3. Journalism--Political aspects--United States. 4. Mass media--Economic aspects--United States. 5. Mass media--Ownership--United States. 6. Mass media--Economic aspects. 7. Mass media--Ownership. I. Title.
 PN4888.O85.A55 2010
 338.4'307173--dc22
                                          2010026758

Hampton Press, Inc.
23 Broadway
Cresskill, NJ 07626

Contents

Acknowledgements

While writing this book, the author has acquired numerous personal and academic debts toward many colleagues, friends, institutions, and experts.

In the first place, I must look back to my doctoral work between 2001 and 2005. That research, and the doctoral dissertation that resulted from it, which was defended in 2006, laid down the theoretical foundations of this book. The many persons who contributed and helped me during that period are the first to whom I must, once again, express my gratitude.

The empirical research of the case studies was, nevertheless, a later undertaking. A great contribution to this was made by the Agència de Gestió d'Ajuts Universitaris i de Recerca (AGAUR) of the Generalitat de Catalunya (the institution in which the self-government of Catalonia is politically organized).This organization endowed me with a grant that allowed me to spend time abroad to study European communication groups. During those stays, many people gave me their disinterested help, and among them I would like to mention Peter Humphreys of the University of Manchester, UK; Cess Hamelink and Julia Hoffman of the University of Amsterdam, The Netherlands; Jacques Guyot, Philippe Bouquillion, and Christian Pradié of l'Université Paris 8, France; Jean Marie Charon of l'École d'Hautes Études en Sciences Sociales, Paris, France; Michel Diard of the Syndicat National des Journalistes, Paris, France; and Sune and Vanni Tjernström of the University of Kalmar, Sweden.

For writing some of the chapters, in particular, I have enjoyed tremendously valuable help. Chapter 1 is a revision of a section of my doctoral dissertation that I would never have completed without the appraisal by Miren Etxezarreta, Professor of Applied Economics at

Universitat Autònoma de Barcelona. Doctor in communication and specialist in the structure of communication in the United States, Ana Isabel Segovia of Universidad Complutense de Madrid helped me with the revision of Chapter 4, and Professor of History Daniel J. Leab of Seton Hall University, New Jersey, contributed, albeit unwittingly, to the revision of Chapter 2. To all of them, one more time, my gratitude.

Nevertheless, it goes without saying that any errors and imprecisions that this work may contain are attributable exclusively to the author.

I also want to express my gratitude to the translator of this text, William McGrath, for his competence and utmost collaboration, and I would like to point out that this book exists due to the support of Universitat Pompeu Fabra (UPF) in Barcelona, which has financed part of the translation and the final stage of the research, taking me into its academic bosom with enormous generosity. I owe this fact, not exclusively but very especially, to Professor of Communication Theory Miquel Rodrigo, head of the Department of Communication at this university, and to Jaume Casals, Professor of Philosophy, also at UPF. To both, my warmest thanks.

Finally, I cannot fail to express my gratitude to the International Association for Media and Communication Research (IAMCR) and to Hampton Press for having made the publication of this book possible, and to Robert W. McChesney for the prologue. And my thanks, too, to family, friends, and colleagues who have given me their support during these last years of my work, among whom I want to mention especially Carlos Jiménez Villarejo, a former anti-fraud senior prosecutor of Spain, who backed this book before anybody else.

Preface

Robert W. McChesney

*University of Illinois
at Urbana–Champaign*

In this book, Nuria Almiron presents research and critical analysis in the tradition known as the political economy of communication. The political economy of communication is the field of people in this latter camp. Political economists of media do not believe the existing media system is natural, inevitable, or impervious to change. They believe the media system is the result of policies made in the public's name but often without the public's informed consent. They believe the nature of the media systems established by these policies goes a long way toward explaining the content produced by these media systems. Political economists of media believe that assessing policies, structures, and institutions cannot answer all of the important questions surrounding media, but they believe their contributions are indispensable to the comprehensive study of media.

Political economy of communication endeavors to connect how media and communication systems and content are shaped by ownership, market structures, commercial support, technologies, labor practices, and government policies. The political economy of communication then links the media and communications systems to how both economic and political systems work and how social power is exercised in society. Specifically, in the United States and much of the world, what role do media and communication play in how capitalist economies function, and how do both media and capitalism together and separately influence the exercise of political power? The central question for communication political economists is whether, on balance, the media system serves to promote or undermine democratic institutions and practices. Are media a force for social justice or oligarchy? Equipped with that knowledge, what are the options for citizens to address the situation? Ultimately, the political economy of communication is a critical exercise committed to enhancing democracy. It has emerged and blossomed during periods of relatively intense popular political activism, initially in the 1930s and 1940s and then decisively in the 1960s and 1970s.

The political economy of communication is often associated with the political left because of its critical stance toward the market and because some of its most prominent figures were and are socialists. For many of the major figures in the field, changing the media system was part and parcel with changing the broader economic system to produce a more humane and equitable society. But the "project" of political economy of media, to the extent that it can be defined, grows directly out of mainstream liberal democratic political theory. Nor is this purely theoretical: The condition on which the entire U.S. constitutional system rests is that there must be a viable and healthy press system for self-government to succeed. Hence, the mission statement for the political economy of media is clear: What structures and policies generate the media institutions, practices, and system most conducive to viable self-government?

The field of political economy of communication has grown dramatically since the 1960s for reasons that in the "Information Age" approach being self-evident. Few people doubt the importance of media, of journalism, of entertainment culture, of communication in general, for shaping the world in which we live. Moreover, media are a central part of the capitalist political economy, the center of the marketing system, and a source of tremendous profit in their own right. Media do not explain everything, but understanding media is indispensable to grasping the way power works in contemporary societies. It is worth repeating that political economy of media does not come close to explaining everything about media, not by a long stretch, but what it does do is essential for scholarly analysis to be comprehensive and accurate.

Yet despite the rise of the political economy of communication to some prominence in recent decades, the field has struggled with an identity crisis in the past generation due primarily to the emergence of neoliberalism and the Internet.

Neoliberalism, put crudely, refers to the doctrine that profits should rule as much of social life as possible, and anything that gets in the way of profitmaking is suspect, if not condemned. Business good. Governments bad. Big business very good. Big government very bad. Taxes on the rich bad. Social spending aimed at the poor and working class even worse. Take care of number one, and everyone fend for yourself. There is no such thing as "society," only individuals in fierce competition with each other, and their immediate families, the only permissible freeloaders. Property and profits *uber alles*. Put this way, neoliberalism is simply capitalism with the gloves off.

Neoliberalism became ascendant in the 1980s and is associated with Reagan and Thatcher. It seemed to be cemented with the overthrow of communist regimes by the early 1990s and the notion that we had reached the "end of history." There Is No Alternative, as Margaret Thatcher famously intoned. In this environment, the political economy of media was thrown for a loop. What was its purpose if all societies were best run by the market? What was the point of studying and criticizing commercial media if that was the only plausible system and the system toward which all nations were rapidly and inexorably moving?

During the long neoliberal era, if one may generalize, the political economy of communication gravitated toward research that was less concerned with the connections between the broader capitalist economy and the communication system and spent more time examining specific industrial structures and policies and how they affected content. There was also a turn toward more historical research. Crucial issues such as the tendency toward crisis in capitalism, the rise of financialization as a salve to stagnation, and the important and growing link between financialization and media industries were simply unexamined in a dedicated sense.

Neoliberalism came crashing to earth with the economic and political crises of our times. Its promised shibboleths of increasing prosperity, freedom, and human happiness appear like so many bogus PR slogans, even a sick joke. With the demise of neoliberalism, scholars and activists are beginning to revisit the idea of imagining a more humane and democratic social order, one where profits for the few are no longer the highest social priority, but there is still a very long way to go, especially in the United States. Combined with the elimination of the old communist model as the alleged "alternative" to contemporary capitalism, humanity is now beginning a process of experimentation in democratic social structures that has not been witnessed for generations, especially in Latin America. The importance of this work cannot be exaggerated. There is a crucial role for political economists of media in this process because communication systems are at the heart of both developing economies and political systems. It is where much of our work in the coming generation will be directed.

A crucial area of research that has been too long neglected has been studying the connection between the media and communication industries and the broader capitalist economy. Professor Almiron has done trail-blazing work in this volume doing exactly that. She has masterfully traced the relationship of the "financialization" of contemporary capitalism and linked it to developments in communication. Her research is both original and incorporates a rich appreciation of the scholarship in the field. Although largely overlooked or glossed over in the past, the connections between communication and high finance are striking and of singular importance. They force all scholars and citizens to take a much harder and more sober look at our media system and at our economy. This book will serve as the opening salvo in what one hopes will be a generation of critical research on this all-important topic. It is imperative that this research be done if we are to understand our current predicament and develop workable policies to get us to a better place.

Introduction

As Michael Dawson and John Bellamy Foster said more than 10 years ago, one of the great myths of our time is that organized capitalism is being displaced by a new electronic-republic era thanks to an information and communications revolution, the greatest revolution ever (Dawson & Foster, 1998). Indeed, as many scholars have shown since (outstandingly summarized in Mosco, 2005), almost every wave of new technology, including information and communications media, has brought about declarations of radical social change. These claims have been so powerful that they have recurrently created widespread historical amnesia, making people forget that history is strewn with plenty of unfulfilled myths about technology. As Dawson and Foster put it, what history truly reveals is that every technological revolution in communications, no matter what potential for democratization it may have had, hasn't overridden the logic and power of capital. On the contrary, technological revolution "has lent itself to the growth of new monopolies of information when inscribed within existing systems of social and economic power" (Dawson & Foster, 1998, pp. 52–53).

What media history really shows, despite technological revolutions, is a continuing process of commodification throughout the development of capitalism (Mosco, 1996; Schiller, 2007). This process has experienced many critical junctures (or periods in which the old institutions and mores collapsed; McChesney, 2007), whose consequences have brought about much criticism in some countries since the beginning of the 20th century: "A century of radical media criticism" in the United

States, as Robert W. McChesney unfolded in his 2004 compilation with Ben Scott (McChesney & Scott, 2004), and the rise of critical media schools in Europe and Latin America.

How the commodification of culture and information have accelerated during our own historical epoch has been largely studied by these critical scholars to reveal monopolistic practices, hypercommercialism through advertising, audience and property concentration, industry-oriented communications policies, consent manufacturing through biased messages, and several other important issues related to the role of information and culture as commodities. All of these issues have been, and still are, essential to understanding why revolutions in communications, despite all their potential, instead of overriding the logic of capital have become a tool for its dominance.

We can see this very clearly by looking at the claims that have accompanied all technological myths, including the current digital myth. According to these, history, politics, ideology, space, and time have come to an end. Actually, almost all technological myths are variations on the "end of" myths (Mosco, 2005): the end of politics, the end of ideology, the end of history, and the end of space and time. Today, the digital myth includes the end of capitalism as well. Nevertheless, as could be seen in the financial crisis of 2007–2009, capitalism is more likely to collapse because of its own structural contradictions than because of a technological revolution.

The "end of" theories have been denounced by many critical authors in the last decades as being the intellectual fallacy underpinning policies that do not serve the public interest. In Europe, Spanish journalist and critic Manuel Vázquez Montalbán claimed that global communications have been hijacked by the proponents of "end of" theories. At the same time, this appropriation impedes the development of the emancipatory virtues of social communications (Vázquez Montalbán, 2000). In that sense, the role of communications and the media lies more in the pursuit of private interests than in a benefit to democracy. But this instrumentalization of communications and the media is nothing new, although most histories of communications fail to mention it.

THE INSTRUMENTALIZATION
OF COMMUNICATIONS THROUGHOUT HISTORY

In fact, all communications, whether individual or collective, have a persuasive goal regardless of any underlying goodness, logic, or social usefulness. The history of communications can be explained, from a liberal point of view, as democratic social attainment, although there may be other, more critical, approaches. But in any case, communications manifest themselves as an instrumentalization, although the goals and character of the instrumentalizing agents may vary.

The fact that every act of communication is performed to attain some sort of effect has been understood by humans since they began to talk. Therefore, we have had theories of argumentation for more than 2,000 years, if we take Aristotle's *Rhetoric*, 337 BC, as the starting point. Thus, since the first state or officialist journalism, on through doctrinaire, political, informational, sensationalist, propaganda, and opinion journalism, all the history of journalism is the history of an instrumentalization. This instrumentalization by whatever power was hegemonic at each moment, allowing the social system to have a conditioning effect on the communications system rather than the other way around despite what technodeterministic theoreticians—eminently conservative (as showed in Almiron & Jarque, 2008; Mosco, 2005)—have been expounding since Marshall McLuhan.

As Vázquez Montalbán (2000) reminds us, in the ancient world, epistolary communication (i.e., the use of the mail as an instrument of access to the news) was restricted to dominant minority castes. Both pharaohs and priests used persuasive communications and the monopoly of information to create states of opinion favorable to their interests. Legal and structural control of communications (through edicts, laws, privileges, and monopolies) is as old as the first communicative actions.

Although in sacrosanct classical Greece there was a great degree of freedom of expression, actions were common against drama (which was considered dangerous), against sophists (let us remember the burning of Protagoras' books), and against conversation (as shown by the death sentence against Socrates). Later on, Rome institutionalized repression more effectively. Romans whitewashed walls as a support on which information could be *uploaded* (painted). But only official information was allowed: Clandestine writing on walls, whether whitewashed or not, was forbidden and punished. Rome developed, as had Greece and Macedon during their own imperial expansion, a system of communications that served exclusively the purposes of the state, be it republican or imperial. Afterward, the excesses of Christianity would make political and social repression by Rome seem small by comparison, but the fact is that the death penalty for the spreading of information considered slanderous or injurious was still in force in the first century BC.

After the classical era, the control of social communications would be optimized by Christian unitarianism, whose defense of orthodoxy through the persecution of heresy would extend for almost 1,000 years— from the fall of the Roman Empire in the 5th century AD to the 15th century. The disintegration of Rome into medieval atomization favored uncommunication and the manipulation of information.

The power of the Christian Church was established, in fact, on the foundation of apologetics and apostleship, the principal means of communication during the feudal era. As Vázquez Montalbán (2000) reminds us, this ironclad control of communications was effective and persuasive enough to create a new set of universal values—built on the Christianization of the conventions and mores of ancient and popular culture—that permitted social uniformization. "The Church applied its spiritual utilitarianism to communication, thus truly transforming it into persuasion" (Vázquez Montalbán, 2000, p. 36). It could not have achieved this without securing the monopoly of culture and communication. The Inquisition, established in 1184 through Pope Lucius III's bull *Ad abolendam* and imposed in Spain by the Catholic Monarchs in 1478, constitutes the epitome of communicational control, the ultimate agency for the repression of freedom of expression. European monarchs would delegate on the Church the main repressive functions starting in the 15th and 16th centuries and well into the 17th century. Although it no longer was an exclusive instrument, the Inquisition functioned as an ideological apparatus of the state—as the heir to the spirit of the counter-reformation—until the 19th century.

After the introduction of Gutenberg's printing press (1456), Renaissance princes and kings hurried to invoke their rights (royal privileges) to control printers, who could only exercise their profession by royal authorization. After the protestant Reformation, the wars of religion reactivated this control even more. Concessionism (printing under royal concession) and the license system (censorship prior to publication of a work) structured the activities of this incipient sector. This strict system of licensing by royal prerogative (that prevented independent discourse on political or state issues) determined the functions of the early press, which was from the onset under royal-court censorship.

Gazettes became instruments of promotion and support of the acts of absolute monarchs, and the messenger or post systems that were already becoming available to private individuals, and therefore had the potential of bypassing censorship, were quickly incorporated into the concessionist regime. It is obvious that royal/ecclesiastical censorship could not control the contents of all letters, the transmission of all *accounts* (embryonic chronicles), the publication of handwritten newsletters or almanacs (the first purely informative documents), or impede the distribution of libels, either handwritten or printed. But it is no less evident that royal printing presses and publications directly controlled by royal power were hegemonic (because they had access to greater resources and support) and that, from the onset, strenuous efforts were made to impede the diffusion of public opinion that was either critical or in opposition to power. In this sense, Theofraste Renaudot's *Gazette de*

France, published in 1631 by order of Richelieu, is the "indubitable start-ing point of *state journalism*" (Vázquez Montalbán, 2000, p. 85). However, it is well known that the first private handwritten news services, such as the *avvisi* and *Zeitungen*, arose to meet the information needs of the social strata that were closest to power and/or that were ascending, especially nobles, merchants, and bankers. The importance of information, pure and simple, as a political, commercial, and econom-ic instrument was soon understood by those in power, and the develop-ment of social communications would always remain linked to this instrumental usefulness. This was so even after the collapse of the *Ancien Régime*.

Both monarchy and religion made use of the press to vehemently defend their positions of power, as did the bourgeoisie to invert the power balance. The development in England of a bourgeoisie of landowners, merchants, and industrialists, which was the first step toward parliamentarism, made for greater freedom of the nascent press in that country as early as the 17th century, when it duly reported the struggle between Parliament and the King. However, the rise of the new social class did not emancipate the press: An arguably more combative journalism arose, but it was ideologically aligned to one or the other side of the struggle.

The effects of the 1688 English revolution on social communications were intrinsically linked to the character of the change achieved. Although they represented a break with the medieval regime, they did not democratize the press. To be precise, as Vázquez Montalbán (2000) points out, they reproduced in the press the same democracy for nota-bles that existed in the political realm. The Libel Act passed in 1792 clearly protected bourgeois individualism—in the United Kingdom, the political harm that could be caused by a piece of information was above the right to inform until the 19th century. Although the new political cli-mate allowed for criticism in the form of political satire and although pub-lic information would eventually become democratized—albeit it would still require one century to bring its costs down—the new rising class also "sought in the indoctrinating and formative press the spread of the ideas that served to legitimize its historic ascension" (Vázquez Montalbán, 2000, p. 112).

The French Revolution would give rise to a wider set of ideas regard-ing respect for public opinion and political participation by the masses, and it would do so mainly due to the critical awareness that pamphlets, gazettes, and clandestine pasquinades ignited among the different stra-ta of the bourgeoisie. It must be remembered that this happened despite the proverbial scorn felt by intellectual encyclopedists toward those early journalistic texts, considered by them a minor genre, uncultivated and irrelevant. Thus, Vázquez Montalbán (2000) summarizes the process by which revolutionary principles were extended: The illustrated high bourgeoisie and certain sectors of the critical nobility sought in the writings of Enlightenment thinkers an ideological underpinning for their historical awareness; those writings were made known among a wide layer of the lesser bourgeoisie through leaflets and legal or illegal publications; and, finally, the common people had access to these ideas through public readings, songs, almanacs, and satirical short stories. In this way, Rousseau and Voltaire reached the masses without, obviously, being directly read by them, but rather through the vulgarization of their ideas in the popular press and literature, so strongly despised by both thinkers.

How this mediated and directed illustration of the masses came about is analyzed by Haim Burstin (2005) in *L'invention du sans-culotte*, a text in which *sansculotisme* is defined as a creation of the revolutionary Jacobin avant-garde whose purpose is to secure the allegiance of the common people and utilize this adhesion politically. Thus, the *sans-culotte* was an invented figure, an ideal created by the revolutionary elite to contain the people, and it served to generate a "compatible" and acceptable popular participation. The *sans-culotte* was the connection between the intellectuals and the illiterate populace. The growing awareness by wide sectors of the poorer social masses was the consequence, then, of a cascade of events that the bourgeoisie made efforts to channel for its own benefit, even before July 14, 1789.

The French Revolution is, in this sense, one of the most emblematic moments of the frustrated power of communications. The press flourished as it melded and guided the people before and after the revolutionary outbreak, but afterward this manifest potential caused the revolutionary power to unleash a ruthless repression of the press. When the Revolution became institutionalized, both the feudal counterrevolution and the revolutionary fervor of the populace were feared in equal measure. To conjure this fear, first the Directory and later the Consulate and the Napoleonic Empire gradually mutilated the freedom of a press whose situation under Napoleon, according to Vázquez Montalbán (2000), "and especially in its stage of decay, was much worse than under the Ancien Régime" (p. 131).

Freedom of the press as first formulated by the Declaration of Rights of the State of Virginia (1776) and by the French Revolution's Declaration of the Rights of Man (1789) should be thus viewed as a confirmation of the power that the bourgeoisie recognized in both public opinion and the social communications that generate it. The pact among the bourgeoisie, the aristocracy, and the people came to an end when the feudal structure had been fully demolished. Bonapartism put its seal on the demise of this agreement when it consolidated fundamental attainments at the cost of revolutionary regression.

This retraction became more pronounced in the post-Napoleonic stage prior to the 1848 revolution, with the surge of reaction in all continental countries in response to the events in France. Starting in 1848, through the second half of the 19th century and until the 1920s, there was a boom of infrastructures basic to communications, especially steam and electricity. The railroad and telegraph gave enormous momentum to the press, but the motives for this were commercial and industrial rather than democratizing. Capitalism, which propelled nascent industrialism, also battled for freedom of expression, but this struggle was in reality a battle for competitiveness and the market. Thus, when the journalistic enterprises born during the second half of the 19th century won this battle—because they proved that they needed a certain amount of independence to ensure their business—social communications passed from one submission to another: from being subject to the Church, the Court, and the state to being subordinate to the market.

Not even the United States, the first nation to consign in its constitution the right to freedom of expression, was exempt from this communicational utilitarianism. As Paul Starr (2004) points out, although conditions in the 16th and 17th centuries in America were quite different from those in Europe, the public sphere created by the rapid expansion of the printing press, the postal service, and newspapers in North America was also at the service of political interests. The French monarchy exported to Quebec its censorship and informational repression in its entirety, whereas British colonies experimented with greater freedom to impose their own communications policies. In Massachusetts, the Puritan colony developed, starting in 1630, a potent network of communications and schools, but also an ironclad control of the press and of all printed works in its efforts to model society according to its rigid religious criteria. During the same period, in Pennsylvania, the Quakers, who had had ample experience in clandestine printing in England, started out by repressing independent publications of any kind. The first newspaper in the colonies issued on a regular basis, the *Boston News-Letter*, created in 1704, was not an official newspaper like the gazettes of London and Paris, published under the sponsorship of their respective governments, but nevertheless sought the prior approval of the governor in Boston and, just like the gazettes in European courts, avoided any kind of confrontation with authority. The *Boston News-Letter* would be the model to follow by the rest of the early journals published regularly in the American colonies.

During the first half of the 18th century, as happened in Europe, the fragmentation of political elites and commercial competition ended the dominance of official journals in America and opened them to political debate. Nevertheless, the continuing dependence of the printers of American publications on the authorities (through printing contracts, advertising, and key official information) prevented true freedom of the press. As Starr reminds us, faced with political and economic pressure, newspaper publishers during the first half of the 18th century stayed away from all criticism of the authorities. This position changed starting in 1765, when the press began to get involved in political debate, although this was done exclusively in the service of politics. From that moment on, the press was no longer an instrument of "Anglicization," in Starr's words; it became a means of cohesion of the budding nation, an instrument of "Americanization."

The postal service and the network of newspapers created in British America provided the infrastructure for the creation of a protonational public sphere, and printers began to identify their interests with those of resistance to Britain. The leaders of the revolution of independence, in turn, started to identify their cause with that of the press. This press at the service of revolutionary ideals, or what amounts to the same, American independence, which greatly relied on the press, was what caused the leaders of the revolution to elevate freedom of the press to the status of a fundamental right of the nation.

Afterward, when the bourgeoisie had become politically and economically consolidated as a power throughout the modern world, by the mid-19th century, it subjected social communications to its own service as the ideological apparatus of the state. However, journalistic enterprises, whose foundations were made secure by the growth of readership and the appearance of advertising, launched a fierce final battle to forge the rules of liberalism in the field of social communications, as Vázquez Montalbán (2000) reminds us. It was at that moment when the liberal theory of the press as the fourth estate was developed. At the same time, the great news agencies were born (British Reuters, French Havas, and German Wolf), geographically established in accordance to the political-economic influence of their corresponding countries and exercising an information policy subject to the interests of the state.

The birth, during the following decades, of radio, cinema, and television conformed to the same logic. All of these media contributed to break barriers and traditions and in themselves were revolutionary, but they also made an enormous contribution to what Vázquez Montalbán (2000) terms "the disarming of the critical consciousness of the masses" (p. 162). The propagandistic function of radio and cinema during the two world wars was noteworthy on both sides.

The ideological use of the media in the era of mass communications would become evident with the inception of research on the subject during the 1930s. The momentum generated by those studies created a dominant current in research that would not be surmounted until the 1960s, with the impact of the social crisis experimented by American society. The main proponents of this research in the United States —

which had become the planetary hub—and its objectives had little to do with freedom of expression and respect for public opinion, the foundations on which the liberal theory of social communications had been built, but rather its concern lay in the masses as consumers of information. The underwriters of the research (the new audiovisual media, the political system, private foundations, and the armed forces) promoted empirical-quantitative studies to sell audiences to advertisers; they launched research on the formation of public opinion and its underlying mechanisms to help the "governmental management of opinion," in the words of Harold D. Lasswell (1902–1978); they encouraged the study of audiences and the effects of mass communications to develop mechanisms of intervention in the public sphere; and they supported studies on propaganda. As Vázquez Montalbán (2000) puts it, it is evident that it was not "about orienting the market but about profiting from its disorientation" (p. 208).

These demands produced what Paul Felix Lazarsfeld (1901–1976) termed *administrative research*, which arose from the alliance of interests and wills between the communications industry and American research centers during the 1930s. As a matter of fact, this administered structure is still extant, with slight modifications, not only in the United States but also in Europe, for the study of digital information and communications (Almiron & Jarque, 2008). The Internet presents as much revolutionary potential as all the social communications media that arose earlier and offers enormous spaces for alternative, critical, or opposition discourses. Nevertheless, as happened in the past, the emancipatory possibilities of the new medium are becoming overwhelmed by the dramatic imbalance of forces and resources between the promoters of the liberal theory, homogenizing and hegemonic, and those that advocate theories critical toward the dominant discourse.

The lucrative usefulness given to social communications, because they were organized into a business structure, constitutes a different stage from communications in the precapitalist era, but it is still a subordination to a force other than the common interest.

FINANCIAL CAPITALISM AND THE CRISIS OF JOURNALISM

The liberal bourgeoisie that has emerged triumphant in the capitalist era, along with the current communications emporia that concentrate power and interests without precedent, constitute the clearest evidence that the battle for the freedom of the press, which has raged since the Middle Ages, has become a mere instrument for the ascension of a new dominant elite that has in the liberal theory its ideological justification for staying in power.

This liberal theory narrates that the political process of democratization in Western societies was propelled by the development of modern media. According to James Curran (2002), this thesis is organized around two key arguments: (a) journalistic enterprises struggled to liberate themselves from government repression and control, and (b) free media empowered the people. This narrative states that the media brought information about public issues to the attention of a wider audience, thus fomenting a culture of democracy. At the same time, the media empowered the people by submitting authority to critical scrutiny and by representing public opinion before the government. It is a story "of progress in which the media became free, switched their allegiance from government to the people, and served democracy" (Curran, 2002, p. 7).

However, when the media belong to increasingly concentrated enterprises, with interests more and more diversified—and farther away from journalism—with ever-deepening dependencies and corporate and financial alliances, and with messages that become progressively more homogenous, the fantasy of "the goodness of the liberal organization" disintegrates or, as Vázquez Montalbán (2000) states, "enters a definitive crisis" (p. 215).

The crisis of journalism as an activity with social responsibility is not, as we have seen, new. Journalism can be considered to have always been in crisis, starting from the moment it had to confront a set of ideal values with the historical construction of a profession and an industry ever subject to the instrumentalization of dominant classes, whether these were religious, political, or economical. It is, in fact, a structural endemic crisis, a historical contradiction that—and this is the main thesis of this text—is becoming deeper in the heyday of financial capitalism.

In the context of current financial capitalism, the contradiction between the emancipating potential of the media and their unprecedented capacity to impose uniforming truths is bigger than ever. Nowadays, despite the magnitude of the digital technological revolution, the media that are critical toward the capitalist system still lack the conditions to balance or exercise any sort of control over the dominant communication flows. On the contrary, financial globalization and the values and priorities espoused by it have all but accentuated even more the crisis in values undergone by journalism regarding credibility, independence, and social responsibility.

From this evidence, this book suggests that we have entered a sort of postcorporate media era, a new stage in which financial capital plays a leading role within media corporations and in which corporatization and commodification aren't enough to explain where the media, journalism, and communications are heading.

Indeed, the main contradiction within journalism throughout the 20th century was its commodification, what some have termed corporate journalism, in that the liberation from its former yokes submitted journalism to a new kind of subordination. It is evident that submission to the dictates of the market prevented the realization of the emancipating precepts of communications, just as submission to the Church or absolutist courts had done in former periods. This corporatization of communications companies is not, however, the ultimate characteristic that thwarts the system of media in living up to its social potential. Financialization, or the dominance of financial economy over real productivity, represents the last step of this ongoing process of failed potential. Financial capitalism, the latest stage of the dominant economic organization system in the world, exacerbates the contradictions within journalism.

The present text incorporates the financial dimension into the critical analysis of the political economy of communications, a dimension that has been neglected in the context of the critical study of the structure, activities, and organization of the communications media in contemporary democracies. The aim of these pages is to contribute new elements to the discussion of this historical *crisis* of journalism—and, insofar as is possible, to also provide arguments to confront and help resolve the weakness of contemporary Western democracies—exposing the current factors that prevent the media and the practitioners of journalism from living up to the social responsibility to which everybody—proponents of liberal or critical theories, pragmatists or skeptics—agrees to ascribe. For this purpose, the book's thesis addresses essentially the following issues.

In the first place, Chapter 1 provides a context for the financial system, explains the interpenetration between productive economy and financial economy, and describes financialization and its role in productive economy, which includes cultural industries, among them communications groups that own news media firms.

Chapter 2 deals with the historic relations between the financial system—especially banking and stock exchange markets—and the media system, the different stages in the evolution of these relations, the parallel development (toward concentration and oligopoly) that both sectors have experimented worldwide, the financialization process of the media industry, and the increasing dependency on information on the part of the financial system. It also provides a set of tools for measuring the financialization of media owners.

Chapter 3 analyzes the world's top news media owners and the degree of financial dependence and financial logic dominant within them. We take a glance over the world's media industry in 2009 and provide data about the financialization of capital structures, corporate goals, and corporate governance bodies.

Finally, in Chapter 4, a reflection is made on the consequences that the financialization of the major communications groups has on journalism.

When this book was first devised, the main expectation was to provide a critical compilation of up-to-date information on the evolution of corporate media in modern democracies in the context of the last stage of financial capitalism. Actually, almost every key subject had already been raised elsewhere: Financial prevalence in current economics has been largely discussed among critical and nonorthodox economists; corporate media, the commodification of culture and information, and its consequences on journalism have been extensively dealt with in the work of critical scholars, mainly political economists of communication; and data on financial institutions in the ownership and boards of directors of media firms are being collected regularly—although usually isolated for specific frameworks—by media-management and corporate-governance researchers. All of them have done a stupendous job producing a large amount of data to compare with and learn from. Of course, all of them have been a great source of inspiration and knowledge for this book, which is why I would like to take this opportunity to express my gratitude. I am deeply indebted to all the authors mentioned in the pages that follow. At the same time, nevertheless, I somehow felt that the picture as a whole was lacking: the connection among data and the critical theories within the underlying and ubiquitous context of late capitalism. This context is nothing but financial capitalism, the current scenario where the chronic crisis of journalism exacerbates.

Financial capitalism is the background music that orchestrates everything. The majority of people cannot explain why and how it works, and most of the time they have difficulty understanding how it affects their lives. However, they do know that it has a deep impact on them. In 2008, the world's economy entered one of the worst scenarios of crisis since 1929 due to global financial turmoil. Suddenly, although not unexpectedly for many critics, the international context offered a true opportunity to realize the impact that financial capitalism has on our everyday lives. The fragility and instability of global financing was fiercely evidenced, as well as its ties with local economies. In this context, one of the most recurrent sentences we heard was "the impact of the crisis on the economy, on industries, on firms." In the case of the media industry, the impact of the crisis on advertising was one of the main topics to explain what was occurring to the sector. But as we see in the following pages, major media conglomerates were idols with feet of clay when the 2008–2009 crisis emerged. The strategy of growth based on profits and revenues that haven't been earned yet, that is, on borrowings or fictitious capital—as the whole world economy has being doing during the last century—was at the core of the crisis, and not the opposite—a somehow spontaneous unmotivated crisis that was at the core of the industrial failures.

Therefore, the goal of this book is to address something that hasn't been attempted yet: to not merely try to denounce the weakness of the foundations on which the media industry is building its empires, but to help understand why the news media industry experienced such a troubled time when the crisis emerged.

Last, this book joins those who demand more transparency. There has been a call for transparency after every episode of turbulence in the economy in recent decades. It was also demanded following the big debacles of 2001–2004 (Enron, Parmalat, WorldCom). At that time, light was again thrown on misleading management in media companies (e.g., the accounting irregularities in Vivendi Universal and Time Warner). In 2009, it was clear that all the corporate failures, irregularities, and bad management at the end of that year—and of the many preceding decades—were by no means a contextual issue but rather a structural trend. This trend pushed the world economy into the 2008–2009 scenario. For many of us, it is undeniable that if capitalism fails, the solution is not more capitalism. But this is not the place to discuss economics, but rather to show the whole picture regarding news media producers (i.e., how a key column of democracy has added financialization to corporate subordination). Therefore, once again in history, journalism finds itself unfree and with its hands tied.

1

Financial Capitalism and Financialization

Finance is only a branch of economics, the branch that deals with matters related to money and capital markets. It is also the branch of economics that John Kenneth Galbraith denounced to be founded on one of the most well-known frauds of all economics' frauds (Galbraith, 2004): the pretense that capital markets are under control and predictable. The onset of crises and recessions hinges on too many variables (national governmental decisions, financial institutions' measures, and corporate and individual actions mainly, but also political relations among countries). The combination of all of them results in what Galbraith terms *unknowable*. Because the unknowable is impossible to know, any claim to the contrary is a fraud.

Despite the unpredictability, uncertainty, and lack of responsibility shown by financial markets throughout their history, this area of economics has become nowadays the dominant field in resource allocation, management, acquisition, and investment. But the supremacy of the capital sphere (finance) over the industrial sphere (production) is not a characteristic of present-day economics only, but rather an attribute inherent to the evolution of modern capitalism.

In this chapter, we look at the primary purpose of the financial system, at financial capitalism and financialization, at the role played by the banking system, and at how the financial dominance or financialization of the economy affects all branches of production in the modern world, including the cultural industries to which the news media belong. Finally,

I will address the claim of some modern economists to the effect that financial dominance has been brought to an end by the information and communications technologies (ICTs) revolution.

WHAT IS THE FINANCIAL SYSTEM AND WHAT IS ITS PURPOSE?

Nowadays, orthodox economic theory considers that the financial system of a country is, in general terms, the aggregation of institutions, means, and markets, whose primary purpose is to channel the savings generated by economic actors with a surplus to borrowers or economic actors with a deficit. In other words, the financial system's role is to transform savings that would otherwise not be used by having institutions take them as deposits in exchange for the payment of an interest so that these same institutions can in turn lend them, also for an interest. The economy functions on the basis of allowing the surplus money of savers to be used by public or private investors, and that main function is performed, according to neoclassical theory, by the financial system. The purpose is to ensure that financial resources are allocated effectively, that is, that the economic system has access to the financial resources it needs, appropriate not only in their volume or amount but also in their nature, terms, and costs (Parejo, Cuervo, Calvo, & Rodríguez, 2004).

However, this is not the only function of a financial system according to the dominant economic paradigm. According to this view, the financial system is also expected to contribute to the monetary and financial stability of a country. Monetary authorities develop, by means of their structure, active policies for the purpose of ensuring that stability. Stability, from the point of view of orthodox theory, is understood to be the absence of major crises in the various institutional groups that make up the system (private banks, savings banks, insurance companies, etc.), as well as the attainment of a stable evolution of the main monetary and financial macro dimensions (Parejo et al., 2004: 21).

But also classical economic theory affirms that, when a financial system performs its functions adequately, it is not limited to serving as a conduit for financial resources between savers and investors, but also contributes, through its own structure, to facilitating the generation of further riches (by generating a greater volume of liquidity that it then channels toward the productive activities that require it). Economic development of countries is thus accompanied by a parallel development of their financial system. Most orthodox economists recognize that, apart from public investment, the main flow of resources destined to productive investment, in countries with market economies, takes place through the financial system.

This is roughly the description of the financial system that can be found in most economics textbooks and that constitutes the most widespread approach in theoretical terms. However, this definition overlooks a major part of the financial system that has become its dominant trait: money creation. In other words, financial organizations loan more money than they receive in deposit. This happens from the moment at which they discover that they only need a minimum of reserves in deposit to satisfy the routine demand of cash payments. Mike Hall (1992), for instance, considers this omission very important:

> The orthodox account is repeated over and again in all the textbooks, yet analysis reveals that, among other faults and omissions, it fails in its central objective—it does not explain the creation of bank money— [...]: it [fails] to explain how banks create money, and [fails] to analyze money-creation deriving from the repayment of loans. [...].

> So far as the accumulation of bank-capital is concerned, the failure on the part of the orthodox account to analyze—or even mention— the amortization-circuit is a major omission, because, of course, one of the most important ways in which bank-capital increases itself, and centralizes control over the total social capital, is through the appropriation of newly-created value in the form of loan-repayments and interests. (Hall, 1992: 104–109)

This money-creation capacity has several consequences, among which is the emergence of great quantities of fictitious deposits—capable of causing the bankruptcy of the financial entity in periods of crisis (or in periods in which the demand for payments is higher than the actual reserve of deposits)—and of what some authors have termed "fictitious capital," whose analysis is not addressed by classical or neoclassical economics. It is in this sense that Marx frequently stated that during a crisis capitalism is forced to abandon "financial fictions" and return to the realm of cash to the eternal truths of the foundations (Harvey, 1982: 296). However, it was authors subsequent to Marx, such as Rudolf Hilferding, who used the term *fictitious capital* as a more concrete and institutional concept, with the purpose of describing the historic fact of the unification of productive and banking capital under the hegemony of the latter (Carcanholo & Nakatani, 2000: 151–170).

This is what makes the orthodox approach insufficient, if not fraudulent, in its efforts to describe reality, insofar as it is incapable of explaining the divorce between real economy and financial economy (in great part because it does not take into account the important consequences of the trait that it overlooks—money creation). For that reason, it is necessary to add to the objective function of redistribution, which doubtless should be pursued by the financial system, the critical vision contributed by nonorthodox theoreticians, which leads to a definition of the financial system that is much less instrumental and more committed to reality. According to this point of view, the financial system is more a system of domination of social production than a tool for the rational distribution of the yield of this production, thus establishing a connection with the critical current initiated at the start of the 20th century by Rudolf Hilferding, who considered the dominance of the financial system as the highest degree of economic and political dominance (Hilferding, 1910/1985).

The financial system should thus be understood as the a priori system designed to optimize the allocation of capital in society—that is, to put capital at the disposal of productive economy. Capital is to be understood as the two dimensions of finance capital defined by Serfati: the resources that keep the form of money and that are valued in the form of money (turning thus into capital), taking the form of credits, property rights, and so on; and the entities (banks, insurance companies, pension funds, investment funds, etc.) and institutions (stock exchange market and other capital markets) whose function is to centralize money in the form of capital to make it profitable (Serfati, 2003: 59). This system, as will be seen, operates in the opposite sense: subordinating industrial economy to finance capital.

FINANCIAL CAPITALISM

Modern finance came about in the late 19th century as a result of the emergence of a new configuration of capitalism based on the separation between ownership and management of companies and a new role for financial institutions. Prior to the 19th century, most financial activity was linked to the financing of public expenses. However, by the turn of the century, a new private financial framework had developed, one that was closely related to the economy. This new framework was the main reason for the two aforementioned transformations: the formation of large corporations, backed and controlled by finance (i.e., by a framework of agents [public institutions and private actors] interlocked in a global network and with converging interests); and the widening of the distance between the workers and their means of production due to the managerial revolution (Duménil & Lévy, 2005: 19–20).

During the first decades of the 20th century, capitalism was extensively modified as a result of the above-mentioned changes and their subsequent consequences: the relatively large autonomy of managers and the dominance of finance over monetary and financial mechanisms. All this, mostly in relation to the development of large corporations in Germany, led Rudolf Hilferding (1910/1985) to define *finance capital*, by which he implied a close relationship between industrial capital and banking capital. According to Hilferding, industrial capital had been replaced as the dominant form of capital by finance capital, with the industrial capitalists having become more reliant on finance capital.

Obviously, Hilferding's was not the first analysis of finance capital, but it was the first, after Marx (in book III of *Capital* Marx had already presented a theory of the *autonomy* of finance), to address it in depth in a study on the interrelation between industrial and financial capital. Prior authors, including Max Weber and August Bebel, had dealt with finance within the analysis of capitalism or imperialism. In 1902, British author John Atkinson Hobson published *Imperialism*, a text that, according to some, even contains a definition of *finance capital*, which is more useful than Hilferding's for the analysis of financial expansion at the end of the 19th century, in that Hobson studied Great Britain (Arrighi, 1994), whereas Hilferding based his analysis on the penetration of major banks into the capital of major industry in Germany starting in the last decade of the 19th century.

In *Financial Capital*, Hilferding dealt with modern incorporated societies, imperialism, the role of trade unions, and, most particularly, the role of banking and financial concentration. For Hilferding, the development of the great incorporated companies is a key to understanding the ever-closer relationship between banking and industry because its main trait, the separation between ownership and management, had important effects in both directions: On the one hand, it increased the importance within the system of banks as promoters of those societies through the stock market; on the other hand, it separated industrial and financial capital, allowing the latter to play the dominant role. "The expansion of capitalist industry develops the concentration of banking. The concentrated banking system is also a major motor for the attainment of the highest degree of capitalist concentration in cartels and trusts," claims Hilferding (1985: 245). The growth of industry could not come about without the banking system, which, by allocating a growing portion of its capital to industry, became the owner of a large portion of the industrial system. This was the origin of financial capital: "I apply the term finance capital to banking capital, that is, capital in the form of money, that thus truly transforms into industrial capital" (Hilferding, 1985: 247–248). Industrial capital, in turn, is productive capital (means of production, workforce, profits), so that financial capital, which is in fact virtual (let us remember money creation, also known as "fictitious" capital), becomes real.

As Pollin (2000) points out, a primary need of any capitalist order is the creation of flexibility—or liquidity—which allows "capitalists" to maximize their opportunities for profitability without having to commit themselves to a particular line of business. Financial markets and institutions satisfy that need, but, as John Maynard Keynes explains, financial markets also encourage short-term speculative behavior on the part of investors because they break the bond between the ownership of an enterprise and the management of its productive activities as the means for the attainment of a profit (Pollin, 2000: 133).

According to Pollin, there are two main forms of interconnection between productive and financial economy: the systems based on banking structures and the systems based on the capitals market. This author concludes that the greatest integration among financial and nonfinancial enterprises in the systems based on the banking structure constitutes an inherent advantage as opposed to the more unstable systems based on the capitals market. But he also discovers that this greater efficiency does not impede banking structure-based systems from being the less democratic or egalitarian: "The tight and entwined relationship between major companies, banks and bureaucracies offers opportunities for favoritism in the allotment of credit" (Pollin, 2001: 69).

Whatever the interconnection model, with the expansion of industry, the banks' power grows and a conservative ideology arises, entirely opposite to liberalism, whose description in Hilferding's words, seems to portray exactly the global hegemony exercised by U.S. capitalism after World War II. The quotation is long, but we feel it is illustrative. It is important to remember that it was written in 1910:

> Finance capital does not want freedom, but domination; it has no regard for the independence of the individual capitalist, but demands his allegiance. It detests the anarchy of competition and wants organization, though of course only in order to resume competition on a still higher level. But in order to achieve, and to maintain and enhance its predominant position, it needs the state which can guarantee its domestic market through a protective tariff policy and facilitate the conquest of foreign markets. It needs a politically powerful state which does not have to take account of the conflicting interests of other states in its commercial policy. It needs also a strong state which will ensure respect for the interests of capital abroad, and use its political power to extort advantageous supply contracts and trade agreements from smaller states; a state which can intervene in every corner of the globe and transform the whole world into a sphere of investment for its own finance capital.
>
> Financial capital, lastly, needs a state that is strong enough to carry out a policy of expansion and to acquire new colonies. While liberal-

ism was opposed to state-intervention policies and wanted to ensure its own domination against the older power of aristocracy and bureaucracy (...), financial capital requires an unlimited policy of strength (...). (Hilferding, 1985: 372)

At the end of the industrial-expansion and banking-concentration process, a few financial entities hold in their hands most of social production and have become an oligarchy (later on, during the period between the world wars, Keynes would refer to it as the *Parliament of Banks*). The consequences are manifest: Economic power means, at the same time, *political power*, according to Hilferding (1985), and the stronger the concentration in the economic sphere, the more limitless will be the domination that it will exercise over the state. Therefore, for Hilferding, financial capital in its perfection means the highest degree of economic and political power in the hands of the "capitalist oligarchy." The proof of the triumph of financial capital is the triumph of its promoters (the "imperialist domain"), who were none other than the Anglo-Americans (Tabb, 1999: 3).

Looking back to Hilferding is useful because it allows us to understand the origin of the current relations between productive economy and financial economy. Afterward, there were various authors, especially during the second half of the 20th century, who recognized that what happened 100 years ago paved the way that reaches to today. This is how Paul M. Sweezy (1994) expounds it:

Financial capital, once cut loose from its original role as a modest helper of a real economy of production to meet human needs, inevitably becomes speculative capital geared solely to its own self-expansion. In earlier times no one ever dreamed that speculative capital, a phenomenon as old as capitalism itself, could grow to dominate a national economy, let alone the whole world. But it has. [...].

In all the advanced capitalist countries, the last two decades of the nineteenth Century witnessed an intense process of concentration and centralization of capital [...] (cartels, trusts, holding companies, giant corporations) aimed at eliminating cut-throat competition and getting control of their price and output policies. [...] By the turn of the twentieth Century what had been the small-scale, predominantly domestically oriented capitalism of the nineteenth Century became the monopolistically controlled imperialist system of the twentieth. (Sweezy, 1994: 2–4)

But these early stages, dominated by private finance, faced major instability when confronted with the Great Depression and World War II. In the aftermath of those two events, "national economies, even those in which markets played a very powerful role, were placed under the ultimate control of governments." At the same time, international economic relations were placed under the control of the new postwar financial institutions: the International Monetary Fund (IMF) and the World Bank (Crotty, 2005: 77).

So, over a period of almost 30 years, modern finance was "held in check by regulations, capital controls, the power of labor and the welfare state." But the Keynesian revolution (the global prosperity that characterized the quarter of a century following the end of World War II in 1945, the so-called *Golden Age* of modern capitalism, which was dominated by the belief that market economies needed strong social regulation to function properly) succumbed to its own inherent contradictions. Between the late 1960s and the beginning of the 1970s, this framework came to an end (Epstein & Jayadev, 2005: 46–76), and "international governance becomes the conduit for the greater dominance of finance capital" (Tabb, 1999: 3).

In the 1960s, the world of the Euromarkets, a huge surplus of dollars seeking to avoid domestic regulation and control, started circulating outside the United States and with them offshore tax havens emerged. The rise of the Eurodollar market was, according to many authors, a key moment in the creation of the financialization of the world economy (Dickens, 2005: 210–219).

In the 1970s, economic instability exploded with two crises over OPEC oil prices, the collapse of the Bretton Woods fixed-exchange rate system, and the buildup of excessive debt in the Third World. By then, the scenario was ready for a makeover: "Falling profit rates and a moribund stock market in the USA triggered a powerful movement, led by business and, especially, financial interests, to roll back the economic regulatory power of national governments." It was the advent of, first, monetarism and, later, what is usually referred to as neoliberal globalization (Crotty, 2005: 77; Seabrooke, 2001).

Another 30 years have gone by since then, during which time the world's economies have undergone profound transformations. Swezzy referred in this sense to the development of a relatively independent financial superstructure set above the world economy and made up of banks and intermediaries that are completely interconnected. The result is that "the real economy, the one that produces goods and services that enable people to live and reproduce, is owned by a tiny minority of oligopolists" (Sweezy, 1994: 8). For this author, the inverted relationship produced between the real and the financial economy is the key to understanding the current global trends. As Hilferding before, Sweezy recognizes the ultimate political power of economic power: The real power of corporations and governments, he states, is in the hands of the financial system.

More recently, Carcanholo and Nakatani (2000) went further and affirmed that "speculative and parasitic capitalism" that characterizes the last decades "is the tragedy of our time" (Carcanholo & Nakatani, 2000: 169). That is so insofar as productive economy is completely subordinated to speculative economy, "the speculative logic of capital over its circulation and reproduction in international space" (Carcanholo & Nakatani, 2000: 153) defines the current capitalist stage. This is what Giovanni Arrighi (1994) terms the change from the material-expansion phase to the financial phase, particularly accelerated starting in the 1960s, in whose substratum this author also detects the power struggles that underlie financial expansions.

Thus, from the 1980s, the hegemony of finance is such that some authors talk again of the "autonomization" of the financial system and of "capital resurgence" (Duménil & Lévy, 2001). The growing importance of the capitals markets, the increase in the cost of credit, and the changes in the pattern of public spending are interpreted as expressions of the triumph of the financial sphere over the productive sectors of capital and labor. This renewed autonomization of finance has its nucleus in the systems of private pensions by financial capitalization that began to develop after World War II in the Anglo-Saxon countries and Japan (Chesnais, 2001). It is precisely in those private pension systems partly or wholly financed through the stock market that the tremendous risk and social impact of this financialization become evident. As has already happened (let us remember the Enron case), a bankruptcy in the funds that underwrite these pensions can leave thousands of people pensionless.

This is what makes all these authors affirm that the current role of financial economy within global economy is one of domination, in that it is a fact that capital valorized in the form of financial investments and with common interests with corporate profit appears as the dominant portion of capital, the part that is able to set the pace for the forms and tempo of accumulation. The effects of this domination on the productive nonfinancial economy are clear: The formation of the financialized regime has caused the financial markets to replace the economic policies and collective negotiation that characterize fordism. In addition, the interpenetration between finance and industry is greater than in any previous historical period, so that negative financial phenomena (such as the stock-market crashes) have unprecedented consequences over the real economy, by weakening the lending network designed to finance industrial and real-estate activities. The financial crisis starting in summer 2007 is an example of this strong interrelation.

Starting as an American financial crisis in August 2007—when a loss of confidence by investors in the value of securitized mortgages in the United States resulted in the so-called subprime mortgage crisis (Schechter, 2008)—in a few months the world financial system was affected in its entirety by a liquidity crisis that prompted substantial injections of capital into the financial markets by the U.S. Federal Reserve, the Bank of England, and the European Central Bank. Despite these aids by the public sector, in September 2008, the crisis deepened as stock markets the world over crashed and entered a period of high volatility, and a considerable number of banking, mortgage, and insurance companies went bankrupt in the previous and following weeks or had to be rescued by public or private actors (Northern Rock, Bear Stearns, Indymac, Fannie Mae, Freddie Mac, Merrill Lynch, HBOS, Lehman Brothers, and others). Shares worldwide experimented record falls, and Wall Street had its worst year since 1931.

Although America's housing collapse triggered that crisis, the financial system was vulnerable because of intricate and highly leveraged financial contracts and operations; a U.S. monetary policy that made the cost of credit negligible, therefore encouraging such high levels of leverage; and what has been called a "hypertrophy" of the financial sector. The resulting credit crunch produced a great impact on the real economy, and a period of true economic recession started at the end of 2008 due to the financial turmoil.

WHAT IS FINANCIALIZATION?

Nowadays, practically all economists accept that one of the basic traits that defines contemporary capitalism is the role played by finance within it, although only the critical view accepts that this role causes extreme poverty and injustice. This has caused some authors to speak of the financialization of the economy.

Among the first to use the term *financialization* were the French authors André Orléan (1999) and François Chesnais (2001), the latter terming current financial capitalism a "regime of accumulation dominated by the financial" and a "financialized regime of accumulation." André Orléan has also described the financialized economy as *creditor power*: "The abstract power of money is transformed into actual power over production, investment and the workforce" (Orléan, 1999: 194). This creditor power adopts two forms according to Orléan: banking power and financial power. These in turn correspond to the two channels through which financing of enterprises is carried out: "On the one hand, banking credit; on the other, negotiable documents such as commercial paper, obligations and stocks" (Orléan, 1999: 195), although the latter are in fact managed mostly by banking entities. Both forms answer to lenders' need for liquidity, whether they be banks or financial markets. Liquidity is what bestows great power on the macroeconomic level in that "the financial lender bases his strength on the permanently-wielded menace of withdrawing his capitals and taking them elsewhere" (Orléan, 1999: 209).

It is in this context that Orléan speaks also of corporate financialization — "the purpose is to redesign the organizational architecture of the firm according to strictly contractual principles" — and of a patrimonial, rather than citizen, individualism in contemporary societies (Orléan, 1999: 193–259).

At about that time, British professor Ronald Dore also provided one of the first definitions of corporate financialization: "The increasing dominance of the finance industry in the sum total of economic activity, of financial controllers in the management of corporations, of financial assets among total assets, of marketized securities and particularly equities among financial assets, of the stock market as a market for corporate control in determining corporate strategies, and of fluctuations in the stock market as a determinant of business cycles" (Dore, 2002).

What this definition means in practical terms is summarized by José Manuel Naredo (2004): "Equilibrium in the balance of payments of rich countries is shifting no longer from trade balance to income balance, but rather from the latter to short-term capital balance and to the workings of the foreign exchange market" (Naredo, 2004: 62).

This situation is a total inversion of the premises that should be served by the financial system. As Isabelle Hallary (2003) explains, the recent developments of globalization and liberalization in financial markets have not favored productive economy: It is not productive investment that benefits from the development of the capitals market, but rather it is the stock market activity that profits from the abundance of funds looking for a destination. Companies provide the market with financing in that the access of capitals into the markets does not translate into an increase in capital, but eventually stimulates the search for financial surplus value at the expense of real investment. The failure of the financial system's objectives is clearly reflected in the fact that the indicators of economic and financial activity are increasingly out of phase: Corporations are financialized (taking stock value as their main reference of results), and the deregulation of the financial system allows reference credit to finance nonproductive activities and even many firms to destine a part of their profits not to productive investments but to financial speculation. This paves the way for the illusory pretension that assigns money the property of being, by itself, a generator of value in the realm of production (Hallary, 2003: 85). The consequences for one of the two great precursors of the current financialized regime cannot be more eloquent:

> [...], the liberalization of the financial system in the United States has not fulfilled the promises of their more ardent defenders. It has not favored in a special way the financing of productive investments. It has not improved the allotment of capital and, on the contrary, has often deviated the same capital toward uses whose social usefulness is questionable. It has not improved the financial situation of companies, which are, in fact, more indebted. Neither have they reduced the cost of financing, which has actually increased. On the other hand, financial globalization has fully satisfied the demands of the owners of the capital, restoring to them an economic and social power that had weakened in the 60s and 70s. (Hallary, 2003: 90)

The statement that the economy is nowadays financialized, dominated by finance, also means that, on both national and international planes, the economic regime is organized to allow investors to appropriate financial income in the most regular and secure conditions. Financial markets "have been elevated to the category of institutions responsible for the distribution of income between the workforce and the capital." Thus, the most flagrant effect of financial liberalization has been the considerable transformation of the distribution of power and wealth. "In the first place, the reform of the financial system has devolved the power of companies to shareholders and lenders. [...] Making use of their great power, the owners of capital have brought about a new orientation in the distribution of wealth. A redistribution of value added has been operated to the detriment of salaries and to the benefit of capital [...]" (Hallary, 2003: 87).

Although the industrial sector, as represented by the great transnational groups, still holds a relevant place in the economic system, industrial capital no longer sets the pace of the general process (Chesnais & Plihon, 2003: 47, 49). The pace is set, rather, by financial institutions, at the forefront of which, due to their enormous capacity, are the nonbanking institutions (insurance companies, pension funds, hedge funds, etc.), which operate as fund managers on behalf of their dispersed clients. But it is necessary not to forget that many of these nonbanking institutions are fiduciary subsidiaries of major banks.

Actually, the banking system is still fundamental and continues to be at the core of the mechanisms for money creation and, in a large measure, at the core of the mechanisms "which guarantee the transformation of liquid cash-capital into illiquid financial assets" fundamentally benefitting financial capital (Serfati, 2003: 69). Financial disintermediation and the emergence of institutional investors have financialized banks' activities to the utmost, forcing them to take on ever greater risks. This is another main trait of financialization.

More recently, and in what probably is the most important collective work on financialization so far, *Financialization and the World Economy*

(2005), Gerald A. Epstein, editor of the book, asserted in his introduction that financialization was one of the three main features of the profound transformations that world economies have undergone in the last 30 years. While the other two features, neoliberalism and globalization, have received much attention, the phenomenon of financialization is a relatively new subject of study about which there is not even a generally agreed-on definition.

As Epstein summarizes, many authors usually apply the term in a quite narrow sense: to mean the ascendancy of value to shareholders as a mode of corporate governance; to refer to the growing dominance of capital-market financial systems over bank-based financial systems; to refer to the increasing political and economic power of a particular class grouping, the rentier class, in line with Hilferding's approach; and also to mean the appearance of new financial instruments in financial trading.

Broader and more comprehensive definitions, nevertheless, are much more interesting and accurate descriptions of what is going on in the current world economy. Epstein's definition in the book mentioned earlier is one of the most inclusive: He describes financialization as "the increasing role of financial motives, financial markets, financial actors, and financial institutions in the operation of the domestic and international economies" (Epstein, 2005: 3). Alongside this definition, we must also quote Greta Krippner's (2005) prior contribution, for which financialization refers to a "pattern of accumulation in which profit making occurs increasingly through financial channels rather than through trade and commodity production."

Last, it is necessary to point out, as the authors quoted remind us, that the financialization of the economy is not the product of chance, but rather responds obviously to the success of certain initiatives. Just as capitalism "is not simply an economic system, a form of organizing material production, but also (and even above all) a means of social domination, a form of organizing power" (Chesnais, 2001), the dynamics of financial globalization are also considered the result of energetic initiatives carried out by a well-defined set of economic interests (Duménil & Lévy, 2001). For Serfati (2003), "the potential that financial capital possesses nowadays is not, in any way, the spontaneous result of the free play of the forces that operate in financial markets, but rather it is due to government policies oriented to the satisfaction of lenders' demands" (Serfati, 2003: 69). William K. Tabb's (1999) words, written years ago, are still perfectly valid: "Again the problems are political and not economic — if indeed we should make a separation between the two. The assertion that economic laws are binding is always an assertion of the hegemony of a certain type of economic reasoning, one with a political content" (Tabb, 1999: 13).

The political character of the economy becomes evident in the analysis of the processes that, more recently, have accentuated the process of international financialization.

THE FINANCIAL GLOBALIZATION PROCESS AND ITS CONSEQUENCES

As numerous authors have described exhaustively (Arrighi, 1994; Brenner, 2002; Chesnais & Plihon, 2000; Epstein, 2005; Palazuelos, 1998; Seabrooke 2001), the boom in the late 1990s, as well as the origins of the process of financial internationalization (or, at least, of the unprecedented degree of financial internationalization achieved at the end of that decade), have their roots in the crisis at the end of the 1970s and the rise of neoliberalism and the free-market doctrines of Milton Friedman and the Chicago School of Economics.

A particularly interesting approach is Giovanni Arrighi's (1994) theory of the long 20th century, which states that the current phase of financial globalization is nothing but the third stage of one single capitalist era made up, first, of the financial expansion in the late 19th and early 20th centuries, in the course of which the structures of the old British regime of accumulation were destroyed to create the new American empire; second, of the material expansion of the 1950s and 1960s, during which U.S. domination brought about a worldwide expansion of commerce and production; and, third, of the current financial expansion, during the deployment of which the old American regime is being destroyed and substituted by a different regime.

The old regime that was extinguished was the post-World War II Bretton Woods system of fixed international exchange rates and the dollar peg to gold. The demise of fixed exchange rates was one of the most important impetuses to the rise of financialization but not the only one. Another key factor brought about by the financial scenario of the late 1960s and early 1970s was the recycling of petrodollars (as a consequence of the deposits by leaders from oil-exporting Arab countries, the major banks in developed countries experienced a great volume of liquidity that would result in a boom of international loans). In addition, other aspects that contributed to forging the current situation were *the disorganization of raw-materials markets* (that was to cause instability in prices, types of contracts and intervening agents, and increased intermediation for speculative ends); *the privileged position of transnational corporations* (which would erupt into international financial markets and whose claims would clash with the restrictions imposed by national regulations in exchange policies and capitals movement, thus turning them into one of the main voices calling for liberalization of international financial movements and encouraging them to disintermediate their financial operations in respect to banks); and *budget deficits* (the search by governments for cheap and noninflationary forms of finance caused further banking disintermediation) (Palazuelos, 1998: 18–25).

The context of the international recessive and inflationary crisis of the early 1970s favored indebtedness (by companies, Western governments and nondeveloped countries, as well as by the international agencies that channel financial help to underdeveloped countries) and generated consequences that configured the later scenario.

Although the dynamics of internationalization during the last decades intensified the trends that had been developing since the 1950s and 1960s in the process of capitals globalization (in its three forms: commerce, finance, and investments), the aforementioned factors accelerated them, bringing about several effects: an expansion of international financial markets, a supremacy of the dollar (that would continue to be an international monetary reference), the consolidation of the main international financial agents (major international banks, transnational firms, governments, central banks, and new nonbanking financial companies), the growing interrelationship of capitals, and a persistent instability of financial markets (Palazuelos, 1998: 25–37). This is what Chesnais (2004: 27) summarizes as the three Ds: *déréglementation*, *décloisonnement*, and *désintermédiation*—derregulation, liberalization, and monetary disintermediation—of national financial markets and investment.

Probably the best references to understand the huge transformation the world economy has experienced in the last three decades are the figures generated by the explosive growth of financial markets. The conversion from fixed international exchange rates to floating exchange trading in stock markets triggered an exponential rise of these markets the world over, which leapt from US$18 billion daily turnover in the early 1970s to US$590 billion in 1989 and US$3.2 trillion in 2007, according to the Bank for International Settlements (BIS) (the 1970s figure being an estimate of Excelsior Worldwide Corp.). Actually, every survey published by the BIS since 1989 reports unprecedented growth in this rate, and it is well known that an important portion of the foreign exchange transactions are speculative (some authors estimate it at about 70% to 90%).

Other financial markets have exhibited similarly explosive unprecedented growth since the 1970s: equity (stock) markets trading, government securities trading, futures trading, corporate debt trading, state and municipal bonds, options trading, mortgage derivatives, and OTC derivatives in general.

The futures markets hold an outstanding position in this trend. Founded in the mid-1800s, all futures trading were solely based on agricultural commodities until the 1970s. But after the end of the dollar gold-backed fixed-exchange rate system in 1971, contracts based on foreign currencies began to be traded. After the deregulation of interest rates, futures contracts based on various bonds/interest rates also began to be traded. Nowadays, the financial futures contracts (based on interest rates, currencies, or equity indices) dominate the futures markets.

Futures markets are only one of the most common type of derivatives. According to BIS, activity in the OTC derivatives market continued to expand at an even faster rate than foreign exchange markets—to US$4.2 trillion in average daily turnover in April 2007. Related to this, one of the most notable features of financialization has been the development of overleverage (more borrowed capital and less owned capital), which was one of the main causes of the financial crisis starting in 2007. Derivatives instruments are financial instruments, the price or value of which are derived from the price or value of another financial instrument. The initial purpose of those instruments was hedging and risk management, but they became widely traded financial assets on their own.

To synthesize, it is now evident that from the crisis the 1970s and the consequences that followed, two circumstances derived: first, the conversion of the financial sector into one of the main sources of profit for a great number of firms—financial or not—and, second, the fact that world economies as a whole have come to be run fundamentally by parameters of behavior that correspond to financial activities and that the latter have become "a permanent source of economic instability on a global scale" (Palazuelos, 1998: 14).

This process, which bears a clear Anglo-Saxon stamp, mainly American, means for Robert Brenner (2003) the restoration of "patterns of capitalist development reminiscent of the time prior to World War I" (Brenner, 2003: 14), insofar as a number of economic policies were implemented that, aided by the application of technological advances to the operation of financial markets, have given rise to the necessary elements for the globalization of financial relations to take place effectively.

The fact that such financial globalization supported by conservative national leaders and orthodox economists ("liberalization and deregulation of their financial systems have been accomplished at a rapid pace under the direction of the WMF and the World Bank under the political pressure of the United States"; Chesnais, 2004: 28) had consequences for economic growth and social welfare that were in fact the opposite of what was expected did not halt the process. Neither was it thwarted by the manifest overcapacity that liberalization had generated by allowing any firm whose stocks were highly priced to be financed, even if its profitability and potential for future profit were low or even extremely low. This happened starting in the mid-1990s, especially in the technology, media, and telecommunications industries, which were hailed as the sectors of America's *new economy.*

Thus, with their high stock prices as their only reference, a great number of new or young enterprises were able to find financial resources with an ease that was spectacular. That was how, on the basis of practically free financing, these companies benefitted from the extensive deregulation in the sectors of the new economy, hardly worrying about where their profits or the demand for their products would come from. But as Brenner (2000) also explains, "since the investment boom was not based on an increase of real or potential profit, but in companies' access to practically free financing provided by the disinformation proceeding from the stock markets," all of this could only lead to a scenario of "overinvestment that spread the situation of overcapacity and falling profit rates far beyond the industrial sector" (Brenner, 2003: 15).

Therefore, both commercial and investment banks committed themselves to the industry of that new economy (investment banks in exchange for lucrative commissions for their title emission and subscription operations and for their management of mergers and takeovers) so that, when in the spring of 2000 the stock market crashed and the telecommunications and Internet bubble burst, the institutional agents affected were numerous. The immediate result was the implementation, particularly in the United States, of what has been termed *new financial engineering*, through which many major corporations started to manipulate their accounting to exaggerate their short-term earnings and thus be able to maintain the vital reference that kept them aloft: their stock-market rating (let us remember Enron, WorldCom, and Parmalat, to name but the best known).

The consequences of periods of overcapacity are always the same: crisis and a bigger concentration of the sectors affected, in which competitors absorb the bankrupt companies' assets and clients.

Therefore, financialization had profound effects also on the structure and performance of large nonfinancial corporations of the late 20th and early 21st centuries, just as financial capital studied by Hilferding had on the nonfinancial corporations of the early 20th century—when the German Marxist theorist analyzed the transformation of competitive and pluralistic liberal capitalism into monopolistic finance capitalism.

According to Crotty, nonfinancial corporations have been adversely affected by the return of the hegemony of finance through two major changes: "A slowdown in the rate of global aggregate demand [. . .] growth and an increasing intensity of competition in key product markets, on the one hand, and a shift from 'patient' finance-seeking long-term growth to impatient financial markets that raised real interest rates, forced [non-financial corporations] to pay an increasing share of their cash flow to financial agents, drastically changed managerial incentives, and helped shorten [non-financial corporations] planning horizons," on the other hand. This scenario has placed nonfinancial corporations in what Crotty (2005) calls the "neoliberal paradox": that is, simultaneously in a competitive market that makes it impossible to keep or even achieve high earnings, and in a financial market that demands the generation of ever-increasing earnings (with the threat of falling stock prices and hostile takeovers). This paradox affects all capital-intensive core industries with huge economies in terms of scale and scope (Crotty, 2005: 78).

The response of many nonfinancial corporations to the low profits and high costs of external funds that they faced in much of the 1980s and 1990s, as well as to the high returns they observed being made on financial assets and financial enterprises, has been twofold: (a) acquiring financial assets, and (b) creating or buying financial subsidiaries. In other words, they have financialized their activities.

These have been, succinctly, the causes and consequences of the financialization process of the world economy, or financial globalization, whose roots connect directly with the roots of neoliberalism, a connection that leads some authors to accuse the countries that supported neoliberalism, especially the United States, of being the main instigators of the change in the world financial regime through the shaping of international financial and monetary systems (Seabrooke, 2001). Actually, and due to its close connection with the internationalization of capital and the globalization of markets, we can define this return of finance as hegemonic and a form of new imperialism. Especially if we consider the class-struggle claim made by Duménil and Lévy (2005): "It is finance that dictates its forms and contents in the new stage of internationalization; it is not internationalization or globalization that create the insuperable necessity for the present evolution of capitalism." That is, the reassertion of the power of finance is an ideological expression, something devised by, and in favor of, a wealthy social minority, this minority (financial capitalists, rentiers, financiers) being the social elite that owns the financial capital and/or rules the financial institutions (Duménil & Lévy, 2005).

Epstein and Jayadev (2005: 67) have reinforced this idea by showing how the finance elite (financial institutions and owners of financial assets) has been able to greatly increase its share of the national income in a variety of Organization for Economic Co-operation and Development (OECD) countries since the early 1980s. Therefore, because their results suggest that neoliberalism and financialization pay for those owning financial assets, one can "surmise that the rentiers promote policies that fatten their bottom lines." Because these policies do not equally favor the rest of society (in fact, finance attempts to impose the consequences of their risky movements on others jeopardize moderate and healthy growth and employment and deepen crises, or they even create new crises through policies focused on inflation rather than on employment), their imposition is an act of hegemony

THE FALLACY OF FINANCIAL CAPITALISM BEING OVERCOME THANKS TO ICTS

Despite everything asserted up to this point, different authors since the early 1990s—mostly proceeding from techno-utopian and conservative spheres—have been building a story of the end of the economy as was formerly understood in light of the seductive digital myth. Whether to offer the promise of a *new capitalism* or to promise the end of capitalism as the dominant form of economic organization, a theory is set forth that claims that mercantile capitalism, precapitalism, industrial capitalism, and even financial capitalism have been left behind and something has been initiated for which terms are coined that are as vague as they are varied: new economy, digitalism, or digital economy, to name but a few. Nevertheless, as is evident, the rupture that starts this supposed new era does not alter at all the basic mechanisms of advanced capitalism. On the contrary, the history of the last phase of world capitalism is intrinsically linked to an international upsurge of financial capitalism—or financial globalization—which indicates that the financialization of the economy, described by Hilferding in Germany as early as the start of the 20th century, is a consolidated, expanded, and growing reality worldwide at the start of the 21st century.

As a matter of fact, the first acceleration phase of the current process of globalization, during the second half of the 20th century, had financial capital as its main protagonist. This is true to such an extent that the financial dimension is the most extended and important of all dimensions of globalization. Capital is even an integral part of the definitions of globalization, as happens with the one given by Andrés S. Suárez Suárez (2001): "The term [globalization] is applied to the process of progressive integration of national economies in the framework of the world market, to the process of liberalization market exchanges and international capital flow, which continues the trends to openness or liberalization of the foreign exchanges of preceding times [...]" (Suárez Suárez, 2001: 2).

There are two elements that favor this situation. The first one has to do with political will, stimulated by the arrival of certain political leaders to the governments of financially strong countries. These leaders espoused the need to reinstate the free market, which they irremediably associated with economic prosperity (the main ones were Reagan in the United States and Thatcher in the United Kingdom). The second element has to do with the exponential growth of technological development experienced in highly developed countries, especially in communications and transportation. There are other causes of the acceleration of economic globalization during the second half of the 20th century, such as the role of the World Trade Organization and major multinational corporations, and the acceptance of American cultural values throughout the world, but none is as powerful as the first two.

As to ICTs, their main impact over the world's economic organization has not been, up to now, to overwhelm financial capitalism, but rather to aid in its acceleration and expansion. This statement is easily corroborated through some of the main legacies of financial globalization (such as tax havens and clearinghouses) and through the simple comparison of current financial magnitudes with real economy data.

ICTs and Tax Havens[1]

The integration of financial markets at such a speed and scope ("a quantum leap," according to Blecker, 2005) would have been completely impossible without new ICTs. But the greater speed, connection, and data control that ICTs allowed was not exploited, paradoxically, to create a more transparent system—essential for legal business—but, rather, to escape from the transparency itself. Indeed, the phenomenon of capital internationalization in such a way accelerated in the 1970s was going to experience an unprecedented splitting at the same time when a new system parallel to the legitimate one was born: tax havens.

Tax haven is the popular denomination by which the offshore financial centers are known, where *offshore* is a euphemism for "located in a lawless land" (or with a relaxed legal regime). Tax havens—also born in the 1970s—peaked around the 1980s, this peak being associated with the suppression of legal impairments, exchange controls, and the development of telecommunications, which have intensified the international movements of financial capitals. Their growth has been fostered by the flows of digital information, which allow the easy and inexpensive transfer of money and data in real time (Hernández-Vigueras, 2005, 2008).

After many hindrances—due to the opposition of many countries—at the end of the 1990s, a group of strong countries within the OECD agreed that offshore territories serve essentially for tax evasion and capital laundering. In 2000, OECD finally identified 35 countries and territories that should be considered tax havens (Organization for Economic Co-operation and Development, 2000). This figure would increase and change later depending on the classifying organizations and according to a degree of permissiveness. The absolute permissiveness is found in countries such as the Bahamas, the Cayman Islands, and the British Virgin Islands, where neither financial audits nor presentation of accounts in any public office are required, even the communication of profits or the identification of the society's managers and/or shareholders. There, the legislation to repress transactions and laundering of money arising from crime is only recent. Less permissive tax havens are Andorra, Barbados, Jamaica, or Monaco, where specifications of obtained profits, the register of social accounts in public registries, and the compulsory identification of the managers are all now required.

As the Tax Justice Network (TJN) reminds us, data on the value of wealth held offshore are hard to come by because neither governments nor the international financial institutions seems either able or willing to research the global picture. Some investment banks and financial institutions had been sporadically providing data in recent years, but the flow of publicly issued information seems to have been drastically cut down after some nongovernmental organizations (NGOs) (as was the case with Tax Justice Network) used these data to denounce offshore permissiveness. Nevertheless, the figures that are known show a clear expansion of tax havens parallel to the expansion of financial globalization and neoliberalism.

The BIS, an institution controlled by banks, estimated in June 2004 that offshore bank deposits totaled US$2.7 trillion out of US$14.4 trillion total bank deposits. This means that approximately one fifth of all deposits were held offshore that year. However, this figure relates solely to cash and excludes all other financial assets, such as stocks, shares, bonds, real estate, or gold (typically controlled through offshore companies, foundations, and trusts that do not furnish—that is why they are off-shore—annual accounts) (Tax Justice Network, 2005).

According to data released by Merrill Lynch and Cap Gemini, TJN estimated the 2005 figure for assets held offshore by high net-worth individuals to be US$9.7 trillion, which represented more than 30% of all liquid financial assets held by that group. From this, TJN calculates that the overall tax loss resulting from wealthy individuals holding their assets offshore was US$255 billion that year.

The role of the banking system in this phenomenon is also clearly visible within the sector records themselves. In 2000, Merrill Lynch calculated that at least half of the US$6 trillion located in offshore centers was placed in banks located in tax haven countries (Merrill Lynch/Cap Gemini Ernst & Young, 2001). That is, according to the estimations of the banking system, a third of the financial assets of high net-worth individuals (people with more than US$2 million in financial asset wealth) can be found offshore, and banks manage at least half of them.

Financial entities have thousands of branches sited in tax havens. Most of these are not offices from unknown banks, but delegations or branches belonging to the world's main financial companies. Their existence, and the whole existence of offshore regimes, is due to political reasons (no government has proven to a have real interest in fighting this phenomenon) and to the deployment of ICTs, including the lack of transparency in their use, permitted also for political reasons. It is possible to state that new technologies have been, and still are, working in the service of the greatest possible profit operated by agents whose final objective is to evade legislations with poorly liberalized tax systems.

However, to speak about difficulties in the control of capital movement and the impossibility to control movements, transactions and intangible flows can only be an ignorance-related fickleness. Nothing is more tangible than the electrical impulse that forms the digital bit of information. Indeed, ICTs (essentially computing and telecommunications), which set up electronic banking transactions in the second half of the 20th century, did not subsume the banking system within the virtual shadows. Instead, they put the very key to transparency in our hands. The fact that all the transactions are conducted electronically does not mean that they can be hidden from public opinion, but rather that they are under a greater control; an absolute control in fact. Nowadays everything remains recorded in electronic registries. Although these electronic registries can be erased, manipulated, or altered, this is at the expense of leaving a footprint. Never before has a similar tool to control such complex systems been available.

ICTs and Clearing

Therefore, it is not a paradox but common sense that the same technology which allows parallel opaque financial systems to exist may be the key to change this state of affairs. This is the main lesson to extract from an important investigation embodied in two books that have had hardly any impact on public opinion: *Révélations* (Revelations) (2001) and *La boîte noire* (The Black Box) (2002). Both books were written by French researcher and journalist Denis Robert, with the help of an insider from one of the two big cross-border clearing societies, Ernest Backes, co-author of *Révélations*. Denis and Backes describe a long and dense investigation proving, among other things, that the weakness of the criminal financial system stems from the strength of the system—that is, from the use of ICTs. To understand this, we must first talk about the contemporary history of the financial systems and the meaning of clearing.

During the early 1970s, several banks established around the world decided to associate and set up an interbanking cooperative. At that time, they were only 100 (today they add up to more than 2,000), and their objective was to create a system to facilitate international banking exchanges, which would be called clearing. Denis Robert explains it in this way:

Let's go back some decades. When an insurance agent from Chicago wanted to sell part of his company's capital to a Greek ship owner, how did he do it? He went to see his banker, let's say the Bank of New York, and charged him with the task of selling the bonds. The banker took a plane to Athens, where he was going to meet with the ship owner's banker, for instance the Greek subsidiary of the ABN AMRO Bank. Clearing allows, on one hand, to save time, and therefore, money. It is not necessary to travel. From then on, a central organization has guaranteed the happening of the exchange. The basic principle is trivial: bankers from different countries should join to create a confidence area where the banking exchange will be registered and guaranteed. Unlike the stock exchange market, which brings together the different elements of a transaction, a clearing company is an infrastructure apparently passive. It takes care of registering and guaranteeing the modification. The bonds do not move, only the name of the owner is changed. (Robert & Backes, 2001: 22–23)

The clearing system, also known as *compensation systems*, was meant to bypass the minimum 2 weeks that the foreign buyer had to wait before the bonds arrived (e.g., a Rome bank buying IBM shares from a bank in New York as requested by a client). It was aimed at avoiding time and money costs (the shipment had to be insured, and precious time was wasted while the bonds were physically traveling).

The first clearing society, Euroclear, was created in 1968 in Brussels and was founded by an American bank, Morgan Guaranty Trust Company of New York, which at the time was the biggest private bank in the world. The second clearing society appeared in 1970, called Cedel (now Clearstream, a company owned by the German stock exchange), as a reaction from the European and American banks that had not participated in the creation of the first clearing society.

These are the only two current transnational clearing societies. Euroclear and Clearstream allow their member institutions to exchange titles (shares, securities, etc.) to balance their accounts after performing operations at their own risk or on behalf of their clients. Their success was such that all current important international transactions are now dealt with by one of these two societies exclusively. A compulsory step that involves "the almost real time recording and storing of a footprint of a transaction in codified documents" (Robert & Backes, 2001: 24).

Although these are the only two clearing systems at a cross-border level in the world, clearing systems exist at the national level in almost every country. Their tasks are limited to domestic compensatory operations of capital exchange, and the amounts of money shifted around by the national societies cannot be compared at all to those of the international societies. In 2007, the total number of international transactions processed by Clearstream rose to 176 million, while the value of assets held in custody on behalf of customers rose to approximately EUR 10.5 trillion.

In summary, since the 1970s, clearing "has learned to make itself discretely essential" (Robert & Backes, 2001: 40) and has been progressing in close association with economic liberalization. "Clearing has contributed to the foundation of what economy and financing journalists have christened as the Global Village (much later after bankers and clearing users started using this term). A Village where power and information centers are interconnected" (Robert & Backes, 2001: 41). Currently, there is no important international transaction that is not channeled through one of these two big companies, Euroclear and Clearstream. The clearing system has become, in the words of a Clearstream ex-official, "the world's notary" (Robert & Backes, 2001: 244).

Sure enough, the rulers of the clearing societies are the new world's digital notaries. Every single international or national financial transaction is registered there, and anyone trying to avoid the clearing societies risks ending up outside the world's banking system. That is, international clearing systems are the mechanisms of mutual confidence created by banks so they have a chance to play on the world's financial field. It is an organized system that has accompanied the explosion of financial markets, and here is the big discovery by Denis Robert: Clearing has superbly adjusted to the interest of some key groups.

Robert concludes that these systems are an ideal method for money hiding and laundering, and this is the way they are being used. Thanks to a perversion of the clearing systems, states Robert, fraud opportunities at the international level are made much easier, making them practically undetectable. But, even if undetectable and invisible for public control, they still exist and can be prosecuted. Robert and Backes describe details of this with a wealth of evidence. They reveal how both clearing societies use the undisclosed accounts system (created for a particular legitimate use) to hide certain transactions. Transactions carried out in these undisclosed accounts represent, according to Robert and Backes, a tremendous opportunity for those seeking "maximal discretion in the global village" and succulent profits for the clearing society.

In summary, both researchers claim that clearing societies, in addition to being used for the objectives they were intended—to facilitate international transactions, thus providing the conditions for financial and economic globalization by the end of the 1990s—are used as a means for organized crime.

Indeed, although Clearstream and Euroclear were created to speed up the exchange of equities and to avoid the physical transfer of titles and money, this would not have been possible without the fundamental role of ICTs. Essentially, computing and telecommunications enabled the creation of clearing societies, which in turn guarantee their management. All clearing societies keep records of every single transaction performed. Even if they tried not to do so, it would be absurd because this is their safety guarantee against their most influential clients. It is the use of this sophisticated technology that makes these societies trustworthy; it is precisely their technology that allows managing the complexity of the system and keeping it under control. Any judicial or criminal inquiry about international crime would be able to progress drastically if it had open access to the registries of these two big societies.

ICTs are related to such a degree to the creation and maintenance of the financial world core that the main instrument of these clearing societies is itself a technology company: The Society for Worldwide Interbank Financial Telecommunication (SWIFT). SWIFT was created by the main shareholders of the two international clearing systems (a group of 239 European and North American banks) in Belgium in 1973. Currently, it belongs to more than 3,000 banks and connects more than 7,600 financial institutions. The aim of creating SWIFT was to provide clearing societies with an instrument for extra fast transmission of cash in every currency. Nowadays, nearly all the banks in the world are connected by means of this system. SWIFT is the technology platform that links all the world's financial institutions and that is used by the two big clearing societies.

However, the clearing societies and SWIFT are not the only links in the chain for those wanting to launder money. An accomplice entry bank that is ready to risk accepting doubtful funds must be involved. But this is not a problem thanks to tax havens. Robert and Backes (2001) go further in stating that "tax havens would not exist without large trading banks and without the international clearing societies belonging to these large trading banks" (Robert & Backes, 2001: 252). They add that the growth of offshore systems is nearly paralleled by the growth of the clearing system.

In short, ICTs enable reliable and safe interconnection of finances around the world. But this interconnection belongs in the private hands of the interconnected agents themselves, which has led to "unsustainable diversions to the detriment of transparency in the markets" (Robert & Backes, 2001: 261). The pretended self-regulation of the financial markets and the agreements among some large banks and multinational companies, trying to hide their benefits, has added to the substantial profits arising from managing gains related to terrorism and drug dealing. This has led to the perversion of the system, which, still working for its legitimate original purpose, has suffered an illicit broadening of its uses.

It goes without saying that ICTs are not to blame for this, but it is rather the result of political decisions. Obviously, at the same time that ICTs are used to propel financial globalization and its perversions, digital technologies provide the solution to the problems created. Actually, clearing societies offer an ideal point of view: They are the perfect vantage point over the financial markets. Technically, and thanks to ICTs, it should not be a problem to claim a tax for international transactions, to control the main financial movements in the world, or to ascertain the whereabouts of large sums of vanished money as long as the international clearing system made its technological platform accessible to magistrates, the police, politicians, and citizens. When a journalistic source speaks about an enormous volume of illegal or crime-related money that is vanished and evades justice, what this source should rather talk about is money "protected within the opacity" in which clearing societies work. Money is not evaded; rather, what have been evaded are legal responsibilities. The reason is simple: Clearing—the real functioning of the markets, the technological foundation for world finances— is an absolute unknown. This issue has been mentioned here as a means to point out the extent to which ICTs are contributing to strengthen, rather than to defeat, the logic of financial capitalism despite all the promises of the digital myth.

Virtual Economy Versus Real Economy

Finally, the main evidence of the fact that financialization has consolidated and expanded, rather than having been overridden, in today's world economy lies in the current financial market figures that have already been mentioned here and in the comparison of financial turnover data with real economy figures.

We have seen that in the past 20 years, from the beginning of the 1990s, financial markets (equity or stock markets; securities trading; all kind of derivatives such as bonds, futures, mortgages, options, or swaps; corporate debt; foreign exchange trading; etc.) have experienced dramatic growth. Derivatives, for example, have played a role in commerce and finance for thousands of years. The term *derivative* refers "to how the prices of these contracts are derived from the price of some underlying security of commodity or from some index, interest rate, exchange rate or event" (Dodd, 2005: 149). What makes current derivatives different from the ones that date back to 12th-century Venice is that today the size of derivatives markets is enormous and by some measures, according to Randall Dodd, exceeds those of bank lending, securities, and insurance. From BIS data, we can observe that OTC derivatives' (OTC refers to the Over the Counter market) global market turnover rose 232% between 1998 and 2007, leaping from US$1.3 trillion to US$4.2 trillion. From BIS data, we can also observe that global foreign exchange market turnover leapt from US$0.8 billion to US$3.2 billion from 1992 to April 2007, a rise of 265%. The extent to which this massive increase in the volume of derivatives and foreign exchange trading can be accounted for by speculative activity is surmised by comparing the figures for the volume of world trade, which shows no equivalent increase. Another usual comparison is done with gross domestic product (GDP). For instance, in the United States, the country with the largest use of financial markets, GDP growth between 1998 and 2007 rose only 57%, from US$8,747 to US$13,807. The U.S. mortgage giants Fannie Mae and Freddie Mac were the world's largest end users of derivatives and were also the first to collapse in the financial crisis starting in mid-2007.

But the pace of financialization is also spectacular in developing countries. In India, for instance, market capitalization was about US$150 billion in 2004 and leapt to almost US$1 trillion in 2007, a huge rise especially considering that in 2007 India's GDP rose by the same amount. That means that the ratio between market capitalization and GDP (the percentage of GDP that represents stock market value) was 100%. Typically, a result greater than 100% is said to show that the market is overvalued. In 2000, according to statistics at the World Bank, the market capitalization to GDP ratio for the United States was 153%, a sign of an overvalued market. Then the dotcom bubble burst, and in 2003 the ratio was around 130% again.

Other ways of calculating the percentage of speculative activity, and by doing so observing the degree of financialization of the real economy, is comparing total financial market turnover with GDP. This is a difficult exercise because of the large amount and complexity of financial market products, but the attempts applied to countries such as the United States show a dramatic drop of GDP as percentage of financial turnover. In the 1960s the U.S. GDP represented around 50% of total financial turnover, whereas in 2007 this percentage fell to less than 5%.

For many, the financial crisis starting in 2007 and the economic crisis that followed was a surprise of unexpected brutality. Actually, the degree, extent, and scope of this crisis, unknown at the moment of this writing, will probably be one of the best evidences of the degree, extent, and scope of financialization in the world economy. But as Blecker (2005) put it clearly: The question is not the extent of financialization, huge as it evidently is, but the lack of control or attention to it when "large parts of conventional international economic theory, in both the trade and finance branches, need to be abandoned for inconsistency with the realities of globalized finance in today's world economy" (Blecker, 2005: 200). Again we are not facing an issue that needs an economic or technological solution, but rather a political one. Let us put it as Leonard Seabrooke did:

"Greater financial internationalization has been facilitated by technology but states still regulate finance and are able to impose controls." The consequences of not doing this are far reaching. We will see in the following pages what they are and what the dominance of finance throughout the recent history of capitalism and financialization mean, in particular for the news media industry (see Almiron, 2007).

2

Finance and Information

The history of the media has been deeply linked to the history of banking from the beginning. As we pointed out in the Introduction, the elites— among them the early bankers—were the first to finance and use newspapers. It was not by chance that the first European newspaper was published by a family of bankers, the Fugger, in the 16th century in Augsburg, Germany. Nor was it a fluke that in 1856 bankers Heinrich Bernhard Rosenthal and Leopold Sonnermann, Germans as well, founded the *Frankfurter Geschafsbericht*—later to become the *Frankfurter Allgemeine Zeitung*—with the purpose of providing information on the stock market. Again, it was no accident that some of the first and most important news agencies should specialize in financial information. Reuters, for instance, was founded in London in 1851 by a German immigrant with the sole purpose of transmitting stock market quotations between London and Paris. It still remains the main agency specializing in financial information and one of the most profitable news agencies (merged with Canadian Thomson in 2008). The course of some of the largest journalistic empires, such as American Dow Jones and British Financial Times Group—created in 1884 and 1888, respectively—is a reflection of the fact that the economics of information and information on economics are two aspects that are profoundly intermingled in corporate media history (Arrese, 2003). Bankers were the first clients of the international news agencies in the 19th century and still are great purchasers of specialized information.

So far, however, these facts have not generated cross-studies—either multidisciplinary or transdisciplinary—on both sectors, finance and information, to thoroughly address these relations. For various causes, the connection between the financial and media systems has long been avoided or approached by few authors only in a tangential manner. Nevertheless, because of its preeminent role in advanced capitalism and because of its many intersections, this is a subject worthy of an extensive multidisciplinary analysis.

The interest for such a study is manifold. In the first place, it is necessary to document the linkage between the global system of commercial communications media and the economy of global financial capitalism. In-depth research on the relationship between both sectors is scarce, and whatever lines of research address it do so only partially. The cause for this is rooted in both technical reasons and tradition. Multidisciplinary studies as such are traditionally scarce in the social sciences, especially so if they involve financial subjects whose technical difficulty is not only the second cause for the lack of such studies, but also the main reason for their limitations, as banking secrecy and confidentiality hinder independent researchers from accessing a great many data. In the second place, research about two actors that are among the modern capitalist system's main industries is, in itself, of interest, and more so at this time, when the process of growing financialization in the economy as a whole is placing the media's principles and values of social responsibility ever farther away. This interest, obviously, increased after the 2007–2009 financial crisis, with its impact on all branches of the real economy.

Paradoxically, the very process of financialization could motivate greater information transparency regarding the structure, results, and strategies of the media system. Although the lack of public data in the sphere of finance is not completely neutralized, information sources are doubtlessly and considerably increasing—the presence of media firms in the stock market is multiplying the need for more transparent information concerning them, and information and communication technologies (ICTs) facilitate access to the new information thus generated.

Third and last, because of the evidence regarding major links between the financial and the media systems and, at the same time, because of the scarcity of multidisciplinary studies that address both realms transversely and in depth, there seems to be an evident need for evaluating these connections, not only quantitatively but also qualitatively. The purpose would be to determine what the dependencies generated by such relations are, and who they are generated on, and to discover whether it is possible to speak of a convergence of shared interests or whether subordinations of interests or some needs that are greater than others can be detected.

In short, the necessity of such an analysis derives from the necessity of rethinking journalism as a "democratic craft," as G. Stuart Adam and Roy Peter Clark (2006) point out in their book. It is a craft with an important place in the architecture of democracy and that has, as was the case with ICTs, a vantage point and a platform for promoting democratic values.

THE HISTORICAL LINKS BETWEEN MODERN FINANCE AND MODERN MEDIA

We cannot deal with the financialization of the media industry today without going to the roots of the relationship between finance and information.
The origins of modern communication are tightly tied to the origins of modern finance, that is, of modern banking. From the 17th to the beginning of the 20th centuries, the constitutive choices about modern media (chiefly the press, postal and telecommunications networks, cinema, and broadcasting) took place in the context of larger political and economic transformations. One of the biggest changes during this period was the creation of a modern banking system.
In the late 15th and 16th centuries, several private and state postal networks (to which the development of newsletters, the antecedents of newspapers, was closely related) were created. The more enduring postal services were developed directly under state authority, but by the early 1600s European state authorities, although maintaining their monopoly, started opening their postal services to the public. Through these private and public networks, postal services supported the creation of news networks. The first elite to have direct access to such information was a mixture of merchants, diplomats, nobles, and bankers. In fact, financial and commercial exchanges were what primarily pushed for news exchanges — they still do so to a considerable extent. Also, we must not forget the original link between trade and banking: Country banks were typically founded by the most prosperous traders in their locality. The first big bankers (Hans/Jean-Konrad Hottinger, 1764–1841; Jacques Laffitte, 1767–1844; Jules Paul Benjamin Delessert, 1773–1847; Casimir Pierre Périer, 1777–1832; James Mayer de Rothschild, 1792–1868; etc.) were mostly and firstly merchants, the so-called "merchant-bankers" (Ackrill & Hannah, 2001: 33; Bouvier, 1992: 48; Starr, 2004: 31).
Newsletters had been a conventional form of correspondence since Roman times, but in the late Middle Ages newsletters among well-known trading and banking families began to cross frontiers regularly with the same goal as many business newspapers and media outlets of today: to transmit important information about the markets and to analyze that information. The owners of an important financial house in the German

city of Augsburg, the Fugger family, were the publishers of the first and most important newsletter of that kind in the 16th century, but there were many other early bankers pushing for news publishing.

In England, one of the communities with the longest experience of publishing in the 17th century (although clandestine due to the persecution they suffered by reason of their beliefs) were the Quakers, who also used this expertise in the foundation of Pennsylvania, 1 of the original 13 colonies that formed the United States. From the 17th to 18th centuries, the Quakers were also one of the main private banking communities in England. The Quaker community built on several trust networks that helped them to progress, as the information network extended to north European and transatlantic trade that gave a fundamental advantage to English Quaker bankers (Ackrill & Hannah, 2001: 23–58; Starr, 2004: 52–54).

In the early 19th century, the Rothschild family laid the foundations of their fortune in two ways: the commissions earned on the transactions related to the financing of the British war effort against Napoleon, and speculation regarding the exchanges preceding and following wars and depressions, as well as by the accumulation of interest. The Europe-wide network of messengers and carrier pigeon stations, gathering critical information for their investments, which they set up before the telegraph era, was a key element of their success. Later, in the mid-19th century, the foundation of the British Empire's news agency, Reuters, was also based on pigeons and financial information. Reuters started functioning in 1850, using carrier pigeons to forward stock-market and commodity prices from Brussels, where the Belgian telegraph line ended, to Aachen, where the German line began (Read, 1992).

Actually, the clearest precedents of the printed press were newsletters and courier services created in response to the commercial and financial needs of several big merchant bankers. Some of these even directly founded the first modern newspapers, as was the case with German bankers Heinrich Bernhard Rosenthal and Leopold Sonnermann, who in 1856 launched the *Frankfurter Geschafstbericht*, a newsletter devoted to stock-market news and later converted into the *Frankfurter Allgemeine Zeitung*. Nor should we neglect the common historical and cultural links between the first bankers and the first successful mass producers of news, the founders of news agencies. Hannah Arendt, in her demystification of the common anti-Semite myth of "Jewish bankers," traced the relationships between European Jews other political-economic classes and the nation-state. She argued that Jews, being outside and left aside from other classes, depended on the nation-state for protection, while nation-states depended on Jews for their financial dealings. Arendt showed how this dual dependence spawned an exaggerated notion of Jewish power, which in part led to modern anti-Semitism. However, in doing so, she also showed how the Jews became state bankers (a few Jews, like the Rothschild family, even played a significant role as international bankers), financial consultants, peace treaty collaborators, and news providers. This last point is supported by the fact that all the major founders of news agencies in the 19th century were Jews: Julius Reuter, Charles Havas, and Bernhard Wolff (Arendt, 1951).

The relationship between the information and financial industrial sectors set up in the 19th century is best reflected by the alliance laid down between modern colonial empires and news agencies. It is no coincidence that in the mid-19th century London simultaneously became a financial center and a news center. As Donald Read stated in his history of Reuters, in 1851, London constituted the focal point of the rapidly developing international economy because the City of London provided services for the commerce and industry not just of Britain and her empire but of the whole world. "Julius Reuter was to add significantly to that centrality by making London the news centre of the world" (Read, 1992: 14). The German and French empires also built the same tight connection between their economic expansion and their national news agencies. The three of them functioned as institutions of their respective empires, being protected by them and contributing to their spread and consolidation. Their first and most important clients were bankers. They still are (although bankers currently represent a wider and more diverse community of people in the so-called financial elite).

Bankers were also one of the first groups to ask for the end of the monopolistic state service in the electrical telegraph era in 19th-century France. A telegraphic fraud committed in 1836 by two French bankers reopened this debate in the heart of Europe and attested to the relationship between the emergence of the stock markets and telegraph news. The two French bankers had been illegally using the public service to send information about the stock market in the French city of Tours in order to access news before it appeared in the newspapers (Flichy, 1997).

FIRST USAGE OF ELECTRICAL TELEGRAPH

Country	Stock Market	Trade	Domestic	Others
France (1851)	38%	28%	25%	9%
Great Britain (1854)	50%	31%	13%	6%
Belgium (1851)	60%	19%	10%	11%

Source: Flichy (1997)

As the table shows, the transmission of stock-market news was the first major usage of the electrical telegraph. According to Flichy, half of the traffic of this new medium was only for use by the stock market, the telegraph supporting the emergence of the stock market:

> Therefore, the links between the stock exchange and the electrical telegraph are tight. During the 1940s, in England, the railway boom heavily increased the activity in the London stock exchange and, at the same time, a dozen province stock exchanges were born. Circulation of information among these sites was provided by the newborn telegraph. (Flichy, 1997: 70)

The marriage between the commercial telegraph and the financial sectors was threefold: Bankers funded the construction of new lines, bankers became the main users, and bankers pushed the financial news business through them. They were not the only actors, but they can be considered the key ones.

Furthermore, the role of the telegraph in the construction of the economic imperialism of the 19th century is not ideology-free:

> [The electric telegraph] falls within the development of the capitalist market era, in mid-XIX Century. It contributes to the growth of financial markets, and also of trade. This main use of it is not a coincidence, [...]. It is, particularly, in tune with the economic theories of the moment: English liberalism, Saint-Simonian trends in France. It falls within the context of both coasts of the English Channel, within the movement of ideas in favor of free trade. (Flichy, 1997: 72)

Two of the largest and most successful current news media brands were also born in the late-19th century. Both were publishers of business and financial news and information; in fact, they are believed to have been the creators of financial journalism. In 1884, Dow Jones, the *Wall Street Journal* publisher and the entity responsible for several widely used stock-market indexes, was founded. In 1888, the *Financial Times* empire was born. Their history and achievements again reflect the deep connection between information and finance.

The state-owned, politically controlled, and partisan press that progressively and, in that order, mainly arose in the above scenario from the 16th to the 19th centuries was radically modified with the turn of the 20th century. Throughout the 19th century, journalism had gradually been shifting to a full-fledged commercial system while the logic of industrial capitalism finally created the modern mass media in the 20th century, with its huge corporate conglomerates. Advertising now paid the costs of publishing, providing much more revenue to publishers than subscriptions or newsstand sales. The barriers to entry into the media markets rose sharply, while competition fell off in different intensities and ways depending on the country. The big-business publishing of the new era meant many different things for the press and the new broadcasting media that joined the old media, but one of the biggest changes was its increasing dependence on the financial sector (McChesney & Scott, 2004: 1–21; H. Schiller, 1989).

The global communication networks that have expanded throughout the planet (from submarine cable, to telegraph lines and the telephone, at first, and the current satellite and wireless digital telecommunications later) have been and are highly capital-demanding. Hence, throughout the 20th century, moving up the technology-productivity-value-added ladder meant, for all media companies, becoming an increasingly capital-intensive company—and internalizing the "liberal paradox," as Crotty has defined it. That is, the obvious contradiction between the "necessary lasting investment in production," with its specific financial risks, and "this absolute freedom of movement demanded by finance," which increases the fragility of finance and the economy. The oligopolistic and monopolistic trends introduced by industrial capitalism first and then by financial capitalism tightened the links between the news company and the banking system by persuading media companies to increase competitiveness and raise capital needs, which increases financial dependence, while financial funding markets became more and more impatient and demanding in the short term. This scenario has brought the media industry into a new stage of financing needs and goals (Crotty, 2005: 41).

THE NEOLIBERALIZATION OF CULTURAL AND COMMUNICATIONS INDUSTRIES

In the early 1980s, Cees Hamelink (1984) had already depicted the embryonic financialization of modern late 20th-century media corporations, although he did not yet use this term. Hamelink's contribution showed significant financial influence and dependence in the transnational information industry of the late 1970s,[2] an influence and dependence larger than those existing in other industrial activities. In his research, the Dutch professor found a highly oligopolistic scenario for the transnational information and banking industries of that time. According to him, the increasing funding and information interests and needs of the information and banking sectors, respectively, revealed both industries to be on the path to convergence in three respects: (a) *Technological*: What Hamelink terms *digital transfer* of all manners of information affects deeply both the information industry and the financial system. The financial system is an important consumer of new information technologies, and the information industry is a supplier of them. (b) *Operative*: Corporations in the information industry sell financial information and several banking services, whereas banks offer various information services. (c) *Financial*: Corporations in the information industry need large-scale financing, and banks provide them with credit. In addition to the lender–borrower relationship, major banking institutions own stock in the information industry and in many cases are represented in companies' boards of directors.

This convergence of interests, especially on the operative and financial levels, led Hamelink to conclude that banks were in a position to exert a decisive influence over fundamental issues in the policies of informative corporations. The most important consequence of this is that the finance sector controls information resources through fund assignment (Hamelink, 1984: 140).

From this derive two types of control that banks can exercise over the information industry. *Operative control* makes reference to the control that is exerted over the everyday operations of a corporation. Much more important is *control over information resources through fund allotment*. In this type of control, influence is applied through the power derived from the capacity to assign or withhold the funds that the firm considers necessary. In this respect, Hamelink stated that control through fund allotment has a decisive influence over the market and over society as a whole, and, therefore, from this standpoint, the interdependence between banks and the information industry adopts the form of domination of the former over the latter. How does this affect the media's production and distribution? The effect, according to this author, is threefold:

(a) *On their existence and operation*. Because the activities of the information industry are highly capital-intensive, to be granted funds by banks is determinant for the existence and future of the elect. Therefore, the power of banks resides in their capacity to determine the number of media that can exist at any given moment according to the support they decide to grant them.

(b) *On their degree of concentration*. According to Hamelink, perhaps banks do not have too much influence over the information produced by each medium, but they certainly do in deciding which media they support financially and, therefore, what kind of information attains greater circulation. The high levels of concentration in the journalistic industry are, therefore, directly related to the close links maintained between the banks and the information industry.

(c) *On their autonomy and diversity*. The concern about the interconnections between banking and the information industry is not limited to the fact that the former contributes greatly to the oligopolization of the latter, but also extends to the information content and the limitations to journalistic independence produced by such interconnections. Hamelink states serious doubts as to the autonomy and diversity that the information industry can maintain being linked so to the banks.

This early work does not yet mention the financialization of the media system, of the cultural industries, or of the news media firms, but it is the first study that refers to and delves widely into the emergence of the mechanisms of correlation and convergence between both industries— media and finance. The massive needs of financing that liberalization and privatization would require in the years to come was to turn this tendency toward convergence identified in the late 1970s into a consolidated and much more complex reality 30 years later. The banks' capacity for influence through fund assignment and finance's dominance over information would be transmuted, as will be seen below, into financial logics intrinsic to the modus operandi of major media conglomerates. Financialization internalizes financial logics to convert them into strategy. The dependence on the financial system that this generates in the corporation is evident, but it is a dependence that nowadays requires a more complex analysis that goes beyond external dominance on the part of financial capital.

Deregulation, Liberalization, and Concentration

Financial and economic globalization, its financialization and the new neoliberal logic applied during the second half of the 20th century by the governments of the world's major nations, with few exceptions, have led cultural and communications industries down the path of conglomeration that has modeled every other industrial sector during the last 50 years, including, most particularly, the banking sector. Although the United States was the first to conglomeratize its telecommunications and communications media starting in the late 1950s, the model was transplanted in the mid-1960s to the Western European countries. Japan and Latin America were to experiment with a similar but more acute process. In all cases, the dynamics would be threefold: concentration of the market and diversification, and internationalization—to a smaller or greater degree—of corporations.

   The causes for the above, as described by the diverse currents of authors, are numerous and diverse: technological convergence, globalization, industrial synergies, the deregulation and liberalization of markets, the emergence of new industries, shifts in the advertising market, greater competition, and even the demands of consumers or the opportunities for new services. If these are closely analyzed, it becomes evident, however, that a great part of these causes, if not all, have to do with public-policy shifts and technological change. Both phenomena are intrinsically inter-connected and, as shall be seen below, linked to financialization in that both political decisions and technological implementation are character-ized by an unprecedented ascendancy of the financial logic at their core.

Nevertheless, it is necessary to point out differences among coun-tries. The communications liberalization process started, indeed, as a U.S. phenomenon. In that country "with a classical alliance between the state and the major private groups," deregulation meant giving monop-olies access to new technologies and new markets. This implied "natu-rally, a gradual easing of the regulations that the FCC (Federal Communications Commission) had been constructing over the last decades for classical media, and a new philosophy of pluralism among multimedia groups, whose potent activity on multiple supports would be the greatest guarantee of diversity" (Bustamante & Zallo, 1988: 17).

As is well known, deregulation in the United States was based on the dominant belief in that country, although not shared by all its citizens, that the mere technical multiplication of supports and products, even if concentrated in the same hands, guarantees pluralism and diversity. Although the liberalizing process was adopted in Europe following prac-tically the same patterns, this idea did not have equal strength in the European continent. There, intellectual resistance to the American per-spective was based on the growing evidence that pluralism could not be maintained only by mere technological diversity of supports, channels, and media (Llorens, 2001: 123–142). In spite of this, the liberalizing model also became dominant in Europe. The breach that allowed its entry was, doubtless, the fiscal and ideological crisis of the welfare state, which, starting in the 1970s and 1980s, lay open many fronts on which an attack could be mounted against the intervention of the state in soci-ety (bureaucratization, dirigism, inefficiency, and restrictions to free trad-ing, among others). In general terms, in what concerned communica-tions and culture, the state in Europe "has been retreating from its role as operator or direct manager, to reappear as just one more actor in the market competition or, simply, to entrench into an arbitration role or as a platform to encourage consumption" (Bustamante, 2003: 36).

Deregulation opened the door to a greater commodification of culture that, in an increasingly globalized context, eventually became synonymous with two a priori antagonistic concepts: growing competition and growing concentration. Meanwhile, states showed a notable disorientation, if not an alarming certainty, about the infallibility of liberalization as a means to overcome a challenge that is not only technological and economic but also democratic (political, according to McChesney, 2007, 2008)

In this sense, Quirós (2002) states that "the relinquishment of states of the regulation of their media systems in order to ensure plurality, paradoxically wrapped in the flag of free enterprise, battered and badly damaged freedom of the press (always a secondary concern when dividends are at stake). [...]" In this framework were born the great conglomerates or multimedia groups in the three major hubs of world economy: the United States, Europe, and Japan.

The technological revolution and its consequences, such as digital convergence, may also have encouraged concentration. Miguel de Bustos (2003) gives diverse evidence on the perverse effects that this "convergence of telecommunications, broadcasting and computing industries" that was made possible by digitalization has had on the structure of the global media system (Miguel de Bustos, 2003: 227). In this respect, he concludes that digital convergence constitutes a new stage characterized by "a race toward gigantism" and by the diversification that gives media groups "a tremendous power of influence over pluralism," without guaranteeing its economic or corporate stability (Miguel de Bustos, 2003: 245). This was confirmed in the 2007–2009 financial crisis, which soon evidenced the precarious balance on which these corporate structures were sustained. In this line, Dan Schiller (2007) also reminds us that digital convergence is not a neutral process that occurs "through an intrinsic technological imperative." On the contrary, "convergence stems from a trio of complex changes linking science and technology development, industry strategy, and public policy" (Schiller, 2007: 103). The analysis of the development of the U.S. telecommunications system allows this academic to demonstrate that upon this trio, "business users have placed a formative and even a determinant role in the evolution of this infrastructure" (Schiller 2007: 63–79).

Last, in consonance with the above, we should observe the interrelation that deregulation and technological evolution have with financial globalization. The same political ideology that propels the processes of liberalization and privatization in the communications and information sectors also drives financial liberalization. The liberalization of finance has, as well, deep synergies with the technological revolution, which it backs in its expansion and development and without which the former could not have occurred. The process of global financialization has developed as a consequence of processes homologous with those that have impelled concentration in the cultural industries. In other words, the concentration experimented by the cultural industry sectors is closely related with their financialization, and, in turn, this financialization encourages the tendency toward concentration.

Concentration—the increase of the presence of one corporation or of a reduced group of corporations in a given market—is measurable through parameters such as income, profit, the number of employees, the number of media, and the audience share of each corporation. It has been and still is the main trait of cultural and communications industries, which in all capitalist countries have followed the same structural tendencies of businesses in the United States (well described, for instance, by Croteau & Hoynes, 2001). There is only one exception that is unique to the U.S. industry: its massive globalization or internationalization, much greater than that achieved by any other national industry. In concordance with this, the degree of financialization of the U.S. economy also holds an outstanding place and, as we point out later, its media system is also remarkable for the high degree of penetration of capital and financial logics into its core.

THE FINANCIALIZATION OF INFORMATION

As we have seen, the term *financialization* has been studied and developed from the critical perspective within different branches of the social sciences, mainly economics, political science, and sociology. It was only recently that the idea of studying the financialized pattern of accumulation of profit making was applied to the information and communication industries and, thus, to the media system. Doubtlessly, the first in-depth effort has come from the French scholarly community.

One of the first authors to approach this issue is Christian Pradié (2002, 2002a, 2005), who stated that it is not possible to dissociate the operation of cultural industries from the history of capitalism, at least in developed countries. For this author, the end of public monopolies and the development of private sectors in the broadcasting and telecommunications businesses constitute trends that approximate these sectors to the deregulatory movements in financial markets insofar as an increase in the pursuit of capital appreciation in new business is produced. Thus, the broadcasting and telecommunications sectors become "areas of social activity that evolve following conditions that tend to shift their main function into an area of financial placement assignments" (Pradié, 2005: 86).

Therefore, studying concentration phenomena in cultural industries only as economic phenomena is no longer enough, and it becomes necessary to study the financial logics that propel these phenomena. As we do this, our understanding of the economic model of cultural industries increases, and we confirm that this area is indeed undergoing a process of growing financialization.

For Pradié, the trends that drive the increase of capitals put into circulation in the sectors related with cultural industries are basically of three kinds: The first is the *concentration of economic power* through the growing accumulation of capitalist means of production that come under the control of, and become dependent on, an ever-decreasing number of decision centers. The second is the *internationalization of capital* belonging to corporations in the cultural industries. The third is the need to remunerate invested capitals according to the *principles that govern financial markets* (Pradié, 2005: 89).

Economic concentration, internationalization of capital, and industrialization of production in corporations of the communications sector have been studied by this and other authors (Bouquillion, 2008; Bouquillion & Combès, 2007; Bouquillion, Miège, & Pradié, 2003), and the results have been conclusive. In every instance, there is an evident correlation between, on the one hand, concentration, internationalization, and industrialization, and, on the other hand, financialization.

Thus, the greater the degree of corporate concentration is, the larger will be the internationalization of capital and the industrialization of production. By causing the organization of concentrated, internationalized, and industrialized production, the process of financialization produces major industrial shifts that transform the communications sector. What are those transformations? According to Pradié (2005), the main effect of financialization on cultural industries is to inject "into a preeminent part of the activities the traits that characterize quoted companies and the formation of strongly internationalized corporate groups with modes of production subject to productivity rules" (Pradié, 2005: 103). That is, the requirements of profitability are much greater in those corporations. On the other hand, the companies that maintain a degree of independence from financial markets have a small degree of concentration, are less internationalized, and have the means of production that approximate the artisanal and, therefore, have much smaller profitability requirements.

In this sense, Philippe Bouquillion (2005, 2008) reminds us that, from the 1990s, the main financial operations in the cultural and communications industries hold the first places on the financial operations ranking in the history of international finance. These financial macro-operations—that doubtlessly have generated a reduction in the number of independent decision centers and have submerged the markets of cultural industries into an oligopolistic logic—are both the sign and driving force of a new phase in the industrialization of culture and communications. In this new phase, grounded on globalization and financialization, standardization of cultural and intellectual products must increase in order to satisfy the profitability requirements of financial investors.

We must point out that, among the biggest mergers, the telecommunications sector is remarkable for its mergers. Nevertheless, media mergers are also among the biggest in history. As we can see in the following table, this merger euphoria is concentrated in a relatively short period of time, which coincides almost millimetrically with the outbreak of the financial globalization boom.

SOME OF THE BIGGEST CORPORATE MERGERS AND ACQUISITIONS IN HISTORY

Merging companies	Business area (Year of merger)	Transaction value in US$ in billions
Exxon (USA) buys Mobil (USA)	Oil (1998)	240
Vodafone Airtouch (UK) buys Mannesmann (Germany)	Telecomm (2000)	183
America Online (USA) buys Time Warner (USA)	Telecomm & Media (2001)	181
Citigroup is created after Citicorp (USA) acquisition by Travelers Group (USA)	Finance (1998)	140
MCI Worldcom (USA) buys Sprint (USA)	Telecomm (1999)	127
Pfizer (Germany) buys Warner Lambert (USA)	Pharmaceutical (1999)	88
SBC Telecomm (USA) buys Ameritech (USA)	Telecomm (1998)	72
Bank of America is created after Bank America (USA) acquisition by Nationsbank (USA)	Finance (1998)	65
Verizon is created by Bell Atlantic (USA) and GTE (USA)	Telecomm (1998)	71
Verizon Wireless is created by Bell Atlantic/ GTE (Verizon) (USA) and Vodafone (UK)	Telecomm (1999)	70
AT&T (USA) buys TCI (USA)	Telecomm (1998)	70
AT&T (USA) buys MediaOne (USA)	Telecomm (2000)	54
BNP Paribas is created after the acquisition of Paribas (France) by Banque National de Paris (France)	Finance (1999)	Around 50
British Petroleum (UK) buys Amoco (USA)	Oil (1998)	48
Bank of America (USA) buys FleetBoston Financial (USA)	Finance (2004)	47
Worldcom (USA) buys MCI (USA)	Telecomm (1998)	37
Bank of America (USA) buys MBNA (USA)	Finance (2005)	35
Viacom (USA) buys CBS (USA)	Media (1999)	35

Vivendi (France) buys Seagram (Canada)	Media (2000)	34
DaimlerChrysler is created after Chrysler (USA) acquisition by Daimler-Benz (Germany)	Automobile (1998)	33
The new Wells Fargo (USA) is created after Wells Fargo acquisition by Northwest (USA)	Finance (1998)	32
Unicredit (Italia) buys Capitalia (Italia)	Finance (2007)	29
Verizon Wireless (USA) buys Alltel (USA)	Telecomm (2008)	28.1 (22.2 in debt)
Wachovia (USA) buys Golden West Financial (USA)	Finance (2006)	25
Wachovia (USA) buys World Savings Bank (USA)	Finance (2007)	25
Deutsche Telekom (Germany) buys Voice Stream Wireless (USA)	Telecomm (2000)	24
Bank of America (USA) buys LaSalle Bank (USA)	Finance (2007)	21
Bank of America (USA) buys Merrill Lynch (USA)	Finance (end 2008)	19
Bank of New York (USA) buys Mellon Financial (USA)	Finance (2007)	18
Walt Disney (USA) buys ABC (USA)	Media (1995)	18
Santander Central Hispano (Spain) buys Abbey Bank (UK)	Finance (2004)	16
Time Inc. (USA) buys Warner Communications (USA)	Media (1989)	15
Wells Fargo (USA) buys Wachovia (USA)	Finance (end 2008)	13
BNP Paribas (France) buys Banca Nazionale del Lavoro (Italy)	Finance (2006)	11
Hypobank (Germany) buys Bayerische Vereinsbank (Germany)	Finance (1998)	10

Sources: Corporate press releases, finance authorities notes, and press clippings.
Note: Only transactions higher than US$10 billion are provided. Figures vary depending on sources, so this information is provided here only as a reference. Some top banking mergers are missing because of the lack of transparency in Europe about the value of merger transactions or because they were still in course at this writing.

On the basis of a study on financial, industrial, and geographical development of the major industrial groups active in the broadcasting and editorial sectors, Bouquillion describes how the strategies and tactics of these groups, guided essentially by short-term financial goals, can be set independently from industrial logics, whose effects are normally felt in the long term. Thus, it can be observed that financial matters play a leading role in most takeover operations by the leading communications groups and conglomerates. This is why Philippe Bouquillion applies the term *poles* to those great industrial communications groups (Bouquillion, 2008) because their synergies are not industrial but financial. At the same time, the exacerbation of the oligopolistic operation of the culture and communications industries is also inextricably joined to financial issues. Liberalization has been the driving force behind this financialization.

During the 1980s and 1990s, financial liberalization allowed the access of financial capital to sectorial and national communications markets despite the restrictions kept in place as entry barriers. The main, most influential financial actors—pension funds, credit ratings agencies, and financial analysts, among others—began to participate in all the new investment spaces opening up before them that promised good opportunities to make their investments profitable. The area of cultural industries, especially the media, was one of the new spaces in which the major international financial investors started to show interest. Aside from the former patrimonial income, these actors are extremely interested in large-scale corporate operations because they are an important source of revenue for them, mainly in the form of commissions. But in addition to commissions and investments, for the major financial actors these operations constitute a growth in power:

> Their influence over industrial actors increases, particularly their control over management. Once the operation has been concluded, they help define the contours of the new conglomerates. They also orient the great strategic decisions as well as the appointment of key managers. Again, after these operations and once the poles are dependent on financial operations (loans, bond issues, capital increases [...]), they can exercise a permanent influence over major strategic orientations. (Bouquillion, 2005: 119)

For this reason, Michel de Certeau and Philippe Bouquillion speak of *coups financiers* when referring to the great financialized corporate operations because they respond to financial tactics on the part of the actors who carry them out rather than to industrial strategies. Thus, a good part of the major corporate mergers were almost always accomplished through stock package swaps, the benefit of which went mainly to those who promoted them: financial institutions and officers with stock options. (The case of AOL and Time Warner and the purchase of ABC by Disney should be interpreted in this light: They were operations propelled and facilitated by major banking institutions strictly on criteria of financial profitability.) The tangible proof of this is the nil, and often negative, results that the majority of these mergers have had in purely industrial terms, even though they had been justified precisely in those terms (Bouquillion, 2008).

The first analyses of financialization in the information and communications sector were still too dependent on the classical research models centered on the concentration of the ownership of communications groups. *Financialization*, thus, was defined in a narrow sense, as a communications group going public and, by extension, as the participation of international financial actors in the capital of communications conglomerates. However, these studies were already pointing the way to overcome what up to that moment had been their biggest blind spot: the growing financial character of stockholder bases concurrent with a decoupling of corporate management and ownership; the dispersion of ownership itself; the financial profitability of communications assets; the growing presence of international financialization actors, especially American; the influence of financial capital on the industrial management of the major communications industrial conglomerates; and the so-called ownership hard cores.

Of special interest here is the definition given by Philippe Bouquillion of financialization in the case of cultural and communications industries. For the French academic, financialization refers to "not only the growth of the financial stockholder base and its corollary, the dissolution of financial cores in favor of financial markets (stock exchanges), but also to the set of links and dependencies that arise between industrial actors and actors from the financial sphere [banking companies, financial directors, institutional investors, credit rating agencies, etc.]." Regarding these links and dependencies, in the following pages, I attempt to contribute elements for their evaluation, both quantitative and qualitative. But before doing that, we must address the specific process that has led to the financialization of the industries that concern us here.

Media and Forms of Financing

Cees Hamelink (Hamelink, 1984: 96–97) established four great stages in the historical development of mass communications media (to which corresponded four different means of financing): manager-owner stage, separation of management and ownership, expansion with internal resources, and expansion with external resources.

The first stage in the financing of the media system—that of the manager-owner—corresponds to the birth of the communications media industry as a productive sector during the 18th century: "During this period, arose, along with the printing of newspapers, the first medium-scale information industry. In companies, there was a high degree of integration among production, distribution and financing. Ownership and management were combined in the person of the private entrepreneur (invariably a financier, banker or merchant) who founded and financed the medium" (Hamelink, 1984: 96–97).

During the second stage, the manager's role was still performed by the proprietor, but the processes of production, distribution, and financing were already differentiated. This phase ran from the first decades of the 20th century to World War II: "With the birth of massive-circulation media on a national level the need for external financing grew and management and financing became distinct. Diverse sources of external financing arose that had no direct participation in production, such as government subsidies and advertising [...], bank financing [...], private groups [...], and the placement of stock among great segments of the public" (Hamelink, 1984: 96–97).

Following World War II and until the 1960s, there was a third stage, the period of expansion with internal resources. This was a period of continuous expansion, especially on a national level, and therefore very intensive in capital resources. It was based on the concentration phenomena through horizontal and vertical integration that took place in the media systems of the majority of democratic industrialized countries. During this stage of growth, financing was increasingly possible through the internal funds owned by the larger corporations.

In the next stage, starting during the 1960s and 1970s and up to 1989, the financing of the media system stopped being possible only through internal funds. This was the period of acceleration of international globalization, in which banking institutions played a leading role.

> It is the period of the transnationalization of the information industry, a process that acquired staggering speed starting in the 60s. This acceleration coincided with the internationalization of banking and with the trend toward concentration of industrial property in general through the shift of stock from individuals to financial institutions and other industrial corporations. The importance of institutional investments also increased remarkably in the financing of mass media. (Hamelink, 1984: 96–97)

Hamelink, who made his analysis in the late 1970s to the early 1980s, pointed out the element that proved to be the defining trait from that moment to the present, and that here we propose as the fifth stage, characterized by the requirement for external financial resources: the new phase of progressive financialization of the media system.

Starting during the 1980s and 1990s, the evolution of cultural industries was progressively characterized by a digital evolution that would be inseparable from it in any analysis and that, as Enrique Bustamante states, is not "a revolution, an abrupt break with preceding history, but rather a continuum" (Bustamante, 2003: 333). It is, in fact, impossible to understand the strategies developed in the digital field without starting at historical processes essential to globalization, such as the media system's deregulation, concentration, and financialization—its close dependency to the stock market, for instance. This is so because, after all is said and done, new technologies cannot erase the central nature of the communications media in modern capitalist society (Garnham, 2000; Lacroix & Tremblay, 1997; McChesney, Wood, & Foster, 1998). Therefore, the fourth stage outlined by Hamelink in 1984 would subsequently, and until the present, take on specific but not unique traits because they were rooted in the same globalizing process in which the so-called digital revolution had its starting point.

This fifth step, to sum up, implies an acceleration of growth and a diversification of the major multimedia groups in an "accelerated commodification" (Schiller, 2007) that became intensified at the end of the last century and that has had considerable consequences in the financial needs of communications groups: the pursuit of accelerated expansion, grounded primarily on external growth (acquisitions and mergers) seriously increases "the indebtedness of the major groups, their financialization and the permanent tension for short-term profits—in contrast with mid- and long-term profitability businesses"—and, as a consequence, there is an increase in "commercial pressure over culture and information" (Bustamante, 2003: 344).

The strong interrelation between news groups and the great banks and other centers of economic power that began with the expansion of the broadcasting sector in the late 1980s and early 1990s was to become ever larger when, at the end of the century, the major communications groups embarked in the "ferocious quest" for diversification in the new networks (Bustamante, 2003: 343). The media system was already a capital-intensive sector during the 1970s and 1980s, but it would become much more so starting in the 1990s.

Stages in Financialization

More recently, the structural role of financialization in the information and communications sector, analyzed by the French authors quoted above, has also produced a theorization of the stages of the financialization of corporations, whose purpose is to measure the weight that the financial economy must have in any general theory of cultural industries. For this purpose, these authors have described the role played by the mechanisms for holding control in corporations in the communications sector.

To explain the heightened concentration movements experienced by the communications and information sectors during the last decades, it was usual to rely on concepts such as the pursuit of *scale economies*, *synergies*, and larger dimensions as a means to enlarge *market power*. Nevertheless, these notions do not take into account the essential financial parameters that lie behind all these corporate moves. This is important because the origin of the capitals involved has determined and continues to determine the various stages regarding the way in which the ownership and control of private property are organized (Pradié, 2005).

According to Pradié, communications corporations can have three kinds of control depending on their degree of financialization. Put another way, there are three main stages of financialization in cultural-industry companies: absolute family control, relative family control, and managerial control. Absolute family control means that the ownership of the organization is exclusively in the hands of family entrepreneurs, thus described because they are not under the obligation of remunerating third parties. Family-owned groups have limited but not nil growth prospects and, especially in the publishing sector and to a much smaller degree in the broadcasting sector, possess a freedom of action congruent with the independence of their capitals (Pradié, 2005: 87). When a part of the funds proceeds from the aperture of capital to the possibilities for financing that the financial markets present, mainly through an expansion of the organization's capital and its going public, these family companies enter a second phase, that of relative family control. This is an intermediate stage because ultimate control can remain in the hands of the family group, as the contribution of external capitals can be only partial. Nevertheless, although the control does not change hands, the corporate strategies must change because aperture to financial markets generates new obligations. "Management of the activities is thus linked to the obligation of a profitability objective, currently situated at around 15% annually above the amount of the company's own funds" (Pradié, 2005: 87).

The relative family control phase is usually very complex and unstable because a relation of strength is established between family and external capitals, which according to Pradié leads to managerial control exercised by the company's management team when the tensions of the former model cause the dilution of family control and a dominant ownership block ceases to exist. This is the stage reached by major financialized communications groups, in which ownership is dispersed but financial capacity is enormous. It is what some term *capitalism without capitalists*, or the substitution of capitalists by the great actors of world finance, whose dispersion leaves direct control to the board of directors, the CEOs, and the parent companies.

Obviously, the evolution described here is by no means homogenous. Corporations at different stages coexist, and some will never undergo this process. Thus, simultaneously there are small or medium-sized companies whose boards of directors are controlled by the owners and where the roles of proprietor and CEO meld. These firms enjoy managerial freedom, but they are not always able to procure the financial resources they need. On the opposite extreme, the great financialized communications groups have at their disposal all the resources originated by the financial markets and are directed by managers who are employees and whose administration must answer to the profitability goals determined by institutions that operate in the financial markets.

It is evident that the coexistence of such opposing forms does not tend toward balance, but just the opposite. The financial capabilities of the more financialized companies allow them to absorb the less financialized ones, and the problems of competing with financialized companies makes the less financialized ones tend to let themselves be taken over totally or partially, as a last resort or simply as a sought-after goal.

In addition to the three categories mentioned above, Pradié adds a fourth one, which he describes as control of a mutual type. It corresponds to those societies neither quoted in the stock markets nor organized into a stockholder-controlled company, but rather based on diverse forms: foundations, cooperative societies, partnerships of journalists, or nonprofit associations. Organizations of these kinds are but a small minority, and most have a low or nil degree of financialization, but there are exceptions. For instance, in the early 1990s, Bertelsmann adopted an atypical form of organization in order to preserve its control and management. All its capital was shifted to a foundation, and a management society was formed to represent the founding family, social organizations, and personnel representatives. The purpose was to avoid becoming a quoted financial value in order to become independent from short-term profitability obligations. Nevertheless, this has not prevented its financialization in that, despite not being quoted in the stock market, its phenomenal growth has been equally capital-intensive. For Pradié, the fact that Bertelsmann is not present in the stock exchanges has kept the German conglomerate apart from the more speculative investor sectors, turning it into a group that is comparable with the major international communications groups. Although it is not possible to disagree with this, we understand that here the financialization must answer to elements other than the presence of part of the capital in the stock market.

In general terms, it is possible to state that groups under absolute family control have the smallest degree of financialization, the groups under relative family control are more financialized, and the ones under managerial control have the greatest degree of financialization. But ownership is not the only factor to be taken into account, as is shown by the fact that groups under managerial control are less financialized than, for instance, Spanish family-owned group Prisa or by the fact that even groups functioning under mutual control may be financialized, as is the case of Bertelsmann. It is necessary to address issues other than ownership or stock-market presence in order to measure the role played by financial logics in cultural industries.

Obviously, nevertheless, the greatest correlation can be found between the major international communications groups and ownership under managerial control in international leaders. As we see in Chapter 3 (this volume), Time-Warner has a high degree of dispersion in its stockholder base, which includes as minority stockholders a large number of investment funds, whereas its board of directors is made up of representatives of major American corporate firms and banks. Vivendi is also a society with high stockholder dispersion and a board of directors constituted by representatives of major French companies and, more recently, great international investors. Disney, in turn, has all its capital distributed among a great number of financial societies. But financialization in all these cases is not due only to the presence of financial actors in their ownership, but also to their financial indebtedness and to the broadening of their corporate purposes, as well as to the links between stockholder cores. Therefore, Pradié concludes that the importance of financial markets in direct financing of direct productive activities allows us to identify two main kinds of national situations: those suitable for financial markets, in which companies' presence in the stock market — intermediated or direct — is the norm (as is the case in the United States and the United Kingdom); and those in which financial-influence cores are formed, in the cases where what develops is bank intermediation and financial links among representatives of boards of directors (as happens in France or Germany; Pradié: 2005: 105). Actually, that can be considered one of the key differences between Anglo-Saxon countries and continental Europe throughout financial history, a difference rooted in the Founding Fathers as stated in the famous quotation attributed to Thomas Jefferson (1743–1826), in which he defined banking institutions as more dangerous to U.S. liberties than standing armies and proclaimed the need to take power from the banks and restore it to the people (allegedly represented in the stock exchange markets).

THE INFORMATION AND COMMUNICATIONS DEPENDENCY OF THE FINANCIAL SYSTEM

This early analysis of cultural industries from the standpoint of their financialization makes it evident that the trend toward convergence between the financial system (financial actors and markets) and information and communications firms that was denounced by Hamelink some decades ago has but expanded. Technological, operative, and financial convergence between the interests of financial entities (mainly banks but also private equity firms, insurance companies, venture capital firms, securitization firms, mutual funds, etc.) and cultural industries can be seen today in all its magnitude, also on the sector in the cultural industries that has the strongest influence over public opinion: the groups that own the news media firms. The major media conglomerates and the world's great financial institutions are tightening their links in a particularly forceful way, as is seen in Chapter 3 (this volume), but the analysis of those links also shows the obligation of avoiding simplistic diagnoses. In 21st-century financial capitalism, it makes ever less sense to speak of domination of the communications media when they are controlled by economic and financial power, and this is so for several reasons.

In the first place, media owners, as happens with the rest of corporate actors in cultural industries, change their structures as they become financialized to adapt to goals and strategies totally subject to financial logic, so that it is not possible to speak of domination from the outside when the logic is assimilated internally. In the cases in which there is a clear trend toward financialization in corporate conglomerates, corporate objectives are based ever less on terms of production and more on financial parameters (future profitability, speculation, and expectations based on virtual references). The point is not that economic-financial power dominates over those great actors of cultural industries, but rather that the industries become an economic-financial power when they assimilate within those logics and become allied with the actors that promote them most strongly.

On the other hand, actors in the financial system, especially banking institutions, despite constituting economic structures that are much larger in size than those made up by cultural-industry actors, precisely because of this gigantism in 21st-century financial and information late capitalism, have multiplied their information and communication needs and interests to unprecedented levels. It is inappropriate to speak of domination of banking actors by third-party actors, but it is inevitable to observe the profound dependency that the major financial conglomerates develop during this stage on the actors that are most influential in the creation of public opinion: the media.

In order to understand this, we must address the historical context. During the last few decades, the financial system has experienced one of the periods of highest corporate concentration and, although this may seem paradoxical, also a growing financialization of banking activity itself. The banking actors, who arose to receive savings and channel them into productive activity, have eminently become intermediaries and actors focused above all on the so-called virtual economy (the one that takes place mainly in the capitals markets and in exchanges based on "fictitious capital"). This concentration and financialization (promoted in great measure by neoliberal policies in the United States, as was exhaustively described by Leonard Seabrooke [2001]) has generated growing information and communication needs in financial-system actors. Parallel to this, competitiveness and concentration in cultural industries, especially in the media sector, have generated new or renewed interests in communication and information on the part of the financial sector. I address in the following sections the specific interests and needs regarding information and communication of the largest financial actors: banking entities.

Information and Communication Needs of Big Banking Groups

By "information and communication needs" of the financial sector we are referring particularly to those deficiencies in information and communication matters that financial actors, especially private banking institutions, have at any given moment, and which they cannot disregard or dispense with because they are essential for success in their activity, and for which they require the participation of communications media. Hamelink addressed these needs regarding the information industry as a whole (with special attention on the then new activities of data processing and telecommunications). We have updated them here in the context of financial late capitalism in the late 20th and early 21st centuries, that is, the stage of financialization of cultural industries and the banking system.

If we focus on the needs of the main actors of the financial system, major private banking conglomerates, we can divide them into the two great groups already mentioned: operational and strategic needs.

In the first place, banking companies are, eminently, administrators of massive quantities of data. The size and breadth of the databases they manage, their access needs, and the geographical dispersion of their activities caused them to be among the first large clients of the information technologies and telecommunications sectors from the

INFORMATION AND COMMUNICATION
NEEDS OF THE BANKING SYSTEM

	Operational	Strategic
INTERNAL	Within the bank	Of the bank
EXTERNAL	Toward clients, the banking community, the authorities	Advertising or creation of opinion

Source: The author, based on Hamelink (1984).

onset. Starting in the 1960s, with the emergence of microcomputing, the banking system's dependency on telematics has steadily increased. Banks have gradually shifted all of their activity into the digital realm, and nowadays they are wholly dependent on their computing and telecommunications systems. What is more, this information and telecommunications dependency affects the banking system globally in the sense that the main forms of international financial connection are computerized and borne by networks that in some instances are several decades old.[3] Indeed, as we have seen, it is possible to affirm that the banking system was among the first to make use of communications over a distance and computer science on a global scale and that these technologies made financial globalization possible.

The banking system's need for equipment and systems for computing and for the establishment and maintenance of private communications networks is probably the banking companies' most important communication and information requirement in operational terms because their correct day-to-day performance depends on it. Downtime in a computer system or in the network that connects banking institutions with international clearing houses,[4] for example, can bring about grave consequences for any organization.

A considerably greater degree of security, control, and speed in the access to banking data have been the main consequences of the integration of communications technology and information in the financial sector, even though this does not always result in greater transparency in the industry, but rather the opposite, as we showed by quoting French journalist Denis Robert's research (Robert, 2001, 2002) in Chapter 1 (this volume).

Although the use of ICTs has always resulted in an optimization of resources, in recent years, the increase in competitiveness has prompted the banking sector to apply the new technologies as a direct strategy to reduce costs. Online banking is doubtless the clearest instance of this.

Second, the need for reliable and secure communications networks and computer infrastructures to manage the massive flows of data generated daily by banking companies does not respond only to an organizational and operational requirement of the banking system, but also, logically, to the day-to-day obligation to be able to keep clients duly informed about everything that concerns their interests regarding managed funds and to the need for control and security in operations in order to satisfy the requirements of the banking community and the authorities. This constitutes the second great operational need that banking institutions have: their mandatory ability to externally supply customers and watchdog agencies with information.

But the banking system is one of the main consumers not only of hardware and software but also of information, of content. As we pointed out in previous pages, and as Hamelink did before, it was not a coincidence that the first European newspaper should have been published by an Augsburg banking family, The Fugger, in the 16th century, nor that in 1856 bankers Heinrich Bernhard Rosenthal and Leopold Sonnermann should have founded the *Frankfurter Geschafsbericht*, later to become the *Frankfurter Allgemeine Zeitung*, with the purpose of informing about the stock market. Bankers were the first clients of international news agencies in the 19th century, and they still are great purchasers of specialized information. What is more, not only do they make use of whatever economic and financial information can be provided by news agencies and specialized press services, but they also have their own teams that permanently draw up political and economic profiles and use their industrial participations to obtain information that is critical for their activities. Thus, banking companies' representatives on the boards of directors of participated companies occupy for them privileged-information enclaves, as the Organization for Economic Co-operation and Development (OECD) recognizes when denouncing the conflicts of interest generated by banking diversification (Organization for Economic Co-operation and Development, 1993: 9). This information requirement is an unavoidable internal strategic need for any banking organization.

Last, but not least, the banking system has a strategic need to transmit information outward about itself in terms of both advertising and creating public opinion. The targets and goals of these information and communication needs are diverse, but their identification is a particularly useful exercise. The targets of the banking companies' public information are essentially three:

- customers (actual or potential),
- the banking community or market (investors, intermediaries, competitors), and
- the general public (media, other industrial sectors, society).

The goals aimed at are mainly three as well:

- informing (about new products and services),
- deciding the strategic information that the market has access to at any given moment (allowing or preventing information leaks), and
- creating and maintaining a desired public image.

Although the first of these goals is the most evident and commercially most important (i.e., supplying potential or current clients with information on products and services), it is the other two that are the most relevant to the organization from a strategic point of view. The virtues and qualities of a certain advertising campaign can be important for gaining new customers, but the determinant aspect is the contents of the offer, the commercial strategy behind it, which in the banking market translates into well-defined concepts: interest rates, commissions, fees, cancellation conditions, and so on. The degree of success in acquiring customers is more a matter of commercial strategy than of advertising strategy, although the latter may be important to make the former known. However, the second and third goals listed earlier are absolutely determinant for the operations of banking institutions.

The great banking companies have been built up in the last few years through acquisitions, mergers, and takeovers, on the one hand, and through investments in diverse areas (some very profitable and others extremely risky), on the other hand. In all of these cases, the information on financial institutions available to the market has been of special importance. This has been so, in our opinion and to the tenor of what has been set forth up to this point, in a double sense:

- for determining the security quotations of banking companies, and
- for determining the degree of uncertainty publicly perceived for the operations.

As is made evident by the legislation currently in force,[5] the vast majority of the mergers, acquisitions, and takeovers undertaken by the banking system in the last two decades at least—to acquire either financial or non-financial organizations—have been performed on the basis of the exchange of securities that represent the equity capital. That is to say, in most operations, no monetary transactions are performed but are done rather through stock swaps. If either of the companies that participate in the operation is not listed in the stock market, the value of its shares is estimated in function of its assets and liabilities. But the large majority of the great operations by banking companies are performed with corporations that are listed, so that it is the securities market that determines stock prices at any given moment.

When the stock market is what determines the value of the exchange in a merger or takeover, any information that flows into the market that is likely to alter the quotation has an enormous importance for the organizations involved in the operation.

Likewise, the merger, acquisition, and takeover processes, as well as the diversification processes, imply a certain risk—a situation involving exposure to danger or loss, according to the Oxford English Dictionary— in theory only financial but in practice also labor-related, environmental, and/or social insofar as bad management of these has an influence on the market's perception. It is not possible to have a completely reliable estimation of this risk because there are always uncertainties that can only be cleared after the operation. For example, according to the study done by Fuentes and Sastre (1998) for the Bank of Spain, the banking mergers and takeovers that took place in Spain between 1988 and 1997, which would give rise to one of the most concentrated banking markets that has generated one of the largest banking conglomerates in Europe and the world, Santander Central Hispano bank, never accomplished the two goals they were mostly aiming for: to expand and increase their level of efficiency. This caused these authors to affirm that it was probably impossible to achieve both objectives simultaneously. In fact, the study by these two researchers proved that banking mergers and takeovers during that period were far from successful in the desired results. Although they stated that the operations had been satisfactory from the point of view of the increase in competitiveness on the part of the banking companies involved, they also recognized that "the mergers analyzed in this study throw no clear results regarding improvements in the profit-generating capacity or efficiency levels of the merged institutions" (Fuentes & Sastre, 1998: 19).

It is true that literature on the results of merger processes is abundant and not always in agreement, but in any case it is possible to state with confidence that the operations that have been at the foundation of the growth and evolution of the banking system in the world's major democracies during the last three decades have not been exempt from risks and uncertainties.

We are not concerned here with evaluating what has been the actual breadth of those risks and uncertainties, but rather we wish to point out that they have existed and that, as a consequence, it is necessary to take into account the importance for financial organizations involved in the operations of the perception by the market and public opinion of those risks and uncertainties at every point of the process.

Information publicly available on those operations and on the global image of the companies involved are factors that have great weight on the development of a certain operation. A judicial probe, for instance, can have negative effects over share quotations. Likewise, publicity of certain data concerning the company to be taken over may increase its selling value. Excessively negative information concerning an operation may even cause it to derail if it were to become public, and the actual causes for many purchases and acquisitions may be evaluated by public opinion (or the authorities) by criteria different from the ones used by the participating companies. In summary, information that flows in the markets regarding a certain operation is capable of having effect on it, and, therefore, it is strategic information for the financial company. So is the image of the degree of solvency, security, and solidity that may be attributed to a corporation. The management of this image and this public information is, therefore, critical for financial firms. In this sense, stock analysts are a key piece because they have a huge impact on companies' stock prices, and their recommendations depend on the information about a company flowing at every moment (Soloski, 2005: 68).

Information and Communication Interests of Big Banking Groups

The evolution of cultural industries during the last three decades, especially of the major conglomerates that own news media, has also multiplied the interests of the financial system, particularly of the banking actors, in those productive sectors. By "interests of the banking institutions in the communications and information sector" we are referring here to those corporate links that banking institutions may establish, in their own interest, with communications groups: ownership, strategic, or industrial links (e.g., links through shares, presence in the boards of directors, agreements or alliances, industrial investments, credit relations, investments in marketing and advertising, and personal relations among shareholders, board members, and top managers).

The needs mentioned earlier serve to explain the two great interests that guide the banking system's penetration into the diverse sectors in which it participates. These interests are also valid for the information and communications sector, and specifically for the penetration of banking companies into news media owners. The interests are mainly of two types:

- *Economic interests*: concerning profit and profitability (based on capital gains, dividends, etc., which may be derived from these operations):
- *Strategic interests*: for being able to influence the decisions of companies in which they have a participation and as a means to have greater and faster access to critical information.

The information and communication sector has increasingly attracted the interest of banking institutions from the onset of the digitalization process in the late 1960s. Telecommunications, computer science, and the media have attracted the economic interest of the financial system on account of their being sectors with great expectations (i.e., promises) for future profitability. Despite this, it is a fact that the banking system's financial interest in the area of the new ICTs—and in the media that converge with them—has not merited the specific attention of too many researchers. However, ICTs in general have merited attention as the recipients of a large part of recent global investments. The issue of the increase in economic productivity due to ICTs has been a recurrent subject endorsed by the highest institutions (World Bank, 2004).[6] Nevertheless, financial companies' strategic interest is probably the least studied aspect. In the early 1980s, Cees Hamelink defined it for the communication and information sector as what determines "the control of information resources through fund allotment," as has already been pointed out (Hamelink, 1984: 149). According to Hamelink, this control has a decisive influence over the market—and consequently on society as a whole—and it consists of four control categories that continue to be valid today:

- *Capital control*: control over the supply of capital that is allotted to a certain company;
- *Shareholder control*: control over the board of directors according to the stocks of a company owned by a financial institution;
- *Control through the customer relationship*: control over the company according to the business volume that the financial institution represents for it (as a customer of its information products or telecommunications services, as an advertiser, etc.); and
- *Control through interconnections at the boards-of-directors level*: Cees Hamelink's description in the early 1980s is still valid today:

Interconnections at the director level are those that exist when a single person is part [of the boards of directors] of a finance company and of a non-finance company. In principle, it is precisely [in the boards of directors] where decisions are made on fundamental matters regarding companies' policies. It is frequent to find bankers in the [boards of directors] of non-financial companies; they act as advisers on the matters they specialize in and as contacts with the financial community to obtain loans whenever necessary. At certain times, they also represent the interests of their institutions, either as creditors or as majority shareholders in the companies. (Hamelink, 1984: 146–147)

In summary, the banking system has important internal or external operational needs related with the communication and information sector, but its strategic needs are those that are directly related to the media. Strategic needs, both internal and external, especially the latter, are also critical needs—banking institutions act as receptors and emitters of information about themselves. Management of both the image of banking companies and the public information that circulates about them is basic for their business in growth and expansion periods. Therefore, banking institutions' economic and strategic interests in the communication and information sector have become stronger during this latest stage of advanced capitalism, which we term *financialized*. The following table summarizes the main interests of the banking system in the media system.

As this table shows, the banking companies' main interest is in productive profitability through classical banking business. That is, banking and strategic interests prevail over productive investments when a finance company enters a communication group's equity capital. This shows that the main interest that a banking company has regarding cultural industries in general, and communications conglomerates in particular, is as manager of capital resources. This function, along with that of making loans, which is characteristic of traditional banking practice, constitutes the real business of banking companies in general, whose annual gains, as is true of any banking organization, proceed essentially from banking fees and interest rates.

The fact that major communications groups have become capital-intensive centers makes them highly coveted banking customers. Banks' participation in large corporations with scarce productive profitability, as is the case of major communications groups, can be best understood by focusing on that interest. Presence in communication groups' boards of

INTERESTS OF THE BANKING SYSTEM
IN COMMUNICATION GROUPS

Type of interest	Means of attainment	Degree of interest
Productive profitability through the banking business	Loans and credits, advanced intermediation, management of banking account	Very high
Speculative profitability	Securities markets (when the company is quoted in the stock market)	Very high
Acquisition of critical information	Presence in boards of directors	High
Participation in decision making	Presence in the boards of directors and capacity for exerting pressure as a customer of the communication group	High
Privileged interaction with other corporate actors	Presence in boards of directors	High
Productive profitability through dividends	Yearly benefits paid by companies of which the banking organization is a shareholder	Low

Source: The author.

directors puts banking groups in a privileged position to participate in the many financing and refinancing operations undertaken by the companies and to manage a part of their assets and resources. Therefore, we can conclude that the participation of major banking companies in the shares of media groups—and in the whole information and communication sector—should not be evaluated so much for profitability in a strictly accounting sense as for indirect profits in day-to-day banking activity.

Due to banking secrecy, these indirect profits are impossible to evaluate with any precision in externally conducted research, but the continuation and expansion of participations with long-term negative profitability allow us to conclude that the indirect profits must be high indeed. In summary, a significant part of the banking companies' interests in the communication and information sector should be interpreted as purely strategic, as a means of attaining tangible banking and financial profits in credit, and the acquisition and management of resources, the operations traditional to banks, and their main sources of income. These interests are more important than their interests as industrial partners or investors.

A good example of this is the study of the last 30 years of the first Spanish banking group Santander Central Hispano (SCH), the world's 12th finance company in assets, and the 9th in the world and 1st in the Eurozone in market capitalization at the end of 2008. This research (Almiron, 2006) showed clearly that SCH's main interest in the communication and information sector is related to banking business *stricto sensu* (loans, credits, initial public offerings, bond issues, bank account management).

Banking companies also have a high degree of interest in the speculative profitability of the companies where they own shares, whereas their interest for productive profitability—purely industrial—is low. Their presence in communication groups also has an eminently strategic interest: to be present in the centers of power through which critical information flows, where decisions are made, and interaction is produced with other corporate actors that have power.

These interests show a greater dependence than is assumed a priori regarding banking companies in relation to communications media. But this does not mean that the latter are not just as dependent or more so, but rather that the former need the latter for their activity. This is so not only in operative terms but also in strategic terms of corporate image, as becomes especially evident if we look at the needs for controlling communication and information flows that the banking system has generated in the last few decades as a result of accelerated growth.

If we take the case of SCH group, its expansion process has been one of the most remarkable in the world. Due to this, its profits multiplied by almost 1,000% from 1999 to 2009. But this accelerated growth has not been exempt—or perhaps this has been the price that had to be paid for it—from numerous setbacks that could have altered considerably the corporation's image and that have tarnished significantly the ethical and good-governance principles that all finance companies, and any other firms, are supposed to be guided by. The breadth and number of these incidents and the considerable weight that they must have had on the company's communications strategy—difficult to assess but not impossible to imagine—have generated a history of the banking group that is completely different from the one that is normally given by the media, annual reports, and financial advisers (detailed in Almiron, 2006).

Therefore, the financial liberalization and globalization process has caused an increase in the needs and interests concerning information and communication for the major actors of the financial system, from both the strategic and operational points of view. The large communication and information conglomerates have become important customers, in addition to partners and investment products, for finance companies, which are as absorbed in the logic of exponential multiplication of profitability as the media conglomerates are. They also are as dependent, or even more so, on the stock-market quotes and the public image of their activities. We must not forget this point in order to complete the analysis of the scenario. However, what we are most concerned with here is financialization of the sector that nowadays has the greatest capacity for political and social influence in the cultural industries, that of communications media or journalistic companies.

TOOLS FOR MEASURING MEDIA FINANCIALIZATION

To measure the degree of financialization of the major information and communication media conglomerates, we should first focus on their main financial needs and interests in the current stage of information capitalism.

FINANCIAL NEEDS OF NEWS MEDIA CONGLOMERATES

	Operational	Strategic
INTERNAL	Corporate efficiency	Self-finance models
EXTERNAL	Expansion	Strategic alliances

Source: The author, based on Miguel de Bustos (2003) and Bustamante (2003).

The first financial need of news media owners that is derived from this scenario logically concerns the strategies that define the business models that allow them to profit from their activity. The trend toward gigantism that we have mentioned, justified by the existence of synergies and the need to face the penetration of international groups into their national territories, is based not only on mergers, acquisitions, and takeovers of other media firms but also on the development of marketing strategies that continually increase costs destined to operations related with the brand and its activity (Miguel de Bustos, 2003: 239–240). In certain cases, they can even be profitable operations, but they always have the purpose of reinforcing the strategic positioning of the media group.

Several of these strategies are carried out with external partners that may be industrial and/or financial but that in all cases must add weight to the project. It is logical that among these strategic partners should often be representatives of the financial system, mainly banks and private equity firms, that provide with their presence in the projects a guarantee of solvency and stability, thus becoming allies or partners of communication groups in specific operations.

The second strategic financial need of media groups has to do, therefore, with their capacity to establish strategic alliances with financial partners of great and recognized solvency. Gigantism, competitiveness, and the financialization of the communication groups—that is to say the progressively larger weight in them of the indicators of virtual economy—generate continual requirements for financial resources in order to achieve the internal corporate efficiency necessary to meet those indicators.

As the authors revisited in previous pages describe, nowadays financial or stock-market strategies prevail when defining a group's situation and operativeness. This implies that indicators such as market capitalization, in the case that the company has gone public or at least has the intention of doing so and has publicly announced it, constitute key elements when assessing what is the best moment to perform an acquisition or any other expansion movement. But even without market capitalization, before getting to the point where they need financial capital for expansion, many media groups need financial resources in addition to those obtained through their activity in order to place themselves in a *position* to grow.

Therefore, the first operational financial need of communication groups has to do with the acquisition of enough resources to place themselves in a competitive position, which often results in a situation in which the group's internal financial resources are not sufficient, and external financing must be obtained to reach the corporate efficiency required by the present-day scenario

Last, as is evident, media groups have high requirements for resources in order to complete expansion processes such as those experienced in the last decades by major conglomerates. The large operations that cannot be collateralized exclusively through internal financing or share swaps—and there are many such—have been guaranteed with external financial resources provided mostly by major banking companies, private or public equity firms, and stock markets.

But this need for external operational financing in order to be able to grow and expand can go much beyond the initial contribution of bank capital or collateral because it has two main characteristics as to its logic: (a) the difficulty of achieving true scale economies, and (b) the enormous indebtedness in which media groups are left due to the expansion processes.

As various authors have shown, expansion processes through a merger (i.e., growth in size) do not automatically imply a growth in income.[7] On the contrary, in most cases, growth after the merger is lower than average for the merged companies' industry, which is only logical given the usual complexity of merger processes. It is true that growth gives these groups more power and capacity of influence over regulators and smaller groups. However, from a financial point of view, the results are far from immediately profitable. What is more, in certain occasions, the merger can even damage the healthy operation of some of the companies in the merged groups. This failure to achieve economies of scale or synergies to multiply income to the extent that size was multiplied can eventually generate new financial needs, as happens with the indebtedness generated by expansion processes, independently of the results they may have produced.

Operative needs of external financing on the part of media groups are not limited, therefore, to resources required for their expansion, but also include the resources warranted by the debts incurred and by the failure of the expansion process to produce good results. This doubtless has been the main source of external financial dependence of the media system during the last 30 years.

From these needs are derived, in turn, the main interests that the media system has in the financial system, which we classify as follows:

(a) Information interests: the financial system as subject of information.
(b) Strategic interests: the financial system as strategic or industrial partner.
(c) Financial interests: the financial system as client, advertiser, and creditor.

In the first place, the financial system and its activities constitute a first-order subject of information for the communications media. Research is still pending that will assess—not only quantitatively but also qualitatively—news coverage about a sphere that has so many connections and links of need and interest interwoven with the media system.

The second great area of interest that the media system has in the financial system has to do essentially with its strategic needs. Financial agents are potential partners and allies not only from the financial but also the industrial viewpoint (as strategic partners) (e.g., in those agreements in which financing the activity requires great negotiating skills, good contacts, presence in the boards of directors of strategic corporations, etc.). The media system therefore has a growing interest in banks and other financial agents it wishes to attract to strategic projects, in which their weight and experience will contribute value added to the operation or will guarantee it outright before public opinion.

The financial system, and more specifically the organizations that make it up, constitute one of the media system's main clients regarding financial information. Another area of research that is still pending is the quantification of the volume of income that financial information—distributed directly to the financial agents—brings to communication groups, as well as its characteristics and peculiarities.

The financial system is also an advertiser important to the media system and, therefore, its client. Again, in-depth research on this relation between the media and financial systems still needs to be conducted.

Finally, and probably most important, the financial system is the main provider of economic and financial resources for the communication groups for their operativeness, development, and expansion. This link is another area that has not yet been studied in depth despite the considerable interactions it can have with the work of the communication groups.

A Set of Tools

This survey of finance-linked needs and interests of the great media conglomerates is meant to portray as faithfully as possible the relations between the financial and media systems during recent decades. This allows us to identify the main instruments that must be measured to evaluate the degree of financialization of the major communication groups. The following table summarizes them. Different authors have conducted research on some of these issues, but the whole picture usually is missing.

That is, to indicate the crucial position of finance at the center of corporate media, we must account for the whole picture, which includes ownership, quotation/market capitalization, indebtedness, corporate goals, other financial tools, and boards of directors.

Of course, capital structure is the first issue to look at. The kind of ownership (whether the company has stayed private or gone public) and the type of private or public shareholders who possess the stock are the clues to a company's primary connection with the financial system. Stock directly held by financial companies (investment and commercial banks, private equity firms, insurance companies, mutual funds, securitization companies, venture capital firms, etc.) is not unusual in publicly owned companies because over the last decade many international financial players, mainly custodian banks (financial institutions responsible for safeguarding a firm or individual's financial assets, typically owned by pension funds or investment funds), have been investing in corporate media public stock, among many other core assets. These entities are committed to institutional investment portfolios and look for the maximum profitability in the shortest period of time. For that reason, the presence of one of these global financial investors in the capital structure of a publicly owned media company means expectations of high profit rates, usually as a result of stock-market quote fluctuations.

Presence in the stock markets is, obviously, the second most important sign of financialization. This is what generates Crotty's neoliberal paradox: Intense product market competition makes it difficult, if not

FINANCIALIZATION OF MEDIA CONGLOMERATES
Elements for its evaluation

TRAIT	CHARACTERISTICS
Ownership	Entry of global financialization actors (commercial banks, private equity firms, insurance companies, venture capital firms, securitization firms (*), mutual funds, etc.)
Market capitalization	Presence in the stock market and distancing between the value of the company in accounting terms and in the stock market
Debt	Growing financial debt with credit companies or capital markets
Corporate purpose	Addition of financial activity to the normal activity
Financial tools	Proliferation of the use of securitization (*), stock options, pension funds, etc.
Board of directors	Influence of financial actors through representatives

Source: The author.
(*) Packaging of pools of loans or receivables with an appropriate level of credit enhancement, and the subsequent redistribution of these packages to investors.

impossible, for most media corporations to achieve high increases in earnings most of the time; but financial markets demand ever-increasing earnings all the time, failing which the fall of stock prices and the threat of hostile takeover must be faced. Thus, financial goals become the primarily obsession of the top staff of a publicly held company. Consequently, the whole corporate strategy is subordinated to short-term profitability targets. Additionally, the company is immersed in a scenario of major instability and of larger fragility that, ultimately, we must not forget, increases competition (every player wants to win the funding race) and generates a wide gap between the virtual value in the stock markets (market capitalization) and the real accounting value (shown in the balance sheet) of a publicly held company.

A wealth of concrete data on ownership of publicly traded media firms has been gathered by different media management specialists in the last decades, mainly on newspaper owners, although more recently the perspective has been widened. As early as 1979, as public ownership increased, the data analyzed by Benjamin Compaine disclosed the rising significance of institutional investors in media ownership (Compaine & Gomery, 2000). Although Compaine's approach was, and has increasingly been, mainly focused on managerial economics, his research was followed by new studies that expressed concern about the consequences of public ownership. Meyer and Wearden (1984), Blankenburg and Ozanich (1993), Picard (1994), Lacy, Shaver, and Cyr (1996), and others built a repository of data, mainly from a managerial approach, about the effects of public ownership on newspaper companies, until Cranberg, Bezanson, and Soloski (2001) published a key work, *Taking Stock: Journalism and the Publicity Traded Newspaper Company*.

In *Taking Stock*, the authors published the results of a study on the organization and behavior of publicly traded U.S. newspaper companies. Their findings were quite clear: Ownership of publicly traded newspaper firms was widely distributed in highly competitive and liquid financial markets whose interests were primarily financial and short-termed; the stock market dictated the behavior of the companies at all levels of the organization; ownership was in the hands of investors not interested at all in the quality of news provided by the firms but in financial returns; investors were mainly concerned with revenues, margins, profitability, and stock performance; publicly traded newspaper firms had created a reward system for executives that assured that policies, decisions, and corporate behavior conformed to the demands of the security markets; board and executive compensations were closely tied to the financial performance of the companies; publishers, editors, and other key members of newspapers were often compensated through bonuses and stock options; corporate control over newspapers was rarely focused on news content but on financial performance; the main aim of newspaper firms wasn't circulation but revenue growth and margin; and the most important short-term strategy for increasing margins was cutting costs (i.e., cutting personnel) regardless of the effect that this could have on the quality of news content. In summary, Cranberg et al. disclosed that the priorities and performance of publicly traded newspapers were becoming the standard by which all newspapers were measured and that stock-market pressures had increased the emphasis placed on revenue, margins, profits, and share price. The results were: lean staffing, low salaries, low efficiency, orientation to advertisers' preferences, and definition of audience in terms of market and advertising aims (Cranberg et al., 2001). That is, newspaper companies were only looking at shareholders' interests, not at public or social responsibilities and interests.

In his 2005 review, Soloski reexamined the ownership of publicly traded U.S. newspapers to ascertain whether the market pressure the firms were forced to live under had diminished or increased. The findings were again quite clear: The situation had become further exacerbated. In 1999 institutional investors owned 69.05% of the shares in the 17 publicly traded newspapers that Soloski and his colleagues studied, whereas by 2004 institutional investors owned 93.16% of the stock in the 15 publicly traded newspaper companies that remained. Not only had institutional investors increased the percentage of stock they owned in newspaper firms, but they had increased their percentage of stock ownership—something that has occurred across all economic sectors in financial capitalism. Furthermore, institutions have been increasingly in "direct, open and frequent communication with management of companies" (Soloski, 2005: 67). To summarize, as stated by Soloski:

> The dangers we identified in 1999 regarding institutional investors owning large blocks of stock in newspaper companies have become even more of a concern. Not only have institutions increased their ownership of newspaper companies' stock, the largest investors have substantially increased their ownership of stock. This means that today a small number of institutional investors exert a significant amount of influence on management. (Soloski, 2005: 73)

In some cases, research shows opposite results, as is the case with Miles Maguire's (2003) work, which reveals that many institutional investors in newspaper companies took a long-term rather than a short-term view. But the same author recognized that this could turn into an imposition of their will, something that would also be negative for the newspaper firm.

Actually, the most relevant work by managerial economics authors has confirmed all these concerns. In 1996, Soloski with Picard warned about the growing influence institutional owners had on publicly traded newspaper companies, and so did a compilation book edited by Picard in 2005 (where Soloski's 2005 review was included). In that text, Picard pointed out the unequal division of ownership increasingly prevalent in U.S. media firms.

Many firms use classified stock that proportionally splits the equity and limits or removes voting rights in one or more categories of the stock thus split. The purpose of this is to reduce the influence of the voting power of outsiders (e.g., institutional investors), but it is typically considered evidence of "poor corporate governance" (Picard, 2005: 6) because a small number of investors hold the power (usually privately) and, therefore, can act in opposition to the majority—what can be considered a perversion of the stock-market ideal.

But the truth is that the ideal stock market, the one that represents ownership by the people, has long since turned into financial ownership (although the financial actors have multiplied, and along with commercial banks we can today find private equity firms, public and private pension funds, insurance companies, venture capital firms, mutual funds, and all kinds of securitization firms). Generally speaking, the main research shows that the more public the firm is, the greater the need and pressure to manage the company in a short-term profit-driven way with many influences on the decision-making process. As Soloski (2005) put it: "Since institutions are in the business of making money, the pressure on management will be to follow policies that ensure financial performance is paramount" (Soloski, 2005: 66).

These words referred mainly to newspaper firms. However, since the beginning of the 21st century, data have also been collected for the big media conglomerates, albeit mainly for the United States. Nevertheless, we must stress here the nonmanagerial approach of this new wave of data gathering. It is worth pointing out the work of some nonacademic associations, which have been feeding most of the critical scholarly research. The Fairness and Accuracy in Reporting Center started in 2000 the Fear & Favor reports, an instructive catalog of instances of pressure from powerful interests on news; it has maintained since then a webpage of data with interlocking directorates of a handful of U.S. media firms (see www.fair.org). At the same time, the Progressive Living organization also published data on interlocked boards in mass media that can still be found online (www.progressiveliving.org). Although not comprehensive and only focused on the United States, these studies were conducted concerning top media conglomerates, not only newspaper firms, and in all cases they denounced that news media owners were highly interlocked with the power elite in the United States. A summary of these research studies, with a useful synthesis of the context that led to this situation, can be found in Segovia and Quirós (2006). In their article, the authors concluded that it is impossible to maintain belief in any kind of autonomy in mass media newsrooms. It goes without saying that all the authors pointed at government policies as the main promoters of the changes that have exacerbated financialization trends in boards of directors.

Third, we must look at indebtedness. Through the last two decades, the financial indebtedness of corporate media increased to represent most of its global debt. Since the 1980s, banks have continued to be the most common suppliers of credit—the other means of raising capital being the stock market. Given that current media groups have developed through a highly capital-intensive growth process, most of them have accumulated an unprecedented banking debt, one of the largest in the whole international economic arena.

This unparalleled corporate media indebtedness is directly related to the financial innovations that brought about the new finance regime that emerged in the late 20th century, which can be summarized by the term *direct financing*. This concept aims to describe a process that is changing the structure of finance in the international political economy through what is also known as financial disintermediation, although it has not removed intermediaries but led intermediaries to expand the variety of financial services on offer to their clients, particularity for security trading.

Thus, direct financing, which has been fiercely promoted by the U.S. government, according to Seabrooke, allows the financial sector to offer more credit to the public and receive more in trading revenues. For commercial banking, that means a radical move: shifting away from bank-held debt and direct bank loans toward security trading and securitization. *Securitization* can be defined as the packaging of pools of loans or receivables with an appropriate level of credit enhancement and the subsequent redistribution of these packages to investors. Investors buy the repackaged assets in the form of securities (or secured loans). Securitization thereby converts illiquid assets (assets that cannot easily be sold) into liquid assets. By this, banks act less as depositories of capital (their traditional role in the productive economy) and more as brokerage houses (as speculators in the finance markets). Companies that make widespread use of securitization (to raise capital from their own illiquid assets through the emission of bonds or titles) or that make intense use of other late 20th-century financial innovations (such as stock options or offshore tax haven regimes) are deeply financialized. The currently increasing financial debt of private corporations and public institutions is one of the main characteristics of the hegemony of the new finance regime according to Seabrooke (2001).

It is also illustrative to look at the other financial tools increasingly used in the last decades by top media firms, such as bonuses or compensations through stock options or pension funds. As Maguire (2005) showed, most companies say they use stock options to attract, retain, and reward talented executives and to align the interests of executives with those of shareowners, but "there is a wide gap between the theory and reality," and to follow the interests of shareholders may not always be the best strategy (Maguire, 2005: 40). Shareholders' interests may be diverse, but they are all focused on financial returns, which most of the time can be considered their main aim. So, aligning the interests of top executives with those of shareholders may lead top executives to focus excessively on stock performance, as Maguire concluded. Furthermore, additional research has shown that highly successful companies over long periods of time do not focus solely on maximizing shareholder wealth (Collins & Porras, 1994).

Another issue that accounts for the financialization of corporate media is, of course, the composition of the boards of directors. Actually, boards of directors, mainly through the study of interlocking directorates, have received enormous attention from scholars since Sweezy (1939) published "Interest Groups in the American Economy"—what has been considered by most the first systematic study of interlocking directorates —and Selznick (1949) first described co-optation as the incorporation of representatives of external groups into the internal decision-making or advisory structure of an organization. A large number of studies have since focused on the financial ties of directorates. Studies of interlocking directorates often focus on co-optation, and ties to financial institutions through directorates have been among the most widely researched issues. Although the United States is the most thoroughly studied case, all other regions have been increasingly considered (Bianco & Pagnoni, 1997; Dooley, 1969; Fitch & Oppenheimer, 1970; Fligstein & Brantley, 1992; Fohlin, 1999; Iwanami, 2006; Kotz, 1978; Mariolis, 1975; Norich, 1980; Ong, Wan, & Hong, 2003). Many of these authors supported in some way the so-called theory of bank or finance control, whose current main argument is that financial institutions seek to profit from debt financing, which leads bank-controlled companies to carry heavy debt loads and to be centered on financial entities. But as Iwanami (2006) showed, this isn't an imposed control because nonfinancial companies have been actively seeking a vertical interlock with banks and other financial institutions to ensure easier access to capital. In any case, most of the studies on interlocking directorates have shown that in all capitalist economies financial institutions occupy central positions in boards of directors and have key influence. As stated recently by Iwanami for U.S. and Japan cases:

> They [financial institutions] exercise a considerable influence on the flow of capital and that of information regarding the availability of capital and investment opportunities. Moreover, general trading

companies, large industrial companies, and banks hold central positions in the Japanese intercorporate networks. They exercise a considerable influence on the flow of capital and that of information concerning strategic decision-making. Enterprises conducting business worldwide hold a central position in the networks both in the U.S. and Japan. Therefore, a sphere of influence exists in the network and the interlocks, which leads to a structural constraint and affects the decision making of individual enterprises. (Iwanami, 2006: 12–13)

As far as media firms are concerned, specific ties to financial institutions through directorates have also received some amount of attention from media managerial scholars (Dreier & Weinberg, 1979; see also An & Jin, 2004, 2005), whereas corporate governance research has usually identified the board composition as one of the most frequently studied governance mechanisms. However, the research focus has been mainly on the financial performance of the studied firms, rather than on their freedom of decision or accomplishment of democratic goals. Nevertheless, An and Jin's (2005) research revealed that ties to financial institutions may lead to more debt financing in newspaper firms, in line with the financial-control theory perspective. This research, thus, supported previous findings from studies not focused only on media firms, which concluded that having representatives from financial institutions on companies' boards not only increased debt-financing, but also protected the ownership interests of the financial institutions. The end result is that companies run conservatively and, paradoxically, with lower profitability (An & Jin, 2005: 15).

Soloski's (2005) research on the boards of directors of newspapers led to the same conclusions. First described in 1999, the situation remained much the same in 2004, with boards of directors of publicly traded newspaper companies coming from the banking and investment communities as well as from industry and with few board members having any journalistic experience.

Finally, and mainly as a result of what has been contended, we must also account for the ultimate corporate goals of media conglomerates: Many media giants have integrated participation in the financial markets as a main regular activity. Thus, they have become financial actors that play with assets in the new international finance arena, rather than focusing on their communication and information aims—or maybe it is that financial activity that explains the communication and information aims of some of the news produced by specific media conglomerates.

3

Financialization in the World's Top Media Conglomerates

In 2002, one of the largest European media empires, KirchGruppe, suddenly went bankrupt and vanished. A complex corporate relationship among media, finance, and politics ended with the collapse of the 46-year-old conglomerate built around films, television, football, and Formula 1 by the German entrepreneur Leo Kirch. It was a dramatic downfall, the biggest corporate bankruptcy in Germany since World War II, and one of the most striking demises ever seen in the media sector worldwide.

The group, up to then seemingly impervious to economic downturns, employed 10 thousand people and had a combined turnover of more than 6 billion euros. Starting in April 2002, one after another, the main holding companies of KirchGruppe announced insolvency, and the conglomerate simply disintegrated. As a result of this, an outstanding list of relevant German banks became direct owners of important media assets, while the whole German media sector was pushed into a profound restructuring. Some years later, the main German financial society, Deutsche Bank, was sentenced to pay for damages and bank secrecy violation—a statement publicly questioning Kirch's solvency by Rolf Breuer, chief executive of Deutsche Bank, a leading backer of the KirchGruppe, had triggered the loss of financial confidence in the conglomerate. Breuer resigned, and the affair evidenced the deep ties that bonded German politics, banking, and big corporations.

This connection was, in fact, no revelation. Kirch's good relations with Bavarian conservative politicians were well known, as was the fact that the latter had aided this group to gain the financial backing of German banks at various times. Nevertheless, the group's debacle threw light on the enormous fragility of the foundations on which corporate giant Kirch was grounded. Of course, it threw light on the consequences of having financialized corporate activity beyond the point of no return.

KirchGruppe was one of the great champions of unbridled growth in the European media sector during the 1990s. The goal of achieving the largest corporate size possible as fast as possible had left it considerably in debt, but political favor ensured the banks' support and the financial strength that in turn guaranteed the favor of politicians, who enjoyed positive media coverage or direct financial support, as was made evident in the case of conservative Helmut Kohl. But in 2001, rumors began to spread that Rupert Murdoch's News Corporation had ambitions to refinance and take control of KirchMedia, the most significant KirchGruppe media holding. To prevent this, Leo Kirch sought to raise more capital to keep the company under his control. Unexpectedly, the previous funders that supported the Kirch debt and growth refused to extend additional credit and even started to demand quick repayment of loans. Actually, it wasn't surprising that Kirch, in its ailing financial situation, lost the confidence of its supporters, but until then the group had been able to keep the support of politicians and financiers despite its well-known financial condition. The point is: Why was confidence lost then and not before or after 2002? The answer has nothing to do with the actual corporate balance sheet but with the unstable and unpredictable balance between political and financial interests that Kirch managed to combine in its favor for a while. The truth is that the same actors that allowed the huge debt and financialization of KirchGruppe to grow were the ones that let it fall (we should rather say pushed its fall) when the balance-of-power relations started to change.

Fowler and Curwen (2002), who studied the case in depth, remind us of the conflict with Springer and the large amount of money owed by the KirchGruppe to Bayerische Landesbank as the key elements of this changing power balance. This bank happened to be at the time a quasi-public financial institution controlled by CSU Chancellor candidate and Bavarian Minister, Edmund Stoiber. Kirch's enormous debt, with Stoiber's Bayerische Landesbank as the main creditor, emerged as "sources of embarrassment for the Bavarian Minister," according to Fowler and Curwen. On the other hand, Kirch had pledged its 40% shareholding in Axel Springer as collateral for a Deutsche Bank loan. For many, the public questioning of creditworthiness of the KirchGruppe by the chief executive of Deutsche Bank at that moment was no innocent matter. Unquestionably, as court decisions confirmed afterwards, the statement played a critical role in the loss of confidence by Kirch's banking creditors. In short, the Kirch issue caused a confrontation among political parties (Social Democrats vs. Christian Democrats), financial institutions (federal- vs. Bavarian-based societies), business interests, and media moguls.

We are not actually interested here in the political-balance forces in play in this story or in what exactly the power balance was that support- ed Kirch and afterward pushed him into bankruptcy. If we are looking back to this case, it is to point out the financial instability on which Kirch found- ed its empire and the strong dependencies and links of various kinds— corporate, financial, and political—that this entailed for the company. According to Fowler and Curwen, Leo Kirch's big mistake was having taken a number of calculated risks based on incalculable financial issues:

> In the first place he took the risk that interest payments would always comfortably be covered by earnings. Second, he took the risk that the banks would always be compliant, and that political pressure would be placed upon them, especially in Bavaria, at times when they became less amenable. Third, he took the risk that he could attract large amounts of private capital via the issuance of put options which he would never be called upon to honour.

Kirch's balance sheet for 2001 showed 5.6 billion euros in bank debt and 2.3 billion euros in other liabilities. Fowler and Curwen found this heavy reliance on bank debt "unusual for modern corporations" at the time. We see in the following pages that the use of debt as the main source of growth, along with the other instruments of financialization we described in the previous chapter, haven't been the exception but rather the rule in modern countries in the media industry.

THE MEDIA INDUSTRY

The above is, in fact, no revelation. John Kenneth Galbraith (1993) reminded us in *A Short History of Financial Euphoria* of the extreme brevity of financial memory in the history of capitalism. That is why finan- cial disasters are quickly forgotten and the speculative episodes of finan- cial euphoria can reproduce over and over again. The key point of the question, according to Galbraith, is that all analyses persistently pre- clude any serious contemplation of the true nature of what is taking place: recurrent episodes of mass insanity.

Galbraith studied all the great speculative episodes of the last three centuries (until the early 1990s) and discovered the recurrence of com- mon features. Two factors especially contribute to and support every episode of euphoria: first is the extreme brevity of financial memory mentioned above, and second is the specious association of money and intelligence: "Money is the measure of capitalist achievement. The more money, the greater the achievement and the intelligence that supports it." Over and over again, the "investing public is fascinated and captured by the great financial mind. That fascination derives, in turn, from the scale of the financial operations and the feeling that, with so much money involved, the mental resources behind them cannot be less" (Galbraith, 1993: 14, 17).

But there is a third common feature no less important. Galbraith's (1993) words couldn't be clearer: "The world of finance hails the invention of the wheel over and over again, often in a slightly more unstable version. All financial innovation involves, in one form or another, the creation of debt secured in greater or lesser adequacy by real assets" (Galbraith, 1993: 19). The invention of the wheel over and over again (i.e., celebrating recurrently someone's genius in discovering and using leverage) could have had in the media companies a strong opponent if journalism had been reporting in the proper way (taking its democratic role as its primary goal). Obviously, this hasn't been the case.

Media conglomerates not only haven't helped unveil the wheel/leverage recurrent invention fraud, but they have had a crucial role in supporting speculative escalations and moods, reinforcing the notion that euphoric moments are well within the norms of successful contemporary capitalism and that the rewards of speculation can be something durable and sane. When the optimism disappears and crisis and recession emerge, they have played a precious role in supporting the Schumpeterian notion, recalled by Galbraith, that the contraction is also normal, tolerable, and even benign.

Media conglomerates, in short, have not helped combat the loss of our financial memory, and they have played a key role in building up personal success stories based on the notion that a good fortune is due to superior acumen; that wealth comes from an exceptional mental aptitude; and that if a lot of money is involved, this must be a serious and superior business. Then comes the crash, and for a while the media recognize the failure. But the cycle starts again (sometimes after a few decades, at other times after only a few years) with the same recurrent pattern: Every euphoric episode "is protected and sustained by the will of those who are involved, in order to justify the circumstances that are making them rich. And it is equally protected by the will to ignore, exorcise, or condemn those who express doubts" (Galbraith, 1993: 11).

Media conglomerates have been among the main supporters of this will, as a consequence of taking as their primary role their commercial rather than their democratic function. Media conglomerates have become key sites for the optimism that is built on the optimism that drives prices up. Media conglomerates have also become financial players and objects in the speculation moods.

Many authors in the last decades have been calling against the "hyper-commercialism" and "accelerated commodification" of the current media age. Among them, remarkably, are political economists of communication, who have been "notable for their emphasis on describing and examining the significance of those structural forms responsible for the production, distribution, and exchange of communication," as Vincent Mosco stated several years ago (Mosco, 1996: 145). In the United States, Robert McChesney and Dan Schiller are two of the most outstanding current scholars to denounce media commercialism.

Actually, the call against commercially focused media isn't new, but rather as old as the birth of professional journalism. This took place in different periods of the 20th century in different countries, but in all places it meant a move from politically oriented to commercially oriented media despite the fact that some press systems remained explicitly partisan. As Robert McChesney observes, that move built into the professional code of journalists a set of biases that not only remain in place today but are stronger than ever: These biases have mainly to do with the selection and sources of stories (incorporating official sources as the basis for legitimate news), with contextualization (massively avoided), and with investigative journalism topics (amenable to the commercial aims of the owners and advertisers as corporate media avoid research on some issues and put stress on others according to their own commercial interests as corporations). That is, "the corporate news media have a vested interest in the corporate system" (McChesney, 2008: 52).

In the previous chapters, we presented the context that transformed this linkage with the corporate system into profound ties with the financial system as well. These ties give us the key to understand the critical role played by the media system in supporting speculative scenarios all through its history. In the following pages, we illustrate this linkage with examples afforded by the main tools that allow us to assess the degree of financialization of media conglomerates (quotation and financial instruments, ownership, indebtedness, boards of directors, and corporate goals). But to start with, we must specify whom we are talking about. The following table shows world media companies with more than US$2 billion in revenues from the news-media business in 2008.

The following list shows top world corporations with more than US$2 billion in revenues from news-media assets (television, radio, Internet, and/or printing media—magazines and newspapers) in 2008.[8] The list includes all major publicly owned media groups (non-state-owned but

The World's Top News-Media Owners
by Revenues (2008) (1)

Corporation (In parentheses: US$ in billions in revenues from news-media divisions when the groups have other main activities)	2008 Revenues (US$ in billions)	Country of origin
1. General Electric Co* (NBC Universal: 16.97)	182.52	U.S.
2. Time Warner Inc*	46.98	U.S.
3. Bouygues SA (TF1: 3.5)*	43.47	France
4. Walt Disney Co*	37.84	U.S.
5. Vivendi SA (Canal Plus: 6.05)*	33.74	France
6. News Corp*	33.00	U.S.
7. Bertelsmann AG** (RTL Group: 7.66 / Grüner + Jahr: 3.64)	21.40	Germany
8. Cox Enterprises Inc* (Newspapers, TV and Radio: 2.20)	15.40	U.S.
9. Viacom Inc*	14.63	U.S.
10. CBS Corp*	13.95	U.S.
11. Thomson Reuters Corp/Plc (2)*	13.44	Canada/UK
12. Lagardère SCA (Lagardère Active: 2.80)*	10.92	France
13. Advance Publications Inc (*)**	7.97	U.S.
14. Reed Elsevier Plc/NV*	7.64	UK/The Netherlands
15. Gannett Co Inc*	6.77	U.S.
16. Clear Channel Communications Inc*** (CC Radio: 3.3)	6.69	U.S.
17. McGraw-Hill Companies Inc* (Information and Media: 1.1)	6.36	U.S.
18. Mediaset SpA*	5.66	Italy
19. Promotora de Informaciones SA*	5.32	Spain
20. Tribune Co (*)***	5.06	U.S.
21. Wolters Kluwer NV*	4.50	The Netherlands
22. Washington Post Co (Newspapers,* Magazines and TV: 1.4)	4.46	U.S.
23. Hearst Corp (*)**	4.38	U.S.
24. ProSiebenSat.1 Media AG*	4.05	Germany
25. Sanoma Oyj*	4.03	Finland
26. Investment AB Kinnevik (Modern Time* Group and Metro: 0.40) (3)	3.81	Sweden
27. RCS MediaGroup SpA*	3.55	Italy
28. Grupo Televisa SA*	3.35	Mexico

29.	Daily Mail & General Trust Plc*	3.31	UK
30.	Georg von Holtzbrinck GmbH** (Newspapers and Business info: 1.36) (*)	3.30	Germany
31.	Globo Comunicação e Participações S.A**	3.20	Brazil
32.	Quebecor Inc** (Newspapers and Broadcasting: 1.31)	3.03	Canada
33.	New York Times Co*	2.95	U.S.
34.	ITV Plc*	2.90	UK
35.	Canwest Global Communications Corp*	2.56	Canada
36.	Independent News & Media Plc (*)*	2.46	Ireland
37.	Naspers Ltd*	2.27	South Africa
38.	Axel Springer AG*	2.26	Germany
39.	Schibsted ASA*	2.07	Norway
40.	Univision Communications Inc***	2.02	U.S.
41.	McClatchy Co*	2.00	U.S.

Source: The author's personal compilation based on the corporation's annual reports and press releases in web pages, except for Hearst Corporation, for which the source was Fortune.org. Different currencies converted to U.S. dollars at April 4, 2009 currency-exchange rates.
(1) Only media conglomerates with relevant assets in television, radio, Internet, and/or printing news media and more than US$2 billion in revenues from these businesses. (2) Merged in April 2008. Pro-forma fiscal year 2008 results. (3) Total sum of Kinnevik's pro-portional part of revenue (Holdings revenues).
(*) Fiscal Year 2007.
Note: * Traded Companies in 2008 (parent and/or subsidiaries)
            ** Private Companies
            ***Turned private between 2007 and 2008

listed in stock markets) and privately owned groups (not listed in stock markets) when information is available.

Large U.S. cable operators (Comcast, Cablevision, Direct TV, Liberty Media, Charter Communications, etc.) are missing from this list because most of them are mainly focused on providing telecommunications services and/or fiction content, and their news content segments don't have revenues that reach US$2 billion. Besides, trying to calculate this figure can be quite risky. Comcast, for instance, declared US$1.4 billion in programming revenues for 2008, but in this figure entertainment and redistribution (of third part content or channels) are dominant. Because Comcast is the larger player in the cable sector, cable operators weren't included, although as a whole they do have a role in providing news content.

Other relevant players are also missing from the list for the same reason. Pearson's media segment, Financial Times Group, had US$0.59 billion in revenues in 2008, while the largest portion of its revenues comes from North American education and international book publishing. BSkyB is also missing because it is included in News Corporation Assets. Virgin Media had US$6.1 billion in revenues in 2008, but only 9% came from its content segment (U.K. television channels and situp channels' portfolio of retail television channels). Hubert Burda's media revenues, in its turn, were slightly higher than US$2 billion in 2008, but the German company, a privately held, family-owned corporation, does not provide enough public data on its website.

As we can see, the largest companies are U.S.-based, the U.S. being the country with the largest amount of big news-media owners in the world. Although the European Union (E.U.) surpasses the United States in number of media corporations on the list, only 3 of them are among the 10 largest corporations by global revenues. It is noteworthy that in 2008, the United States, Canada, and the E.U. countries represented 93% of the group's nationalities shown on the list. Only three corporations aren't U.S.-, Canada-, or E.U.-based: Televisa (Mexico), Globo (Brazil), and Naspers (South Africa). Altogether, the U.S., Canada, and E.U. groups shown accumulate the main brands on every news-media market (television, radio, print, and the Internet) and concentrate most of the audiences and sales in their own areas of activity. The list doesn't include either software or service providers that also offer news (such as Google or Yahoo!). We also omit all kinds of directly or indirectly state-owned companies, as is the case with Gazprom-Media, the Russian media conglomerate owned by Gazprombank, which in 2008, in turn, was owned by Gazprom, the giant Russian gas extractor (the largest in the world and the largest Russian company). Although Gazprom-media was the owner of former independent media companies, the Russian government held 50.01% of the stake in its parent company in 2008.

Among the top 10 media corporations in 2008, we can find the well-known big six U.S. media conglomerates: Time Warner, News Corporation, The Walt Disney Corporation, General Electric/NBC Universal, Viacom, and CBS Corporation. Although we were able to identify up to 17 U.S. media corporate owners with more than US$2 billion revenues in news-media assets in 2008, these six huge corporations concentrate more than 85% of all U.S. revenues. They are the product of successive mergers and acquisitions throughout the 20th century, mainly during the last two decades. We must remember that 50 corporations controlled the vast majority of all news media in the United States in 1983 (Bagdikian, 1983).

The Top News-Media Owners in North America by Revenues (2008)

Corporation	Revenues (US$ in billions)	Difference from 2007 revenues	Revenues from news-media business (*)	Group net earnings/losses	Difference from 2007 (US$ in billions)	Number of employees
General Electric Co	182.52	5.81%	9.30%	17.41 (3)	(21.60%)	323,000
Time Warner Inc	46.98	1.08%	72.00%	(13.40)	–	87,000
Walt Disney Co	37.84	7.00%	62.02%	4.43	(6.00%)	137,000
News Corp	33.00	15.15%	66.40%	5.39	57.24%	53,000
Cox Enterprises Inc	15.40	2.66%	14.29%	n/a	n/a	77,000
CBS Corp	13.95	(100%)	78.00%	(11.67)	–	25,920
Viacom Inc	14.63	8.95%	60.00%	1.25	(32.00%)	11,500
Thomsonreuters Corp/Plc	13.44	8.03%	60.00%	1.94	23.23%	53,700
Gannett Co	6.77	(9.02%)	c. 100%	(6.65)	–	41,500
Clear Channel Comm Inc	6.69	(3.36%)	49.00%	(4.01)	–	22,100
McGraw-Hill Companies Inc	6.36	(6.20%)	16.70%	0.80	(21.1%)	21,649
Tribune Co (**)	5.06	(7.00%)	c. 100%	0.63	(41.51%)	19,600
Washington Post Co	4.46	6.72%	30.87%	0.17	(63.48%)	20,000
Hearst Corp (**)	4.38	(3.10%)	c. 100%	n/a	n/a	20,000
Grupo Televisa SA	3.35	18.55%	81.24%	0.63	1.90%	17,300

The Top News-Media Owners in North America by Revenues (2008) (continued)

Corporation	Revenues (US$ in billions)	Difference from 2007 revenues	Revenues from news-media business (*)	Group net earnings/losses	Difference from 2007 (US$ in billions)	Number of employees
Quebecor Inc	3.03	10.82%	51.47%	n/a	n/a	17,100
New York Times Co	2.95	(7.70%)	c. 100%	(0.06)	—	9,346
Canwest Global Comm Corp	2.56	9.84%	c. 100%	(0.83)	—	2,171
Univision Comm Inc	2.02	(2.15%)	c. 100%	(5.13)	—	4,100
McClatchy Co	2.00	(15.90%)	c. 100%	(0.04)	—	12,100

Source: Annual reports and Forbes.org for Hearst Corporation. Negative figures in parentheses. C, Circa.
Note: Advanced Publications is missing due to the lack of public information.
(*) Television, radio, newspapers, magazines, online news. (**) Fiscal year 2007.

As these data show, the big six U.S. corporations mentioned before, despite the impact of the global economic slump on corporate revenues and earnings, were still by a significant difference the big six U.S. media owners by revenues from the news-media business in 2008: Time Warner (US$34 billion), Walt Disney (US$24 billion), News Corporation (US$22 billion), General Electric (US$17 billion), CBS (US$11 billion), and Viacom (US$9 billion). Nearly all of them have holdings in all main communication sectors (i.e., television, radio, film, print publishing, and the Internet), although we should note that most of them focused their media empires on broadcasting.

Overall, with the remaining big U.S. corporations on our list, this group of corporations includes almost all the top North American news-media brands: the top U.S. networks (ABC, CBS, NBC, Fox, CNN, and MSNBC); the most influential and nation-wide U.S. dailies (*The New York Times*, *The Wall Street Journal*, *The Washington Post*, and *USA Today*) as well as the main local newspapers; the top radio station owners (Clear Channel, CBS Radio, and Citadel Broadcasting); the top Spanish-language media in North America (Univision, Galavision, and Televisa); and the main weekly publications (*Time, Newsweek, Businessweek*, and *Fortune*). Besides other assets in cultural industries and outside cultural industries, it is remarkable that the six top U.S. media corporations are also the owners of five of the six major film studios (20th Century Fox, Warner Bros., Paramount, Universal, and Walt Disney Pictures), not counting other formerly independent film studios that they own as well.

Top 2008 Brands of the Largest North American News-Media Owners

Corporation	TV	Radio	Print	Others in cultural industries
Advance Publications			Condé Nast Publications, Parade Publications, Fairchild Publications, American City Business Journals, the Golf Digest Companies	
Canwest	Global TV, E!	Turkish Radio	National Post, The Gazette, The Vancouver Sun	
CBS	CBS, CW (50%)	CBS Radio		Simon & Schuster
Clear Channel Communications		Clear Channel Radio		Clear Channel Outdoor
Cox Enterprises	Cox Television, Travel Channel	Cox Radio	Dayton Daily News, Atlanta Journal-Constitution, The Western Star	Cox Cable
Gannett			USA Today, The Arizona Republic, The Indianapolis Star, Detroit Free Press, The Cincinnati Enquirer	Careerbuilder, ShopLocal
General Electric	NBC, Telemundo, CNBC, MSNBC			Universal Pictures
Hearst	Hearst-Argyle Television		San Francisco Chronicle, Houston Chronicle, Cosmopolitan, Esquire, O The Oprah Magazine, Denver Post, Salt Lake Tribune	

Company	Print / Publications	Television	Other
McClatchy	The Miami Herald, The Sacramento Bee, The Fort Worth Star-Telegram, The Kansas City Star, The Charlotte Observer, The News & Observer		
McGraw-Hill	Businessweek		Standard & Poor's, McGraw-Hill
New York Times	The New York Times, International Herald Tribune, The Globe		
News Corp	The Wall Street Journal, The New York Post, News of the World, The Sun, The Sunday Times, The Times, News International, Dow Jones	Fox, National Geographic, British Sky Broadcasting (39%), My Network TV	20th Century Fox, HarperCollins, MySpace
Quebecor	Journal de Montréal, Journal de Québec, Toronto Sun, London Free Press	TVA	Vidéotron ltée, Canoe
Scripps	The Times Record News, The Commercial Appeal, Knoxville News Sentinel, Ventura County Star		
Televisa		Televisa, Sky México	Cablevisión, Cablemás
Thomsonreuters			Thomson, Reuters
Time Warner	People, Time, Sports Illustrated, Fortune	CNN, HBO, Cinemax, Cartoon Network, TNT, CW (50%)	America Online, MapQuest, Netscape, Warner Bros. Pictures, Castle Rock

Top 2008 Brands of the Largest North American News-Media Owners (continued)

Corporation	TV	Radio	Print	Others in cultural industries
Tribune Company		WGN-AM	Los Angeles Times, Chicago Tribune, Newsday	
Univision Communication	Univision, Telefutura, Galavisión		Univision radio	
Viacom	MTV, Nickelodeon, Comedy Central	MTV Radio, Bet Radio		Paramount Pictures, Dreamworks
Walt Disney	ABC, Disney Channel, Touchstone TV, ESPN, Jetix	Citadel Broadcasting Corporation		Touchstone Pictures, Miramax Films, Walt Disney Pictures, Pixar Animation Studios, Buena Vista
Washington Post			Washington Post, Newsweek	Kaplan, Cable One

Source: Annual reports.

100

In 2008, Canada was the home country of three big media conglomerates: Thomson Reuters, Quebecor, and Canwest Global Communication. Also in 2008, Thomson Corporation—a Canadian provider of information, software, and services to business and professional customers—acquired the British group Reuters for nearly US$18 billion to create the two top world suppliers of financial information. Quebecor is the largest newspaper publisher in Canada (with Sun Media Corporation, Canada's largest national chain of tabloids and community newspapers, among others) and still a large group despite the bankruptcy of its huge printing segment in January 2008. Canwest is the other leading Canadian media company, with conventional and specialty television networks and the other largest newspaper chain in that country. Canwest has the smallest global revenues amount of the three big Canadian groups, but it is very much more concentrated on news-media business than Quebecor (whose main areas of business are cable providing and telecommunication services).

In Europe, media corporations with more than US$2 billion in revenue from media business were up to 19 in 2008. In the following table, we can see global revenues and other figures in euros for all of them. Taking global revenues as the reference, four big corporations are outstanding: French Bouygues, Vivendi, Lagardère, and German Bertelsmann.

The Top E.U. News-Media Owners by Revenues (2008)

Corporation	Revenues (€ in billions)	Difference from 2007 revenues	Revenues from news media business (*)	Group Net earnings/loss (€ in billions)	Difference from 2007	Number of employees
Bouygues SA (France)	32.71	10.56%	7.95%	1.50	9.08%	145,150 (3)
Vivendi SA (France)	25.39	17.25%	17.93%	2.60	(0.84%)	43,208
Bertelsmann AG (Germany)	16.10	(0.50%)	35.82%	0.27	(33.33%)	106,083
Lagardère (France)	8.21	3.10%	25.70%	0.59	11.05%	30,000
Reed Elsevier Plc/NV (UK/The Netherlands)	5.87	16.36%	31.87%	0.23	(65.61%)	16,000
Mediaset SpA (Italy)	4.25	4.16%	c. 100%	0.46	(9.43%)	6,375
Promotora de Informaciones SA (Spain)	4.00	8.30%	c. 85%	0.08	(56.80%)	13,432
Wolters Kluwer NV (The Netherlands)	3.37	(1.00%)	c. 70%	0.42	0.00%	20,000
ProSiebenSat.1 Media AG (Germany)	3.05	(5.65%)	c. 100%	(0.13)	—	6,000
Sanoma Oyj (Finland)	3.03	3.55%	62.00%	0.12	(50.91%)	21,329
Investment AB Kinnevik (Sweden) (1)	2.91	7.00%	10.38%	n/a	n/a	1,828
Axel Springer AG (Germany)	1.67	0.24%	c. 100%	0.20	32.88%	10,666
RCS Mediagroup SpA (Italy)	2.67	(1.99%)	c. 100%	0.04	(82.61%)	6,628
Daily Mail and General Trust Plc (UK)	2.54	(3.43%)	70.13%	0.18	(86.26%)	17,400
Georg von Holtzbrinck GmbH (Germany) (2)	2.49	10.95%	48.30%	n/a	n/a	14,000
ITV Plc (UK)	2.59	(2.65%)	96.77%	(2.80)	—	5,600
Independent News & Media Plc (Ireland) (2)	1.86	2.30%	c. 100%	0.12	(6.90)	10,100
Schibsted ASA (Norway)	1.56	1.00%	69.00%	(0.10)	—	9,000

Source: Annual reports. Negative figures in parentheses.

(*) Broadcasting, newspapers, magazines, or information online services.

(1) Total sum of Kinnevik's proportional part of revenue (holdings revenues). (2) Fiscal year 2007. (3) Contributors.

Note: British pounds and Swedish and Norwegian kroner converted to Euros at April 4, 2009,currency-exchange rates.

As was the case with U.S. and Canadian conglomerates, top European corporations include most of the main media brands in their respective countries of origin and areas of business. In broadcasting, German groups Bertelsmann (through RTL subsidiary) and ProSiebenSat.1 in 2008 operated a considerable number of television channels and radio stations across many European countries and were the largest European broadcasters—after Vivendi's vain attempt at becoming a pan-European broadcaster with Canal Plus. In the magazines segment, French Lagardère and German Axel Springer have a considerable number of magazine titles appearing as licensed editions in many European countries, while Italian RCS Mediagroup is the owner of one of the largest Spanish media groups (Unidad Editorial). Promotora de Informaciones SA (Prisa), the largest Spanish media conglomerate, has focused its international expansion strategy mainly on Latin-American countries, while UK media groups have done the same toward former British colonies. In the newspapers segment, the most important recent investment in past years had been the Nordic free newspapers *Metro* and *20 Minutes*, with many different local editions across different cities of Europe. The financial turmoil of 2008, with the advertising crisis that followed, severely affected these free papers, exclusively funded on advertising revenues.

We do not inquire here in any more depth into the analysis of the European sector, as we did not for the North American sector, because that is not the purpose of this book. Rather, our purpose is to show the degree of financialization of almost all top news-media conglomerates. The following table points out the main brands accumulated by them in order to show the outstanding news-media assets held by these corporate groups.

Top 2008 Brands of the Largest E.U. News-Media Owners

Corporation	TV	Radio	Print	Others in cultural industries
Axel Springer (Germany)	Hamburg 1 (27%), TV Berlin (27%), dogan TV (20%, Turkey)	Antenne 1 Radio, Antenne Bayern	*Die Welt, Bild, BZ, Sport Bild, Audio video foto Bild, Euro, Auto Bild, Computer Bild*	Schwartzkopff-TV
Bertelsmann (Germany)	RTL (different brands in E.U. countries), M6 (France), Five (UK)	RTL group (different brands in E.U. countries)	Gruner + Jahr (75%)	Random House, Direct Group
Bouygues (France) DMGT (UK)	TF1	DMGRadio Australia	*The Daily Mail, Evening Standard, Metro,* Northcliffe Media, *Mail Today* (India), *Euromoney*	ITN (20%)
Holtzbrinck (Germany)			*Die Zeit, Handelsblatt, WirtschaftsWoche, Der Tagesspiegel, Main-Post*	Macmillan (UK and US); Henry Holt, St. Martin's Press (U.S.), Fischer Verlag, Rowohlt Verlag
Independent News & Media (Ireland)		Radio Mantra (20%, India), Australian Radio Network (Australia), The Radio Network (New Zealand)	*The Independent, The Star, Heraldam, The Belfast Telegraph, The New Zealand Herald (New Zealand), Danik Jagran* (India), *The Cape Times* (South Africa), Conde Nast Magazines	Jagran Engage (India), APN (Australia), CCI (South Africa)

Company (Country)	Television	Radio	Press	Other
ITV (UK)	ITV1, ITV2, ITV3, ITV4			ITV Studios, ITV Global Entertainment, ITN (40%)
Kinnevik (Sweden)	TV3 (also in Denmark and Norway), TV6, TV8, Viasat4 (Norway), TV3+ (Denmark), 3+ (Latvia, Estonia), Nova (Bulgaria)	P4 (Norway)	*Metro*	
Lagardère (France)	Gulli (65%), CanalJ, Virgin 17	Europe 1, Virgin radio, RFM	*Elle, Paris Match, Télé 7 jours*	Hachete, Fayard, Anaya
Mediaset (Italy)	Canale 5, Italia 1, Retequattro, Telecinco (50%, 51%) (Spain)			Publitalia, Endemol, Medusa Film
Prisa (Spain)	Cuatro, +Digital, TVI (Portugal)	Ser, Radiópolis (50%) (Mexico), Radio Caracol (Colombia)	*El País, As, Cinco Días,* Extra (Bolivia), *La Razón* (Bolivia)	Santillana
ProSiebenSat.1 Media (Germany)	Sat.1, Prosieben, Kable Eins, N24 (Germany); Veronica, Net 5, and SBS 6 (Netherlands); TV 2 (Hungary); Kanal 5 and Kanal 9 (Sweden); Kanal 5, Kanal4, 6'eren (Denmark); TV Norge (Norway); VT4 and Vijf TV (Belgium)	Nova FM (Denmark), Radio Norge (Norway), Lamsi FM (Greece), Kiss FM and Magic FM (Romania)	*Veronica Magazine, Total TV* (The Netherlands)	
RCS Mediagroup (Italy)	Veo Televisión (Spain)	Radio 105, Radio Montecarlo, Virgin Radio	*Corriere della Sera, La Gazzetta dello Sport, City; El Mundo, Expansión, Marca* (Spain)	Rizzoli, Fabri; La esfera de los Libros (Spain); Éditions Flammarion (France)

Top 2008 Brands of the Largest E.U. News-Media Owners *(continued)*

Corporation	TV	Radio	Print	Others in cultural industries
Reed Elsevier (UK)			*The Lancet, New Scientist, Cell, Computer Weekly, Broadcasting & Cable, Publishers Weekly, Bizz*	ScienceDirect, Scopus, Gray's Anatomy, Lexis.com
Sanoma WSOY (Finland)	Nelonen, JIM, Urheilukanava, KinoTV, Urheilu+kanava	Radio Aalto, Radio Helsinki	*Helsingin Sanomat, Ilta-Sanomat, The Moscow Times, The St. Petersburg Times, Metro, Kaupunkilehti Vartti*	WSOY, Finkino
Schibsted (Norway)	Kanal 2 (Estonia)		*Verdens Gang, Aftenposten; Aftonbladet, Svenska Dagbladet* (Sweden); *20 Minutes/os* (France and Spain); *Postimees, SL Õhtuleht* (Estonia); *LT, 15 Minutes* (Lithuania); *Moi Rayon* (Russia)	Schibsted Forlag, Metronome Film & Television, Classified Ads
Vivendi (France)	Canal +			Universal Music, Activision Blizzard, NBC Universal (20%)
Wolters Kluwer (The Netherlands)			Professional publications in the health, tax, accounting, corporate, financial services, legal, and regulatory sectors	

Source: Personal compilation based on corporative web pages.

The three remaining corporations with more than US$2 billion in revenue from the news-media business are the most important non-European, U.S., or Canadian private media companies in the world. Televisa (Mexico) is not the largest media company in the Spanish-speaking world (Spanish Prisa had larger revenues in 2008), but it is the largest in the Latin American Spanish-speaking area, with strong assets in broadcasting and television production, in addition to its strong television networks (44% of 2008 revenues). Televisa's are among the world's most exported Spanish-language soap operas. Despite its strength in the broadcasting sector, Televisa is also a relevant magazine publisher (7.5% of revenues). Brazilian Globo media group, a huge portion of whose revenues also comes from soap opera export, has the largest TV-station network in Brazil and, as Televisa, is focused on broadcasting media. South African Naspers is an international media company whose main operations are in pay television (55% of 2008 revenues) and print media (35% of revenues).

How and why all these world media giants have become so oversized has been well explained in many places, and it is not the purpose of this book to focus on this process, which has been based on the U.S. model of communication provision export around the globe and the global needs of top advertisers, whose industries have experienced the same level of concentration and increasingly transnational needs (a good summary can be found in McChesney, 2008: 305–338). But this logic— get very big very quickly in order to avoid being swallowed up—hasn't been free of charge. On the contrary, a huge financial and commercial effort has been made by these corporations to achieve it. This effort has been especially intense in corporations focused on the broadcasting area, but we can also find it in groups still concentrated on the newspaper and magazine segment. While some of them have been able to keep the focus on the news-publishing area after many important acquisitions of assets formerly owned by their competition, others have been expanding into different segments in order to avoid putting all their eggs in one basket—chiefly because this basket, news publishing, is the one that has been experiencing the strongest industrial transformation due to the digital transition and will remain in this transition for years to come. One of the most striking cases, in this sense, is The Washington Post company: While in 1998 about 75% of the company's revenues came from *The Washington Post*, *Newsweek*, and its television stations, in 2008 almost 70% came from the education business (Kaplan) and cable (Cable One). At any rate, in all cases, expansion has meant raising financial capital and deepening ties with financial firms.

In 2008, as the figures in the prior tables show, most of the world's major media corporations were severely buffeted by the financial and economic world crisis, which produced a stagnation or drop in advertising spending (worldwide, the spending increased by 2.6% in 2008, but figures in the most developed countries dropped for the first time after many years of growth) and, above all, generated a strong credit crunch. Despite its apparent strength and splendid growth during the preceding years, the media industry suddenly exhibited high volatility. Jobs were cut, shutdowns were announced, assets were put up for sale, and insolvency threats started to emerge in major news publishing, broadcasting, and Internet companies throughout 2008 and 2009. Before the decline in advertising became truly evident, most listed media quotations had already suffered drastic drops. All the previous euphoria turned abruptly into weakness following the exact pattern that Galbraith described for the financial history of the world.

That was actually the case for all main industrial sectors in world economies during that crisis. On the whole, that is a fairly clear indication of the degree to which all of them were dependent on the most volatile of all elements: financial leverage (i.e., borrowing money for corporate expansion). But a high level of unsecured debt wasn't the only cause for their weakness (as well as the main consequence of the irrational logic of getting very big very quickly). A high degree of financialization of the strategy and goals of the whole media business is what an in-depth analysis of its links with the financial system strongly depicts. Such an analysis explains—or includes elements that need further illumination—why the news-media sector wasn't able to aid in preventing the preceding speculative escalation and mood, and why, on the contrary, they were helping create that mood (and partook of the mood themselves), as has always been the case throughout the history of financial euphoria.

OWNERSHIP AND QUOTATION: THE FINANCIALIZATION OF THE CAPITAL STRUCTURE

To begin with, we must look at the owners of the news-media industry. It is well known that shares in nearly every major media company in the developed world are nowadays traded on one or more stock markets. Almost all corporations on our 2008 list are publicly owned or have publicly owned subsidiaries, with few exceptions, and even in those cases companies are also raising funds from capital markets (Bertelsmann, Globo, Hearst, Hotzbrinck). The reason is simple: Playing in the top media league means becoming capital-demanding, and being listed in stock markets is the fastest way to gain access to capital resources.

What has made news media an industry that requires large amounts of money has been the confluence of two main elements in the past decades: growth pressures due to concentration trends and hi-tech transformation due to technological change. Investment in global expansion and expensive technologies dramatically increased the need for capital, chiefly as a result of the so-called digital convergence, which means that the whole industry needs to redefine its business in the new digital era. What was initially sold as a way to radically reduce costs for traditional media (being able to substitute, for instance, bits for paper) has shown to be, in most cases, a complex and expensive transformation (professional journalists are still needed, probably more than ever, but the repertory of services and products that can be delivered through digital platforms has multiplied the offer). Although the technology now allows the production of all kinds of media content far more easily, to achieve a high degree of competence within journalism and to produce high-quality professional content is the same as ever: lots of experience and effort. Many Internet startups discovered this too late in the Internet bubble of the late 1990s and illustrated the fact that huge amounts of money invested in high technology doesn't automatically produce high-quality news content ("quality" here being not only high image quality and sophisticated possibilities of user interaction). The same applies to satellite and terrestrial digital television and to all kinds of content delivered through new digital platforms.

The wave of initial public offerings for media companies started in the 1960s (Picard, 1994, 2002), but it was in the 1990s and onward that trade in stock markets of top media giants became widespread (at the same time that the growth and concentration of the industry consolidated). With few exceptions, in 2009, all big media companies, including top news-media producers, were listed in stock markets (their parent companies, their media subsidiaries, or both). Although, as Picard observed, traditional media firms overall were not the most attractive investment in the markets, this has not been the case for broadcasting companies. Broadcasting firms have been viewed since they started listing as having the potential for significant growth and future profitability (Picard, 2002). These profit and growth expectations and the oligopolistic scenario of the broadcasting sector worldwide have contributed to the rise of the price of their shares. At the same time, as the media industry increasingly transforms its business model and broadens its methods of distribution—as a main consequence of the convergence that digital technology allows—media companies more and more are becoming cross-platform distributors of content in the digital scenario. However, we must note that in 2008, top media players still got most of their revenues from traditional media. Although increasingly digitized in its internal activities, traditional news publishing through radio, television, and print, and not the Internet, was still the leading revenue source for the majority of media corporations, with few exceptions (e.g., professional information providers such as Thomson Reuters). Most major media players have been trying to expand their business—with different degrees of success, we must add—into as many media segments as possible with the aim of becoming global players in the digital scenario (everybody wanting to be considered a digital broadcaster). It has been this linkage of media firms with leading-edge segments (mainly telecommunications, high technology, and everything connected with digitalization) that has been pushing expectations up in stock markets.

That is why since the 1990s we have seen huge amounts of financial capital flowing to media firms, nationally and also internationally, with many foreign media firms or subsidiaries being listed in the New York Stock Exchange in order to gain access to billions of dollars in U.S. capital (e.g., Vivendi, Bertelsmann, TF1, Canal+, Lagardère, Televisa, Media Capital, and RTL). This consolidation of ownership of media firms through the stock markets has not meant that ownership has been spread into the hands of passive investors while media moguls disappeared. Or we should rather say that it hasn't meant only this because it is true that media moguls have seen their influence reduced (at least in some cases), and many investors are really passive (interested solely in financial returns and not in the quality of the journalism practiced by its investments). But, in addition to this, we must stress the increasing presence of banking and investment firms in media corporations that this kind of ownership has brought to the industry.

Let's look at the six largest U.S. media corporations to begin with. In early June 2008, the six conglomerates' ownership was distributed as shown in the following table.

As is also well known, the majority of large firms' stocks are held by big institutions (namely institutional investors). But what does this mean? Big institutions or institutional investors include pension funds, trust funds, mutual funds, hedge funds, private equity firms, and large accounts in general, and they are often owned by, or related to, financial institutions. Mutual funds, although not holding the majority of outstanding shares, are commonly the most numerous of these institutions. Mutual funds are investment companies classed as *open-end investment companies* by the Securities and Exchange Commission (SEC). That means that they are professionally managed firms of collective investments that collect money from many investors to make investments in securities (stocks, bonds, short-term money market instruments, and others). Mutual funds, as well as the majority of institutional holders, are principally, although not exclusively, interested in listed companies in order to make the greatest return possible in the shortest period of time.

General Electric (GE), owner of NBC Universal, is by far the largest conglomerate of the six with the greatest number of large institutions,

Ownership of Top Six U.S. News-Media Corporations 2008 (1)

Ownership's main traits (2)	GE	DIS	TWX	NWS	VIA	CBS
Free Floating (%)	99.17	92.43	99.68	72.47*	87.80*	86.15*
Institutional Class A ownership or only one class (%)	60.73	64.00	81.97	85.80*	13.04	15.28
Top 10 institutions non MF (%)	19.70	25.27	34.19	45.9*	11.70	14.20
Mutual Funds (%)	6.26	7.63	13.01	1.20*	3.95	1.28
Large class A holders (number)	6,684	3,824	3,594	2,092*	152	153
Institutions	2,257	1,369	1,160	655*	90	82
Mutual Funds	4,400	2,434	2,406	1,421*	58	69
Others	27	21	28	16*	4	2
Institutional Class B ownership (%)	—	—	—	22.88	80.68*	81.62*
Top 10 institutions non MF (%)	—	—	—	13.70	41.20*	39.40*
Mutual Funds (%)	—	—	—	0.87	1.26*	2.09*
Large class B holders (number)	—	—	—	160	2,167*	2,039
Institutions				68	694*	688
Mutual Funds				79	1,458*	1,334
Others				13	15*	17
Board of Directors	0.22	7.57	0.32	40.00	82.00	80.00
Top Shareholder's stake	3.29	7.20	5.10	40.00	81.64	79.80

Source: AOL Finance, MSN Money, Business Week, Yahoo Finance, and SEC.
(1) Figures gathered on June 10, 2008. *Stock without voting rights.
(2) GE: General Electric; DIS: Walt Disney; TWX: Time Warner; NWS: News Corp; VIA: Viacom; CBS: CBS.

which control more than the 60% of GE ownership. At the time of our research in June 2008, among the top 20 GE institutional shareholders we could find divisions of at least six banking entities: Barclays (the first GE institutional shareholder, with 3.94% of shares) and State Street (the second GE institutional shareholder, with 3.28% of shares), but also Northern Trust, Fidelity, Mellon, and Wells Fargo. With this high percentage of institutional ownership and representation of banking entities in the top positions, it is easy to conclude that financially driven shareholders hold the main stock of GE ownership.

In the case of The Walt Disney Company (DIS), institutional investors controlled 64% of the company ownership. Among the top 20 institutional shareholders in June 2008, I could find divisions of at least seven banking entities: Fidelity (the first Disney institutional shareholder, with 4.76% of shares), Barclays (4.03% of shares), and State Street (3.80), but also Northern, Black Rock, JP Morgan, and Mellon. Thus, financially driven shareholders hold the main stock of Disney ownership. Only the presence of a single prominent nonfinancial individual shareholder bucks this trend (Steve Jobs, Apple's CEO, with more than 7% of stock).

Time Warner (TWX), in turn, shows the largest figure in terms of institutional ownership in a publicly held media company: 82% of its stock was distributed among 3,594 institutional owners. Among the top 20 institutional shareholders are divisions of at least six banking entities: Barclays (4.62% of shares), Fidelity (3.80%), and State Street (3.40%), but also Goldman Sachs, Northern, and Black Rock. A mutual fund company, Dodge & Cox, with 5.10% of TWX ownership, is the only investor with more than 5% of shares and is the main TWX shareholder. With such a strong presence of institutional holders and financial entities, we must again conclude that financially motivated shareholders hold the main stock of TWX ownership.

Despite being listed companies, the three remaining conglomerates were privately controlled groups with two different classes of stock: non-free-floating shares with voting rights (class A for Viacom and CBS, and class B for News Corp) and free-floating shares without voting rights (class B for Viacom and CBS, and class A for News Corp). Each one of these media conglomerates has a sole and main stockholder controlling the majority of voting shares and, thus, controlling the boards of directors regardless of the trading movements in the free-floating stock. Nevertheless, the publicly held stock packages without voting rights also represent a group of important financial partners (as they were contributing to the company capitalization) for their respective controlling shareholders, and it is common to find the latter also holding shares in the nonvoting stock. Needless to say, we can also find other interests, including financial ones, among the voting shares that are not in the hands of the controlling shareholder.

In June 2008, around 72% of News Corp (NWS) shares were free-floating shares without voting rights, whereas as much as 86% of them were in institutional hands. As far as the class B shares are concerned, the stock with voting rights (23%) was held by institutions, whereas 40% belonged to an individual shareholder, Rupert Murdoch, through the Murdoch Family Trust. This percentage of control was achieved in February 2008 after the approval by the U.S. Justice Department and the FCC of the stock buyback from Liberty Media, which had until then been the second main stockholder (with 16% of voting shares). This swap between Liberty Media and News Corp meant the exchange of a 16.3% stake in NWS for shares of DirecTV, three regional sports networks and US$550 million in cash.

Among the top 20 institutional shareholders of NWS, we can find divisions of at least six banking entities in both classes of stock: Fidelity, Mellon, Citigroup, JP Morgan, and Barclays, while a mutual fund, Dodge & Cox, holds 12% of class A (nonvoting) shares. The remaining top institutional shareholders are private equity firms and large funds. Thus, financially motivated shareholders also have a vigorous presence in NWS ownership.

Since the 2006 split of Viacom (VIA) and CBS, both companies have been controlled by Sumner M. Redstone through National Amusements, Inc., the firm that controls NAIRI, Inc., the main Viacom and CBS stockholder. Through these companies, Redstone had around 80% of the voting rights in each board of directors. Both firms included, nevertheless, large stockholders in their two types of shares who represent around 80% of Viacom and CBS ownership in the nonvoting shares stock and between 13% and 15% in the voting stock.

Among the top 20 institutional shareholders of Viacom are divisions of at least three banking entities in both classes of stocks: UBS, Barclays, and State Street. The remaining institutions are investment firms and large funds, whereas the second largest investor with voting stock in Viacom is Mario J. Gabelli, with 8.5% of class A shares. Gabelli was also the chairman and CEO of GAMCO Investors, Inc., a New York Stock Exchange-listed company that is a provider of investment advice to alternative investments, mutual funds, and institutional and high-net-worth investors.

Finally, among the top 20 institutional shareholders of CBS, in both classes of stocks, we can find divisions of at least four banking entities: State Street, Goldman Sachs, Credit Suisse, and UBS. The remaining institutions are investment firms and large funds, whereas the second largest investor with voting stock in CBS is again Mario J. Gabelli, with 7.7% of class A shares. According to CBS' annual report, GAMCO Investors, Gabelli's firm, received US$274,120 in 2007 from CBS for investment management services.

According to *Business Week* website analyses in June 2008, the institutional ownership of these six U.S. corporations represented a greater percentage than is typically held for stocks in the media conglomerates industry. In fact, the vast majority of institutional entities, let alone banking-related entities, are also financially driven: Mutual or hedge funds, equity firms, or investment firms are not industrial partners, but rather capitalist partners and, thus, in their investments do not seek to improve the invested firms' industrial know-how, but to maximize their capital investments as quickly as possible. This is true even in those cases where media moguls control the majority of the stock.

We can identify other media moguls/families still in charge at their respective companies in many major listed top media firms (with or without dual classes of shares). The heirs of former Ohio Governor, James Cox, were still in early 2009 the primary owners of Cox Enterprises, a privately held media empire that has its main subsidiary, Cox Radio, listed in the stock exchange markets. The heirs of James A. McGraw, founder of the McGraw-Hill companies, were still on the board of directors of the corporation in the same period. The descendants of Adolph Ochs, who purchased the *New York Times* newspaper in 1896, and Arthur Hays Sulzberger maintained control of the company by holding nearly 90% of the class of stock that counts in the company. It is the same for the McClatchy family, holders of the main controlling stock at McClatchy company, the American publishing firm that in 2006 purchased Knight Ridder, formerly the second largest chain of daily newspapers in the United States. In this last case, under the terms of the agreement, the class B shareholders have agreed to restrict the transfer of any shares of class B common stock to one or more "Permitted Transferees," subject to certain exceptions—a "Permitted Transferee" being any current holder of shares of class B common stock of the company; any lineal descendant of Charles K. McClatchy; or a trust for the exclusive benefit of, or in which all of the remaining beneficial interests are owned by one or more lineal descendants of Charles K. McClatchy. All of this is meant to preserve the control of the company under McClatchy family and its milieu despite shares being traded in the stock exchange markets. Also in the United States, the descendants of S. I. Newhouse still control Advance Publications, a 1922 company ranked as the 41st largest private U.S. company according to Forbes in 2008.

The list goes on. In the Washington Post Company, the heirs of the Meyers-Graham family also kept a controlling stake in early 2009. French Bouygues had a minority controlling stock (19%) in the hands of the Bouygues family. Arnaud Lagardère, the descendant of the family that purchased the Hachette Empire, held also the largest stake (10.7%) of French Lagardère company. The German Springer family has managed to keep 58.5% of the controlling stock in the hands of the founder's widow, Friede Springer. Silvio Berlusconi held a large 36% share of the whole Mediaset, his self-made media empire that controls the main Italian television channels and since 2007 also 75% of Dutch television production company Endemol. The sons of Jan Hugo Stenbeck keep control of the Swedish investment group Kinnevik, owner of a controlling stock of Metro International and Modern Media Times. In Spain, Prisa, the largest media firm of the Spanish-speaking world, was in 2009 still under control of Jesus de Polanco's descendants and their milieu. In the same period, Norwegian Schibsted was controlled by the Tinius Trust, a foundation established by Schibsted's former largest owner, Tinius Nagell-Erichsen, with the express objective of retaining his influence as a major shareholder in the Schibsted Group after his death, which happened at the end of 2007. Finnish Sanoma was controlled in 2009 by Aatos Erkko and other members of the Erkko family (still around 30% after a sale of shares in March 2008), some of the wealthiest people in Finland and descendants of Sanoma's founder. In the UK, Jonathan Harmsworth, fourth Viscount Rothermere, inherited more than 21% of the Daily Mail & General Trust stock. In Ireland, The Independent News and Media had been controlled by Sir Antony O'Reilly and his family for a long time (almost 30% of shares) while an Irish entrepreneur, Denis O'Brien, took a 20% stake in January 2006. In Canada, Thomson Reuters, the company that combined Thomson and Reuters assets and operates since April 2008 under a dual listed company structure with two parents (one in Canada and the other in the UK), was kept under control of the Canadian Thomson family (53%). Still in Canada, the sons of Izzy Asper kept control of Canwest Global Communications, while the Péladeau Group, the Péladeau family's holding, did the same with Quebecor group. The Azcárraga family is in control of Televisa in Mexico.

For all of these media moguls, making their companies public didn't mean losing direct control of them. Nevertheless, even in those cases with large stakes under family control, looking for capital resources in the capital markets has brought to them enormous pressure in terms of financial results. For almost all of them, we could build a story in a similar way as we did for the six top U.S. media conglomerates, unveiling a large list of financial institutions in their ownership. In some cases, only a couple of institutional investors' stakes represent the same amount of voting shares as family owners. In others, family stocks are almost impossible to exceed by the sum total of institutional investors, but the pressure is still there because a decline in quotation means losing the market's confidence, and that can mean big problems when firms are as indebted as most of these are. As the table below shows, in 2009, most of these family-controlled and listed media firms had relevant financially oriented shareholders (around or more than 5% of the stock individually) in their ownership in stock either with or without full voting rights.

Main Institutional Investors in the World's
Top Listed Family/Mogul-Controlled Media Corporations

Company	Family/mogul in control	Institutional investors with largest stakes (country of origin and shares)
Axel Springer (Germany)	Springer	Deutsche Bank (Germany) (8.40%)
Bouygues (France)	Bouygues	Crédit Agricole Asset Management (France) (5.08%) Artémis (France) (2.00%)
CBS (U.S.)	Redstone	AllianceBernstein/AXA (U.S.) (14.30%) Barclays Global Investors (UK) (4.30%) State Street Global Advisors (U.S.) (3.80%)
Canwest (Canada)	Asper	Fairfax Financial Holdings (Canada) (22.4%)
Cox Radio	Cox	Buckhead Capital Management (U.S.) (U.S.) (15.19%) Dimensional Fund Advisors (U.S.) (11.94%) Barclays Global Investors (UK) (6.06%) DFA U.S. Micro Cap Series (U.S.) (5.92%) Vanguard Group (U.S.) (4.65%)
DGMT (UK)	Rothermere Viscounts	N/A
Kinnevik (Sweden)	Stenbeck	Swedbank Robur Funds (Sweden) (7.73%) Alecta Pension (Sweden) (6.19%) Handelsbanken Funds (Sweden) (2.10%)
Lagardère (France)	Lagardère	Qatar Investment Authority (Qatar) (6.46%) Société Génerale (France) (5.5.00) Morgan Stanley & Co International (U.S.) (5.00%)
McClatchy (U.S.)	McClatchy	Ariel Investments (U.S.) (26.23%) Bestinver Gestión (Spain) (16.85%) Chou Associates Management (Canada) (9.60%) Brandes Investment Partners (U.S.) (7.48%) Barclays Global Investors (UK) (6.09%)
McGraw-Hill	McGraw	T. Rowe Price Associates (U.S.) (10.50%) Blavin & Company (U.S.) (3.89%) Barclays Global Investors (UK) (3.83%) State Street Global Advisors (U.S.) (3.76%)
Mediaset (Italy)	Berlusconi	Philadelphia International Advisors (U.S.) (0.54%)

News Corp (U.S.)	Murdoch	Prince Alwaleed Bin Talal Abdulaziz (Saudi Arabia) (7.00%) Taube, Hodson, Stonex Partners (UK) (2.00%)
New York Times (U.S.)	Ochs	Harbert Management Corporation (U.S.) (U.S.) (19.94%) T. Rowe Price Associates (U.S.) (10.06%) Emigrant Savings Bank (U.S.) (4.68%)
Prisa (Spain)	Polanco	Urquijo Gestión (Spain) (4%)
Quebecor (Canada)	Péladeau	N/A
Sanoma (Finland)	Erkko	Ilmarinen Mutual Pension Insurance (Finland) (2.07%) Mandatum Life Insurance (Finland) (1.68%) Varma Mutual Pension Insurance (Finland) (1.60)
Schibsted (Norway)	Tinius Trust	State Street Bank and Trust (U.S.) (13.00%) Foketrygdfondet (Norway) (6.00%) JPMorgan Chase Bank (U.S.) (8.20%)
EW Scripps (U.S.)	Scripps	GAMCO Investors (U.S.) (5.30%)
Televisa (Mexico)	Azcárraga	Dodge & Cox (U.S.) (13.40%) Davis Selected Advisers (U.S.) (8.70%) Cascade Investment (U.S.) (5.50%)
The Independent News & Media (Ireland)	O'Reilly and O'Brien	N/A
Thomson Reuters (Canada/UK)	Thomson	Société Générale (France) (9.08%) Brandes Investment Partners (U.S.) (4.83%) Dodge & Cox (U.S.) (3.70%)
Viacom (U.S.)	Redstone	GAMCO Investors (U.S.) (8.70%)
Washington Post (U.S.)	Meyer-Graham	Berkshire Hathaway (U.S.) (21.31%) Southeastern Asset Management (U.S.) (5.38%) Sound Shore Management (U.S.) (4.01%) Longleaf Partners Small Cap Fund (U.S.) (4.34%)

Source: 2008 Annual Reports, Stock Exchange Authorities, and Online Financial Information Services (AOL Finance, Yahoo Finance, and MSN Money, mainly).

Of course, financially oriented shareholders are also present in the ownership of the remaining top media firms. In January 2009, Vivendi had around 20% of its stock controlled by French banking entities or their investing subsidiaries (Caisse d'Eparge, Banque Populaire, Caisse des Dépôts et Consignations, Crédit Agricole Société Générale, and others), although the institutional investor with the largest stake was a U.S. equity fund (Capital Research and Management Company) with almost 5% of the stock. British ITV, the merger of Carlton and Granada televisions, had American and British financial shareholders as its main institutional investors (U.S. Brandes Investment and a subsidiary of Fidelity Investments held more than 21% of the stock at the time while UK Legal and General Group and Barclays alone held up to 6.46%). Similarly, in 2009, Dutch banking corporation ING Direct held around 5.5% of the stocks of Dutch professional information providers Wolters Kluwer and Reed Elsevier.

Major banking and insurance societies and private equity, pension, and mutual funds have been pervasively investing in media firms especially since the 1990s through capital markets but not exclusively so. Some media firms have seen in the last decade the penetration of financial corporations into their private stocks.

Shareholders of RCS Mediagroup Consultation and Lock-up Shareholders Agreement January 2009

Banking entities	Insurance entities
Mediobanca (14.21%)	Assicurazioni Generali (3.76%)
Banco Popolare (5.95%)	
UBS Fiduciaria (5.95%)	
Intesa SanPaolo (5.65%)	

Investment entitites	Others
Efiparind BV (Pesenti Family (7.75%)	Diego della Valle (Fiorentina soccer club) (5.50%)
Sinpar Societat' Di Investimenti e Partecipazioni (2.09%)	Francesco Merloni (2.09%)
Premafin Finanziaria (5.46%)	Giuseppe Rotelli (3.95%)
Si. To. Financiere (5.14%)	Pirelli & C (5.17%)
	Giovanni Agnelli & C (Fiat) (10.29%)
	Gilberto Benetton (5.00%)

Source: RCS Shareholders Agreement.

The Italian group that owns *Corriere de la Sera* and *La Gazetta dello Sport*—and French publisher Flammarion and Spanish media firm Unidad Editorial (*El Mundo, Expansión, Marca, VeoTV*)—known as the holding RCS Mediagroup since May 2003, is backed by a private shareholders agreement (65% of shares), which includes outstanding banking and other financial entities as main stock holders along with other strong Italian corporations.

German ProsiebenSat.1 Media, one of the two largest commercial TV networks in Europe in 2009, has been owned, since March 2007, by two private equity firms: Kohlberg Kravis Roberts & Co and Permira Advisers Ltd. Both companies created Lavena Holding, which purchased a majority stake of Prosieben through a leveraged buyout. Through the takeover of Luxemburg's SBS Broadcasting In June 2007, a pan-European broadcaster capable of taking on the might of Bertelsmann's RTL Group was created. The deal was financed through a new loan provided by a host of banks led by Bank of America Corp., with ProSieben also using the financing to wipe clean its € 150 million debt. The two private equity firms that own this European broadcasting giant have their headquarters in the United States (KKR) and the UK (Permira), while Prosieben is based in Germany. This case provides a significant illustration of the issue of ownership and capital globalization.

Actually, ProsiebenSat.1 Media wasn't the only media firm taken over by speculative funds in the period 2007–2008 before the global financial crisis exploded. This shows that financial problems in the media firm were much more connected to its own growth and aggressive expansion strategies than to the global financial downturn initiated with

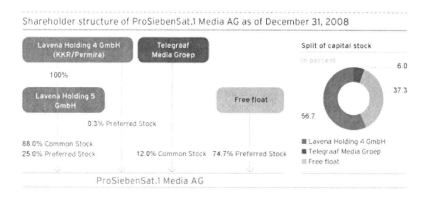

Shareholder structure of ProSiebenSat.1 Media AG as of December 31, 2008

Source: ProsiebenSat.1 Media webpage.

the subprime mortgage crisis in July 2007. In the United States, Univision and Clear Channel Communications were also purchased by financially oriented firms and, in their case, turned private. Tribune Company, in turn, is one of the best examples of the recurrent invention of the financial wheel denounced by Galbraith. The new wheel is, once again, leverage (borrowing). But here a second "innovation" was introduced: employees paying the consequences.

Univision, the largest Spanish-language television network in the United States and Puerto Rico, was sold in March 2007 to a consortium led by Haim Saban's Saban Capital Group (who had previously sold ProsiebenSat.1 to KKR and Permira), TPG Capital, L.P., Providence Equity Partners, Madison Dearborn Partners, and Thomas H. Lee Partners for US$13.7 billion plus US$1.4 billion in acquired debt. The buyout left the company with a debt 12 times its annual cash flow. That's why Univision's shareholders filed two class-action lawsuits against the company and its board members trying to stop the buyout. One lawsuit claimed that the board members structured the deal to benefit only the company's insiders and not the average stockholder. The other lawsuit claimed that the board put its own personal interests and the interests of the winning bidder ahead of shareholders, and it also failed to adequately evaluate the company's worth. In the meantime, more lawsuits were filed, all of this according to Univision SEC filings. The purchasers, for their part, reunited under the new Broadcasting Media Partners, Inc., turned the company private.

In July 2008, Clear Channel Communications, the largest radio broadcasting corporation in the world, was sold to private-equity funds sponsored by Bain Capital Partners, LLC, and Thomas H. Lee Partners, L.P. The sale was explained as the result of the global economic slowdown and its negative impact on Clear Channel ad revenues, but the US$8.0 billion net debt accumulated by the company was by no means a consequence of the global crisis. The impossibility of repayment was. In the irrational logic of financial capitalism, the purchase (US$18 billion) of this highly indebted radio company was executed through a leveraged buyout, that is, with a significant percentage of the purchase price being financed through leverage by six banking societies (Citigroup, Deutsche Bank, Morgan Stanley, Credit Suisse, Royal Bank of Scotland, and Wachovia). The stock of this enormous U.S. radio company ceased being traded on the public markets after the sale.

The case of Tribune Company, the owner of the *Chicago Tribune*, embodies the worst consequences of ownership financialization. The second largest newspaper publisher in the United States (Gannett is the first) was taken private in a complex US$8.2 billion leveraged buyout led by real estate mogul Sam Zell. However, according to media analysts, troubles for Tribune had started before, when the former owners of the

Los Angeles Times, which Tribune Co. acquired in 2000, forced the company to seek a restructuring. Zell's 2007 arrival and the 2007–2008 plummet in advertising income culminated the process, and in December 2008, the Tribune Company filed for Chapter 11 bankruptcy. But the main question surrounding the debt restructuring was what it would mean for Tribune's real owners after the 2007 buyout—that is, its 20,000 employees. As a means of financing the deal and realizing tax savings, Zell achieved a complicated agreement that turned Tribune into an employee-owned society, while Zell himself put up a relatively small amount of his own money ($315 million). In Tribune's most difficult period, speculative investors quickly withdrew. Due to the bankruptcy, billionaire Zell could lose a small fraction of his estimated US$5 billion fortune while Tribune's employees technically owned the company and were the holders of its US$13 billion debt at the beginning of 2009.

Indebtedness was the very problem of major media firms in 2009. In the preceding decade, most of them had based their growth and expansion on leverage. When leverage became unbearable, usually the solution was even more leverage. There is only one thing that keeps this perverse logic going on: expectations. When profit expectations are high, investors of all kinds (long, medium, and short term) hurry in. Expectations had been high in the years prior to the global financial crisis starting in mid-2007. Orthodox economic manuals explain that expectations in corporations are based on quotations in the case of listed companies, but usually reality shows the opposite: Quotations are based on expectations. The confirmation of this is the fact that quotations have been completely disconnected from real accounting results with respect to big companies in the years prior to any financial slump. Instead, it has been the promises, prospects, and hopes of big profits that have kept many quotations exorbitantly high. That is, it has been future virtual perspectives not real material realities that have driven quotations so high. What commonly occurs in financial crises is that suddenly this psychological scenario collapses—for whatever reason (we are dealing with intangible perceptions tied to irrational massive human delusions, as Galbraith noted)—and quotations drop dramatically and massively. At that precise moment, speculative investors retreat, and banking entities suddenly consider unbearable the same debt scenario that only some days before was pushing stock exchange markets up. In 2008, the DJ EuroStoxx Media Index, which tracks the share prices of European media companies, posted a 34.5% decrease. The truth was that drops were ubiquitous and dramatic in the media industry in 2008.

Media Market Capitalization Drops in 2008 (*)

Corporation (place of chosen quotation)	Share Var. 2008
Scripps EW (U.S.)	(94.57%)
McClatchy (U.S.)	(92.57%)
Canwest Global Comms (Canada)	(87.26%)
ProsiebenSat.1 Media (Germany)	(82.13%)
Independent News & Media (Ireland)	(81.50%)
Promotora de Informaciones (Spain)	(78.68%)
Gannett (U.S.)	(78.34%)
CBS (U.S.)	(67.50%)
Schibsted (Norway)	(64.76%)
RCS Mediagroup (Italy)	(59.32%)
Sanoma (Finland)	(56.38%)
New York Times (U.S.)	(56.21%)
Kinnevik (Sweden)	(54.34%)
General Electric (U.S.)	(54.19%)
News Corp (U.S.)	(50.59%)
Cox Radio (U.S.)	(49.66%)
Daily Mail General Trust (UK)	(48.77%)
Viacom (U.S.)	(48.36%)
Washington Post (U.S.)	(47.55%)
Axel Springer (Germany)	(47.50%)
McGraw-Hill (U.S.)	(45.77%)
ITV (UK)	(44.79%)
Bouygues (France)	(41.17%)
Lagardère (France)	(40.85%)
Time Warner (U.S.)	(35.88%)
Televisa (Mexico)	(32.85%)
Mediaset (Italy)	(31.24%)
Wolters Kluwer (The Netherlands)	(29.26%)
Walt Disney (U.S.)	(23.96%)
Reed Elsevier (London)	(16.45%)
Vivendi (France)	(13.37%)

Source: Yahoo Finance historical prices service (January 1, 2008 to December 31, 2008). Negative figures in parentheses.
(*) Quebecor, Thomson Reuters and Naspers are missing due to the nonavailability of the information because of a name change or lack of data in Yahoo Finance.

Finally, we must note that even if a corporation is private, the operation in public stock exchange markets is still possible. This is, for example, the case of Bertelsmann, which is a private company that has been strongly established in the international capital markets starting in 2002. Since that time, Bertelsmann has been using several financial instruments, among them listed bonds. Bonds, like stocks, are securities (a negotiable instrument representing financial value), but while stock holders are the owners of the company, bond holders are lenders to the issuers. Although the vast majority of trading volume in corporate bonds in most developed markets takes place in decentralized, dealer-based, over-the-counter markets, Bertelsmann issues listed bonds in several exchange markets. In January 2009, the company had listed bonds with a total volume of €3.5 billion (alongside private placements) and was one of the largest issuers of Euro-bonds in the media segment. As a bond-listed company, Bertelsmann had credit ratings from the agencies Standard & Poor's and Moody's in the Investment Grade area. Therefore, without having strictly financialized its ownership, Bertelsmann was also exposed to the changing expectations and moods of financial markets.

Everything described above shows how capitalization through exchange markets is still synonymous with strength and is considered a yardstick of corporate and economic power (high market capitalization, or use of securities in general, allows for industrial expansion, buyouts of competitors, avoidance of hostile bids, etc.). Therefore, when the capitalization in stock markets of the top media firms collapsed in 2008, emperor debt, which had no clothes, was exposed as the true problem it really was.

INDEBTEDNESS: LEVERAGE, ALWAYS LEVERAGE

The growing debt of media conglomerates was not a new phenomenon in 2009. Nevertheless, throughout the last two highly capital-intensive decades, this debt has become unprecedented as to scale at the financial level. At the same time, we can observe an intense use of financial tools for raising capital or for recapitalization to the point that they even exceed commercial loans (i.e., the use of financial tools such as public debt, bonds, notes, and commercial paper). Although commercial loans are designed to provide working capital to purchase supplies or finance production or distribution of products, and typically come from a bank and are long term, commercial papers, bonds, notes, and other securities represent a means of raising short-term cash at a rate lower than bank interest rates. Commercial papers or notes are unsecured promises to pay a debt. When access to banking loans is difficult for any reason, companies turn to these securities to refinance debt. Actually, in the first quarter of 2009, the world's volume of market debt more than doubled the amount issued during the same period in 2008. The financial crisis and the subsequent credit crunch were the cause of this increase. The media industry had also been using all these financial instruments abundantly before and after the onset of the crisis.

As is obvious for all crises in capitalism, economic slowdown produces negative effects in corporations' balance sheets, with stagnation or reduction of revenues and losses. In the case of the media industry, the problems of most segments come mainly from a slump in advertising revenues, one of the first variables that reflects the weakening in the economic environment. But sales of media products can also be affected as consumers reduce their expenditures.

A drop in revenues is always bad news for a company in capitalist economies, but when the corporation is indebted or highly indebted, the news is much more than bad. This can be a stairway down to financial hell: Debt repayments cannot be accomplished and a dangerous spiral of refinancing can start (not to mention the dramatic spiral of layoffs and asset sales). It is not impossible to leave this vicious circle if revenues rebound at high and sustained growth rates. Unfortunately, and against what orthodox economists consider as holy logic, there is no logic at all in thinking that exponential growth is possible in a sustained way. Actually it is the contrary because it is unquestionable that, even in the digital era, we do live in a planet with limited resources. Therefore, when corporations are linking their strategies to this oxymoron (sustained high growth rates), in the long term they will always lose the race, although this doesn't keep some people from becoming billionaires on the short or mid-term. Of course, this doesn't mean that corporations can't live for long; some already do, but often they do it at a high cost for the people who don't become billionaires in the meantime (employees, suppliers, stockholders, customers, etc.). In any case, what crisis periods show once again is that highly leveraged corporations are in weaker positions than firms with strategies less based on debt.

Amazingly, growing on leverage is something much prized in prosperous economical periods: Highly leveraged corporations can grow larger and faster, and that's precisely what speculative capital markets appreciate most. As a result, what in prosperity is a value that can even push a quotation to heaven can suddenly become the worst sin when banking and capital markets facilities come to the crunch. Discussing what the biggest problem in crisis periods is, whether drops in revenues or credit-crunch, misses the point and hides the real debate because all attention is focused on the crisis itself. The crisis is treated as the problem, when it really isn't. For many, in fact, the financialized (financial leverage) based economy of current capitalism is the main factor that causes economical stagnation and recession. The crisis wouldn't then be the problem but the consequence. If we want to look at the real roots of the problem, we should rather address the prior period of apparent unstoppable growth. Robert Brenner's description of the U.S. Internet bubble of the 1990s is just as valid for the media industry:

> Belief in the unprecedented potential of the New Economy to increase productivity made for ever-increasing profit expectations, which drove share prices ever higher; the resulting increase of on-paper wealth allowed for record levels of household and corporate borrowing, leading to fast-rising rates of investment and consumption growth; high levels of investment brought about significantly improved productivity performance and helped to dampen inflation, appearing to justify confidence in the New Economy, and so forth. The glitch, of course, was to be found in the ever-increasing chasm that had opened up between expected profits, on the one hand, and actual profits, on the other, which manifested itself in the stock market bubble. (Brenner, 2002: 263)

The Internet bubble burst in 2000, but the 1980s and 1990s had been a really splendorous period for the traditional media industry worldwide as well. Earnings rates and listed stocks had been constantly increasing, at least for the several that survived the concentration trends. As Brenner explained in detail for the economy as a whole during the last decades of the 20th century, debt was the main axis of all this expansion. We can observe it graphically in the indebtedness ratio reached by the world's top media conglomerates in 2008 through the debt/equity ratios.

The debt/equity ratio measures a company's financial leverage, indicating what proportion of equity and debt the company is using to finance its assets. A high debt/equity ratio—more than 1—means that a company has been aggressively financing its growth with debt. The following table shows that the majority of top media owners finished 2008 with a high level of financial indebtedness—an indebtedness that, with few exceptions, had been growing persistently in the preceding years.

Although North American companies have, in general terms, larger portions of debt in notes and other securities than European firms, all firms everywhere are increasingly using these kinds of financial instruments and commercial loans. In addition, we must not forget that the main buyers of bonds, notes, and other securities are investment banks, private equity firms, and other kinds of financially oriented institutions. But we must look at particular debt amounts to realize how large the degree of leverage in the sector was when the financial crisis started between 2007 and 2008. For comparative purposes, I have again included 2008 revenues.

Debt/Equity Ratio of the World's Top News-Media Owners in 2008

Ratio	Corporations
1 or less	Cox Radio, EW Scripps, Kinnevik, Walt Disney, Washington Post.
Between 1 and 1.9	Axel Springer, Lagardère, Mediaset, News Corp, Sanoma, TimeWarner, Vivendi.
Between 2 and 4.9	Bouygues, CBS, DMGT, Independent News & Media, McGraw-Hill, RCS Mediagroup, Schibsted, Viacom.
Between 5 and 9.9	Clear Channel Communications, Gannett, General Electric, ITV, New York Times, Promotora de informaciones, Wolters Kluwer.
More than 10	Canwest Global Communications, McClatchy, ProSiebenSat.1 Media, Reed Elsevier, Tribune (before bankruptcy), Univision (before 2007 sale).

Source: Personal calculation based on financial statements in annual reports.

The World's Top News-Media Owners
With More Than US$1 Billion in Debt

Corporations (2008 revenues, US$ in billions)	Total debt at the beginning of 2009 (US$ in billions)
General Electric (183)	523.76
Time Warner (47)	39.68
Clear Channel Communications (7)	19.50
Vivendi (34)	15.45
Walt Disney (38)	14.64
News Corp (33)	13.23
Tribune (5) (*)	13.00
Reed Elsevier (8)	11.25
Bouygues (44)	11.16
Univision (2)	10.60
Viacom (15)	8.00
CBS (14)	6.97
Promotora de Informaciones (5)	6.70
Bertelsmann (21) (a)	6.04
ProSiebenSat.1 Media (4)	5.37
Canwest Global Communications (3)	4.50
Gannet (7)	4.00
Lagardère (11)	3.48
Wolters Kluwer (5)	3.45

Washington Post (5)	2.40
McClatchy (2)	2.38
ITV (3)	2.26
Independent News & Media (1)	2.18
Mediaset (6)	1.95
RCS Mediagroup (4)	1.94
Daily Mail and General Trust (3)	1.53
Sanoma (4)	1.29
McGraw-Hill (6)	1.27
Kinnevik (4)	1.10
New York Times (3)	1.06

Source: Personal compilation based on corporations' annual reports. Different currencies converted to U.S. dollars at April 14, 2009 currency rates. (*) 2007 Fiscal year. (a) Only from listed bonds and private placements.

General Electric (GE) debt must be considered separately. The total debt of the GE consolidated group amounted to US$523.762 million as of December 31, 2008. Most of its giant debt was accounted for by its General Electric Capital Services Inc. division and its consolidated affiliates' borrowings (98% of total borrowing in 2008), which had been increasing at a regular and growing rate in recent years (58% between 2003 and 2007). Almost all of the GE debt is financial debt, mainly senior debt (unsecured and asset-backed) and commercial papers (U.S. and non-U.S.), while the borrowings payable to banks through loans represent less than 3% of total borrowings. This intensive use of financial instruments by GE meant an increased cost in recent years primarily because of the changes in general market conditions (mainly increased interest rates attributable to rising credit). According to the GE annual report, proceeds from these borrowings were used in part to finance asset growth and acquisitions that were related to their major business segments. On December 31, 2008, GE's media segment NBC Universal had US$8.1 billion in commitments to acquire film and television programming. The strength of the parent company, with US$183 million in revenues in 2008, was something capital markets appreciated greatly, but with such high leverage, it is not possible for revenues to stop flowing in large and growing amounts. This is something that, as history shows, a capitalist economy cannot guarantee in a sustained way.

We must not fail to note that GE debt is mainly due to its third-party financial business activities. At one time, GE Capital was only the financial services unit of GE, but the business grew so much that it became an independent financial unit. This financing subsidiary is involved in a number of financing activities, including credit cards and real estate lending and has had such growing weight inside the whole company that it has become its primary business segment by revenues. This is so to such an extent that at the end of 2008, the financing arm of this conglomerate was eligible for government backing as part of the Temporary Liquidity Guarantee Program unveiled by the Federal Deposit Insurance Corp. to ensure buyers of bank debt concerned with the possibility of not being paid back. The program was initially only available to banks, thrifts, and bank holding companies, but U.S. regulators later expanded the program to other financial institutions.

In the United States, as we have seen, Tribune Company went bankrupt in December 2008 after a leveraged buyout the year before that multiplied its debt by 2.5. Many other media owners were facing major financial problems by the end of that year because of their inability to repay their debt: In addition to the already mentioned Univision and Clear Channel, Canwest, CBS, Viacom, and McClatchy in North America and ProSieben and Promotora de Informaciones (Prisa) in Europe also suffered a rude awakening from the leveraged boom era, while others were also carrying heavy debt loads but still had high revenues in 2008 (e.g., New York Times, Gannet, Reed Elsevier, Bertelsmann, or ITV).

After the leveraged buyout of Clear Channel in mid-2008, its debt experienced the same giant leap as Tribune's, in this case from US$8 billion to almost US$20 billion debt after the deal (annual reports reflected US$15.4 billion in debt proceeds used to finance the acquisition). Considering that the purpose of the sale was, as in the case of Tribune, to save the company from its financial troubles, that kind of deal is something that defies common sense. In the 2008 annual report, the company devotes many pages to explaining the consequences of this growth in debt, beginning with a blatant, "We have a large amount of indebtedness," followed by the detailed explanation of the many conflicts of interests that Clear Channel could have with its new owners (or the societies advised by or affiliated with them) because their business was purely speculative. One of the owners, Thomas H. Lee Partners, had also participated in the leveraged buyout of Univision the year before. We have already explained where Univision's huge debt came from—because its sale to a consortium of investment firms left the company mired in debt and legal trials.

McClatchy's financial position at the beginning of 2009 was not due to any strategy to solve prior financial difficulties but rather to ambitious growth. In 2006, its decision to buy Knight Ridder, a newspaper publisher more than double McClatchy's size, received the applause of Wall Street: It meant growing top-line revenues through an acquisition funded by cheap credit. McClatchy also reduced much of the cost of the purchase by selling a dozen dailies that didn't fit its company profile. Nevertheless, and after more sales and hundreds of layoffs, most of its

US$2.4 billion debt at the end of 2008 was due to that operation. With its main segment, newspapers, as one of the most affected by the crisis, and with revenues going down and the stock collapsing in the exchange markets, the news-media firm's strategy showed its true face as an extremely risky approach.

Actually, the American newspaper industry suffered in 2008-2009 the hangover from the buying fever of 2006 and 2007. Most newspapers remained profitable, but the drop in margins (with the ad revenues decreased) added to a weakened financial position due to the large amount of money borrowed by papers at inflated prices and cheap credit.

Among the six largest news-media owners in the United States, CBS and Viacom were also deep in financial turbulence in 2008. At the end of that year, National Amusement, the parent company for CBS and Viacom, had a US$1.6 billion bond that was due to mature imminently and only US$500 million cash on hand. Actually, to meet debt-covenant agreements, mogul Sumner Redstone was forced by lenders, led by Bank of America, to sell US$233 million of stock in CBS and Viacom some months before (pushing these companies' stocks further down). The whole Redstone family empire is a history of collecting asset after asset. In the limit of surrealism, some media analysts were saying at the end of 2008 that Redstone did a remarkable job of collecting such a number of assets (and controlling them), but that such a high amount of leverage was a surprise. Actually, it shouldn't have been surprising at all.

Still among the top players, Time Warner's debt of almost US$40 billion was pushing the company into several spinoffs of troubled units in order to keep its debt ratio from escalating. First it was Time Warner Cable, and in April 2009 the company began setting the wheels in motion for at least a partial spinoff of AOL, once the undisputed online king. The aim was to remove the debt from AOL's books and to back it up with HBO's assets—the successful premium pay television service.

In Canada, Canwest was in a far worse position in March 2009, when the media started talking about the inevitability of bankruptcy as it was facing critical creditor deadlines that it wasn't able to fulfill. Its US$4.5 billion debt dates back to a quite aggressive growth strategy in all major media segments. In 2000, it acquired most of Hollinger's Canadian media assets and became Canada' biggest publisher of daily newspapers. In 2007, Canwest expanded its television holdings by partnering with an affiliate of U.S. investment bank Goldman Sachs to buy Canadian specialty-TV group Alliance Atlantis Communications. In its 2008 annual report, Canwest explained to its shareholders that the media industry was facing an economic slowdown, investors had begun to migrate away from companies that relied on advertising, and the drop in advertising was the main reason for its problems. The Alliance Atlantis purchase was presented as a significant opportunity they could not afford to miss.

Another Canadian giant, Quebecor, also experienced big financial turbulence in the same period to the point of excluding from its annual financial statements their biggest asset, their printing subsidiary Quebecor World, which filed for protection from creditors in January 2008 (it was carrying a debt load of US$2 billion).

In Europe, Spain's largest media group, Promotora de Informaciones (Prisa), was struggling to keep its position as the top Spanish-language media conglomerate in early 2009. Prisa carried a huge debt due to its aggressive expansion strategy in the previous decades, with heavy investments in multiplatform media assets across Spain and internationally (in Latin America, Portugal, France, and the UK, mainly); and with a broadcasting subsidiary, Sogecable, in an unsustainable level of leverage, although performing magnificently in exchange markets until mid-2007. To escape from this highly leveraged scenario, the company took on more leverage in 2007 while scrambling to come up with enough cash to help repayments of debt. The insanity of the strategy of multiplying debt in order to get rid of debt worsened when Prisa lost the main legal rights for Spanish soccer games, which caused a collapse of its stock. In early 2009, the sale of its digital satellite platform seemed to be the key for the media group to survive and remain in compliance with creditors, mainly banking entities, for repayment of its almost US$7 billion debt. Prisa was the seventh largest European media owner at the end of 2008 but the most highly leveraged pure news-media European company.

At the same time, in early 2009, the German media conglomerate ProsiebenSat.1 Media was restructuring the nearly US$2.4 billion debt held by its holding company, Lavena Holding. The two private equity firms controlling Lavena bought ProSieben through a leveraged buyout to combine it with their other European TV investment, Luxembourg's SBS, which they had bought for €3.3 billion (US$4.35 billion). The aim was to rival Bertelsmann's RTL television network, but a total payout to Prosiebens' shareholders of €270 million in 2006, when ProSieben had reported a net income of only €96.2 million, was already being considered a risky bet at the time—even before the spread of economic turbulence.

In 2009, media companies everywhere were seeing their debt turn into junk status by rating agencies as revenues plummeted and stocks sank. That made it impossible to refinance, the only solution a capitalist economy offers, together with layoffs and cost cuts. We've mentioned here only several examples among the largest media owners; but mid- and small-sized companies, many of them far less indebted than the major ones, were having some of the worst times: In the United States alone, four owners of 33 daily newspapers were seeking bankruptcy protection at the beginning of that year, and media analysts were describing the industry as gasping for survival. Some digital utopists were talking about old-fashioned industries and strategies as the main cause of the publishers' downfall, but the reality was that online strategies, with few exceptions, were still not pumping in revenues in a critical amount. In fact nothing could be enough against such big debt packages. Actually, most of the companies would have made money in 2009 if those loans hadn't had to be repaid.

Nevertheless, the debt crisis in the sector was by no means a newspaper question alone. Media conglomerates of all kinds were selling off assets and refinancing with lenders in early 2009 after the leveraging fever of the previous decade. All of them were facing inhospitable financial environments after years of cheap and easy credit. Despite the advertising downturn, the majority of them would have been making money if they hadn't needed to repay the credits. Actually, what the period really showed was that the media industry was far from being as healthy as capitals markets and the industry itself claimed. The reason for the crisis wasn't the global financial crisis but business strategies based on growing as much as possible as fast as possible regardless of the consequences.

CORPORATE GOALS: WHEN PROFITABILITY COMES MAINLY FROM FINANCE

Up to this point, we have analyzed to what degree ownership and growth have been deeply financialized in the news-media industry. I must now shift to a third element that will help measure the financialization of media companies: corporate goals.

I begin by clarifying the term *corporate goals*. The most extended way of defining the core business of a corporation (which is usually what focuses goals) has always been through the identification of what activities generate the highest turnover, need the highest capital investment, or require the largest work force. This is useful to avoid mistaking the true core business of a corporation. If we take, for instance, General Electric, most people think of it mainly as an industrial company chiefly devoted to the electricity or engine manufacturing business and with important assets in other sectors such as industrial automation, medical imaging equipment, or broadcasting. Nevertheless, revenues (and also debt, as we have seen) show that the financial business arm is the largest GE activity by revenues and also the most leveraged. Of course we can assume that finance is not the core vocational business of GE, but we cannot ignore the weight financing may have in corporate strategy and decision making. So we consider revenues as an unavoidable source of information for identifying core business and, therefore, the main corporate goals of a firm.

Obviously the main aim of any kind of industry in capitalist economies is to make a profit from its business activity. The main business activity of the news-media industry is providing information—or "content," according to market trends that stress that information is a mere product (the product of the media industry), and so proclaim a kind of neutrality in order to avoid old commitments related to the social responsibility of those industries. Therefore, the media industry's main goals should be to maximize profit and the value of the firms through the sale of information. Obviously, a close look at the top news-media owners shows many other interests beyond providing information or content—as is common in diversified and globalized media conglomerates. To what extent these dispersed interests are complementary or contradictory with news provision is an issue considered by many as anything from innocuous to controversial, whereas others clearly see it as harmful. This last position—that the news-media business is incompatible with any other commercial interest if democracy is to be preserved—gains strength if we look at the central position finance may have in defining corporate goals in some conglomerates. We can see this through three different ways in which corporate goals can become financialized: first, financial services become the core business; second, financial information and financial markets become the core business; and third, financial markets activity (speculative activity) is incorporated as a regular business activity.

The first case, financialization of core business, can be found in the most radical example of all top media owners: GE. In 2008, GE's operating business was divided into five segments: Energy Infrastructure, Technology Infrastructure, NBC Universal, Capital Finance, and Consumer and Industrial. NBC Universal accounted for only 9% of total revenues that year, whereas Capital Finance was the largest segment by revenues (37%), followed by Technology Infrastructure (26%) and Energy Infrastructure (21%). The two latter segments included the well-known business of jet engine and gas turbine manufacturing, among others. However, because its main revenue is derived from financial services, we could easily consider GE mainly a financial company with a powerful manufacturing arm. Actually, GE is not only one of the largest lenders in the United States but also in other countries.

This finance-oriented dominance of GE's core business is by no means something new; it has been growing in the last decades, and it is not difficult to find a clear parallel between the success of this GE business segment and the growth of financial markets worldwide since the financial globalization wave started in the 1980s. Thus, while in 1989 the financial segment accounted for only 26% of GE revenues and 18% of profits, the same segment represented 37% of revenues and 50% of profits in 2008.

GE Revenues and Profits from the Finance Segment

Fiscal year	Revenues	Profits
1989	26.34%	18.10%
1991	30.00%	23.11%
1995	37.83%	32.10%
2004	35.33%	38.28%
2008	36.71%	49.58%

Source: GE SEC filings.

The financialization of GE's core business can be recognized in the business definition the company provides for itself in its SEC annual reports. Although GE noticeably avoids defining itself as a financially oriented company, the definition of its financial services business position has been escalating. In 1993, for instance, the company defined itself as "one of the most diversified industrial corporations in the world" and only in a paragraph at the end referred to its financial services segment. In its 2008 annual report, GE avoided the term *industrial* and gave the following definition: "We are one of the largest and most diversified technology, media, and financial service corporations in the world." Actually, and according to its revenues, the right order should be: a company diversified in financial services, energy infrastructure, technology, and media. According to its profits, the right order should be: a company diversified in financial services, technology, energy infrastructure, and media.

In case there was any doubt left, GE's dominant financial profile was confirmed by the U.S. government when, at the end of 2008, it made the company eligible for government-backed financial support in order to cope with the global financial crisis. Therefore, we can plainly state it: NBC, one of the largest television and radio networks in United States, is directly owned by a financial entity.

The second case, financial information and markets becoming the core business, is rather different but still worth mentioning. In this situation, we can find Thomson Reuters—the merger between Canadian Thomson and British firm Reuters, with the Canadian firm leading the operation—and McGraw-Hill, respectively, the 8th and 11th North American media owners by revenues in 2008.

Thomson Reuters' main segment by revenues in 2008 was finance-related information services. Actually, the former Reuters was almost exclusively devoted to providing financial market data (less than 10% of the company's income accounted for news reporting before the merger). Reuters' main focus was on supplying the financial markets with share prices, currency rates, financial analytics, and research, as well as trading systems and so on. This financially focused content, not intended for general information purposes but targeting the financial industry, was also the chief Thomson business. The main customers of the new Thomson Reuters are, as stated in its annual report, "trading floor activities of buy-side and sell-side clients in foreign exchange, fixed income, equities and other exchange-traded instruments, as well as in the commodities and energy markets," (...) "customers in corporate services, investment management, investment banking and wealth management," (...) "financial institutions globally," (...) "media and Business professionals," (...) "legal, intellectual property, compliance, business and government professionals," as well as "accounting firms, law firms, corporations and government agencies" and "government, corporate and pharmaceutical research and development professionals" and organizations "across the healthcare industry." Therefore, the financial system is the main customer of Thomson Reuters.

At the same time, McGraw-Hill, a publishing and education company known for its books and magazines such as *Businessweek*, is also the owner of Standard & Poors (S&P). Actually, S&P is McGraw-Hill's leading segment, accounting for more than 40% of revenues in 2008, whereas its information and media segment only represents 17% of revenues.

S&P is one of the top world credit rating agencies (CRAs). CRAs' main task is assigning credit ratings for issuers of certain types of debt obligations, as well as for the debt instruments themselves. Its aim is to provide investors, issuers, investment banks, brokers, and governments with tools that will let them make decisions with minimum risks in the financial markets and, in doing so, increase the efficiency of the markets (and the volume of capital traded in it). Issuers are very reliant on these ratings, and they use them to back their debt instruments (a good credit rating means an easy and quick placement), as well as to back themselves as issuers (a good credit rating as issuer means more confidence in general from investors). The problem is that the companies the CRAs are rating are also their customers. The model of the dominant agencies is that securities issuers pay for credit ratings. Therefore, to call these agencies "independent actors," as their customers do, is a kind of euphemism to say the least. In fact, the credibility of such ratings was widely questioned after the subprime mortgage crisis emerged in mid-2007 in the United States. S&P, as well as the other CRAs, failed absolutely in their task of controlling the quality of issued debt and other instruments. In the wake of large losses beginning in 2007, CRAs failed to predict losses and instead were assigning top ratings to the issuers and their instruments. In particular, S&P was aoouood of failing to predict the bankruptcy of all the largest Icelandic banks. How the central (and failed) role of firms such as McGraw-Hill in the inner workings of the global financial system can interfere in their activity of providing financial information to news media is something that merits serious concern.

Among those cases involving news media companies targeting the general public (and, therefore, covering financial topics) that at the same time have the financial system as a main customer of their core business, it is worth mentioning the acquisition of Dow Jones (including *The Wall Street Journal*) by News Corp in December 2007. Dow Jones, like S&P, is also an index creator and a provider of financial services for business and financial customers, as well as a financial and business information provider.

In view of this scenario of news-media owners with corporate goals so tightly bonded with the financial system, I cannot fail to mention the third and clearest form of the increasing financialization of corporate goals, that is, when media corporations become financial actors in the financial markets in order to get, from speculative operations, an additional source of revenues and profits. Thus, great corporations become great financial investors that, taking advantage of the great mobility of capital, can even achieve a decrease in their tax loads by making use of fiscal engineering while they become suppliers of capital resources for their subsidiaries and high-risk investors in financial markets. Indeed, these societies view their activity in capital markets as part of their corporate purpose, as is the case of Promotora de Informaciones (Prisa) in Spain. Article 2 section *f* of its bylaws declares as one of its corporate purposes "intervention in the capital and money market through the management of capitals, the purchase and sale of fixed or variable-yield titles or of any other kind, on its own".

Thus, a news-media owner no longer has to compete only in its proper arena—as stated in its business definition—but also in the capital markets, in which it regularly acts as a professional investor. Therefore, a large portion of the company's dedication and strategies is reoriented toward that sphere, in detriment of the strategies that are consistent and in accordance with its line of business.

We have examined the activity of the largest U.S. media firms in capital markets and have discovered intense activity in financial capitals for all of them. For instance, despite its focus on the entertainment and media business, in its 2007 annual report, the Disney Company declared $1.052 billion in profits from sales of equity investments and businesses (3% of its total revenues) and $995 million in equity investments. As has become common among big corporations, in the last decade, Disney made participating in the capital market and financial investments a regular business activity. Again, Time Warner showed significant activity in financial investments, with US$360 million in net gains in 2007,

US$1.045 billion in 2006, and US$1.081 billion in 2005. News Corp had equity investments that were so relevant to its business that changes in the stock market prices, such as the 2008 global stock exchange downfall, could strongly affect the company's final results, regardless of the media and entertainment segments' outcomes, as stated in its annual report. From these analyses, I was able to observe that all big conglomerates had, to a greater or lesser extent, a segment of business that, although not formally declared as such (with the exception of GE), operated at a purely financial level and whose revenues came mainly from buying and selling equity stocks.

In addition, we must not forget that, in the case of the media conglomerates with a majority owner, the private financial interests of these media moguls are also at play. This is the case, for instance, for National Amusements, Inc., the firm through which the Redstone family controls Viacom and CBS. National Amusements is also a listed company.

Finally, the financially oriented roots of corporate goals are arguably obvious in those cases in which private or investment equity firms control the main stake in the capital structure. We have seen, when looking at the ownership, that several big news media are owned by equity or investment firms, as was the case in 2008 of Univision in the United States and Kinnevik and ProsiebenSat.1 in Europe. In these instances, it is as simple as looking at the Risks Factors section of their annual reports to find the lists of incompatibilities or conflicts that this kind of ownership can have for the news-media firm. In this respect, Univision states the following in relation to its financially oriented owners (named "Sponsors"):

> **We are controlled by the Sponsors, whose interests may not be aligned with ours or yours**
>
> We are controlled by the Sponsors, and therefore they have the power to control our affairs and policies, including entering into mergers, sales of substantially all of our assets and other extraordinary transactions as well as decisions to issue shares, declare dividends, pay advisory fees and make other decisions, and they may have an interest in our doing so. The interests of the Sponsors could conflict with your interests in material respects. Furthermore, the Sponsors are in the business of making investments in companies and may from time to time acquire and hold interests in businesses that compete directly or indirectly with us, as well as businesses that represent major customers of our businesses. The Sponsors may also pursue acquisition opportunities that may be complementary to our business, and as a result, those acquisition opportunities may not be available to us. So long as the Sponsors continue to own a

significant amount of our outstanding capital stock, they will continue to be able to strongly influence or effectively control our decisions. (Univision, SEC Filings 2008 Form-10K, p. 21)

As far as ProsiebenSat.1 Media is concerned, the two equity firms that
owned the majority of stock in 2008 are investment-focused firms, so
their main aim is to maximize their investments, whereas Swedish
Kinnevik (actually named Investment AB Kinnevik) was established in
1936 as an investment firm working as a holding company that manages
a portfolio of investments, where media assets (Modern Time Group and
Metro International) proportionally accounted for less than 11% of total
revenues in 2008 and telecommunications accounted for the largest proportion of revenues.

To conclude, and in addition to the cases described above, many
diversified companies have their core business outside the news-media
sector or even outside the cultural industries so it is worth our while to
take a quick look at them.

Segments of Activity of the World's Top News-Media Owners in 2008

Bold: Main source of revenues / *Non-bold*: With activity / *CI*: Cultural Industries

NORTH AMERICAN CORPORATIONS	Television	Radio	Newspapers &/or Magazines	Others in CI	Others Outside CI
Advance Publications (US)			n/a		
Canwest Global Communications (Canada)	53%				
CBS (U.S.)	64%				
Clear Channel Communications (U.S.)		49%			
Cox Enterprises (U.S.)				Cable provider: 57%	
EW Scripps (U.S.)			57%		
Gannett Company (U.S.)			84%		
General Electric (U.S.)					Financial Serv.: 37%
Hearst Corporation (U.S.)			83%		
McGraw-Hill (U.S.)				Financial Info Serv.: 42%	
News Corporation (U.S.)			18.93%	Film: 20.30%	
Quebecor (Canada)				Cable provider: 48%	
Televisa (Mexico)	51%				
Thomsonreuters (Canada)				Financial Info: 46%	
Time Warner (U.S.)				Cable provider: 36%	
Tribune Company (U.S.) (*)			72%		
Univision Communication (U.S.)	77%				
Viacom (U.S.)	60%				
Walt Disney (U.S.)	43%				
Washington Post (U.S.)				Education: 52%	

EUROPEAN UNION CORPORATIONS	Television	Radio	Newspapers & Magazines	Others in CI	Others Outside CI
Bouygues (France)					Construction: 29%
Vivendi (France)					Telecomm: 51%
Bertelsmann (Germany)	34%				
Lagardère (France)				Retail Outlets: 43%	
Reed Elsevier (UK)				Online Serv. 36%	
ITV (UK)	70%				
Mediaset (Italy)	78%				
Prisa (Spain)	41%				
Wolters Kluwer (Netherland)			71%		
ProSiebenSat.1 Media (Germany)	83%				
Sanoma WSOY (Finland)			41%		
Kinnevik (Sweden)					Telecom: 36%
Axel Springer (Germany)			93%		
RCS MediaGroup (Italy)			85%		
The Independent News and Media (Ireland)			81%		
Daily Mail and General Trust (UK)			62%		
Schibsted (Norway)			69%		
Holtzbrinck (Germany)			41%		

OTHERS AREAS	Television	Radio	Newspapers & Magazines	Others in CI	√Others Outside CI
Globo (Brasil)	n/a				
Naspers (South Africa)	56%				

Source: Annual reports except for Hearst Corporation, for which the figure comes from *Advertising Age*, Magazine 300, 2008 edition.
Note: Business derived from Internet sales of the same services or products sold though television, radio, or newspapers/magazines are not considered separately from the core business; however, differentiated online products/services are included in "Others in CI." Mobile and fixed telephony services are considered outside cultural industries (labeled Telecom).
(*) Fiscal year 2007.

In Europe, French corporations represented in 2008 the largest amount in global revenues from E.U. countries, with Bouygues, Lagardère, and Vivendi at the lead. Nevertheless, none of them had news-media business as their main activity, and some had their largest portion of revenues from highly capital-demanding sectors.

Bouygues is a diversified conglomerate whose media segment accounted for only 8% of its global revenues in 2008. As we mentioned, its main business is in construction (Bouygues is a world leader in building, civil works, and electrical contracting/maintenance, as well as in construction of transport, urban, and recreational infrastructure) and real estate segments (it is a major player in property development in France and Europe). Since 1994, Bouygues is also a telecom provider (for mobile, fixed, and Internet communications) while its media business is concentrated in only one activity, but quite a relevant one: TF1 group, France's leading general-interest channel with a 27.2% market share as of December 31, 2008. That year TF1 group accounted for 11% of the Bouygues group net profits, a considerable reduction from the previous years (in 2006 TF1 accounted for 17% and in 2006 for 36% of the Bouygues group net profits).

Lagardère Active, the media division of the Lagardère group, accounted for 26% of global 2008 revenues (a 4% decrease from 2007). Its media activities in 2009 mainly included major magazine publishing (*Elle*, *Paris Match*, and *Télé 7 Jours*), radio stations (Europe 1, Virgin Radio, and RFM), and special-interest TV channels (Gulli, Canal J, and Virgin 17), as well as an active online media segment. Lagardère's diversification outside cultural industries is also relevant with its EADS stake (the European leader in aerospace, defense, and related services), which still amounted to 7.5% in May 2009. But in 2008, Lagardère's main revenues didn't come from media, publishing, production, or broadcasting rights but, by far, from distribution. The chain of retail outlets operated by its subsidiary Lagardère Services (4,000 stores) under internationally known trade names (such as Relay) and brands with a strong local identity (such as Payot in France) accounted for 43% of the revenues that year.

In 2008, Vivendi was a great player in cultural industries (with a music and videogames business) and telecommunications (in France and Morocco). Its news-media assets included Groupe Canal +, a 100% Vivendi subsidiary,[9] and 20% of NBC Universal. Nevertheless, more than half of its total revenues in 2008 came from the telecommunications segment, whereas Groupe Canal+ accounted for only 18% of total revenues.

To conclude, we can see from the previous table that broadcasting is the dominant core business of North America's largest media conglomerates, whereas print news media (newspapers and magazines) is still the dominant segment in the largest European firms. On the whole, almost a third of the firms on our list of top news-media owners have core businesses different from the news-media sector. Therefore, five of the top European news-media owners don't have news-media assets as their core business, among them the largest European media corporations. In North America, eight top news-media owners obtained the majority of their revenues from non news-media assets, and three were directly linked with finance.

OTHER TOOLS: FINANCIALIZED LABOR AND OFFSHORE

Major multinational media corporations have increasingly been using other types of financial tools than debt, as have many corporations operating in other sectors. I briefly introduce two of these tools that have produced important changes and risks—in terms of corporate responsibility—in media firms. I address, first, what has been called the financialization of labor, or of salary, through financialized compensation practices. Afterward, I address the increasing use of one of the main and most harmful fellow travelers of financial markets globalization: the emergence and spread of offshore financial centers, the euphemistic name for what is most commonly known as tax havens.

By compensation practices we mean the use of stock-option plans or salary bonuses based on growth in earnings per share. As we have seen before with Maguire (2005), using stock options to compensate corporate executives is a practice widely extended among listed corporations everywhere—especially in the United States, whose model has been exported abroad—since the mid-20th century but greatly expanded starting in the 1990s. Nowadays, almost all listed media conglomerates have stock-option plans whose main purpose is to "align compensation for executive officers and directors with the interests of shareholders." We can find this statement of intent, or something similar, in many annual reports of top news-media conglomerates. In many cases, this reward, although under modified conditions, is also extended to the rest of the work force (i.e., nondirectors or executives) who have worked for a minimum length of time in the companies. The problem is knowing what the interests of shareholders really are and whether the consequences of stock-option plans really meet their demands and at the same time are beneficial not solely to the financial goals of media firms, but also, and mainly, to their social responsibility in democracies.

Maguire (2005) reached some interesting conclusions in both respects for the U.S. newspaper companies with stock options, and these conclusions are applicable to the major news-media corporations.

First, all companies say they use stock-option plans to attract, retain, and reward talented executives. Nevertheless, all of them vary considerably in the extent to which they use these plans for these purposes. Some had used them merely as a tool for compensating salaries of top executives while others used them as a way of providing motivation at executive or other levels of the organization. Tribune's employee stock-ownership plan can be considered the most extreme case of providing motivation through company stock, where employees owned the company, not partially but fully, after the 2007 restructuring plan—a plan that in Spring 2009 was investigated by the U.S. Department of Labor.

Maguire also showed that there is a wide gap between the theory and the reality of whether stock options lead to better management and stock-market performance. Among the top world corporations we can find, as was the case in Maguire's research, firms with little use of stock options have better financial results than other firms with extensive use of stock option plans. Again, Tribune Company is the most radical example, with the most extreme option plan and filing for bankruptcy a year after it. Of course, rank-and-file employees were not the cause of Tribune's debt. However, before restructuring, the company had approved an incentive compensation plan for top executives based on several financial performance criteria.

Maguire's work also disclosed that allowing executives to acquire substantial stakes in their companies may play a larger motivating role than annual compensation packages. Maguire's work documented rigorously what common sense had been suggesting for a long time: Newspaper CEOs may have reasons for focusing excessively on stock performance as opposed to other corporate activities as a result of their large company stakes. There is no reason to think that this doesn't apply to the major media conglomerates, whose executives are exposed to even higher pressures.

In summary, all top media conglomerates implement compensation plans whose main goal is to align executive and shareholder interests. It can be argued that some shareholders have other interests apart from profits and stock returns, but it is unarguable that profits and stock returns are the main priority for the majority of shareholders. Thus, we don't need to perform more research to conclude that aligning the interests of media executives with those of shareholders means that media executives are focusing mainly on profits and stock returns.

The financialization of the workplace (i.e., the growing use of financial schemes to compensate labor) has nevertheless a further component: the use of pension funds. Pension funds are funds set up for a pension plan—that is, pooled contributions from pension plans set up by employers, unions, or other organizations. All this money is invested in securities and other assets to provide for the employees' or members' retirement benefits. Traditionally, the investment plans of pension funds were conservative, limiting their investment vehicles to government bonds or life insurance annuities. But in the last decades, the average pension fund had been trying to achieve higher returns and thus became much more aggressive investments and, therefore, much more risky instruments as well. Nowadays, pension funds are important shareholders of listed companies, and many workers' retirement depends on the performance of stock exchange markets. Of course, that is also the case for employees in the majority of major media conglomerates.

However, the financialization of labor in media firms through stock options and pension funds is not the last, nor the least, consequence of global financialization on media firms. At the corporate level, the use of offshore financial centers is one of the main signs of corporate embedding within financial logics and structures in all major industries.

In the United States, for instance, more than 50% of publicly traded corporations (a higher percentage if we consider only top-ranked companies) are incorporated in Delaware, a state that can be considered a corporate haven due to its business-friendly corporation law. Main subsidiaries of the largest media owners in the United States are incorporated in Delaware as their 10-K SEC filings show. Something similar happens in Europe: A large number of U.S. media subsidiaries (if not the main parent companies) are incorporated in European corporate havens, such as The Netherlands or Luxembourg. When Asia is the target market, many subsidiaries choose Singapore, whose business success is also due to its tax-haven profile.

In 2008, the majority of GE subsidiaries were based in a tax haven. In the United States, Delaware was the state of incorporation for almost all their subsidiaries, including NBC Universal. Time Warner also had in 2008 many subsidiaries incorporated in Delaware, as well as in other states. That was also the case for News Corporation's parent company and subsidiaries according to its 2008 annual report.

In Europe, ProsibenSat.1 Media is incorporated in Germany, but its owners are investment holding companies with many offices worldwide. At least for one of them, Permira, the parent holding has registered in a tax haven, the island of Guernsey in this case. Actually, the majority of private equity firms are registered in tax havens in order to benefit from no- or low-tax charges on returns and from almost no information obligations.

Similarly, Kinnevik's main shareholders, the Sapere Aude Trust and the Estate of Mrs. Stenbeck, are a foundation registered in Liechtenstein, and a fund sited in Luxembourg, respectively. In addition, Luxembourg was where the holding company had incorporated its media subsidiary Metro International at least until the 2008 fiscal year. Both countries, Liechtenstein and Luxembourg, have been considered offshore havens during the last decades.

The truth is that in-depth research into the presence of big conglomerates in tax havens is a difficult task due precisely to the lack of transparency that tax havens guarantee. Corporate annual reports are almost the only resource to look for subsidiaries registered in places with harmful preferential tax regimes and harmful tax practices as they were termed by the Organization for Economic Co-operation and Development (1998). We tried to conduct research for the largest Spanish media conglomerate, Promotora de Informaciones (Prisa), from 1999 to 2004, and the study disclosed a wide use of harmful tax practices in this period (which is the period of the companies' expansion). In America, we found that Prisa held assets in the Republic of Panama, Delaware, and Florida, which were clearly used for their activities in North and South America. In Europe, Prisa used Andorra, Luxembourg, and The Netherlands for nonresident corporate activities. The Netherlands is the enclave preferred by many U.S., Japanese, and European multinational corporations due to the so-called affiliation privilege, by which holding companies pay no taxes and enjoy other fiscal advantages, all of which sets the Dutch fiscal regime considerably apart from the rest of E.U. countries.

Nevertheless, as we have been able to verify for Prisa and other companies in Spain, subsidiaries in tax havens appear and disappear in the annual reports without any explanation, which is one thing that makes this kind of research extremely difficult to accomplish.

BOARD OF DIRECTORS:
FINANCIERS INSIDE DECISION CORES

As we have seen in Chapter 2, much has been said and written about directorates and the corporate governance of media corporations. Nowadays, the analyses of the world's major media conglomerates confirm the financialization trends of boards rigorously revealed by managerial scholars in the last decades for newspaper companies and by critical scholars mainly for U.S. major media conglomerates—something that is occurring in parallel with the financialization of ownership and the increasing presence of all short-term-oriented financial firms in capital structure, along with banking entities and all sorts of private and public debt-issuing instruments. The capital market pressure on the world's top media conglomerates (owners of the major new media firms) is even greater.

In 2009, in boards of directors and/or supervisory boards (or comparable boards) of news-media owners, we could find directors mainly from the financial system, the industry, nonprofit foundations, and politics.

Former state secretaries or even prime ministers (José María Aznar, former president of Spain in News Corporation), members belonging to the media industry (Springer's Chairman/CEO in Time Warner board), and nonprofit foundations (Rockefeller Foundation in General Electric or Melinda and Bill Gates Foundation in The Washington Post Company) are not the dominant type of directors in news-media conglomerates, although they are illustrative. Nevertheless, the greatest number of directors are coming from the leading advertisers and from the financial system. As far as the latter is concerned, in news-media owners' 2009 boards, there was a strong presence of financial links if we look only at current interlocks and positions of directors.

2009 BOARDS AND FINANCIAL INSTITUTIONS (*)

Company	Financial Members on the board (**)	Interlocks with financial boards (***)
Axel Springer	Oceana Investment Ltd, Trialpha Oceana Concentrated Opp. Fund Ltd, Oceana Fund Ltd, United Trust Bank Ltd, UTB Partners Ltd, Cheyne Capital Management Ltd, Hellman & Friedman LLC	Allianz Italy SpA, Grupo Banca Leonardo, Deutsche Bank AG, Buchanan Capital Holding AG, RHJ International SA
Canwest	Edper Financial Group, Metropolitan Investment Corporation, Oliver Capital Partners Inc, Mackenzie Cundill Investment Management Ltd.	Brookfield Asset Management Inc, Sun Life Financial Inc, RioCan Real Estate Investment Trust
CBS	The Cohen Group Financial Partners, Liberty Mutual Group, Bank of America Corporation	American International Group, Bank of America, Liberty Mutual Group, NSTAR, Bank of America Corporation, City National Bank, The Bear Stearns Companies Inc, Intercontinental Exchange Inc, Popular Inc
DMGT	Stancroft Trust Limited	
Gannet	Brysam Global Partners, GenNx360 Capital Partners, Parson Capital Corporation, Wellington Management Company LLP	NYSE Euronext, Inc, The Asia Pacific Fund, Inc, The Chubb Corporation, SunTrust Banks, Inc
General Electric		The Chubb Corporation, Investment Co. of America, The Mexico Fund Inc, New York Federal Reserve Bank, Partners Group Private Equity Fund
Groupe Bouygues	Artémis, Financière Pinault, Fonds Stratégiques d'Investissement, BNP Paribas, Goldman Sachs International, Groupama, Finama Private Equity, Compagnie Foncière Parisienne	Compagnie d'Investissement de Paris, Financière BNP Paribas, Foncière Financière Participations, Foncière Financière Participations, Scor Holding, Banque de Gestion Privé Indosuez

146

Grupo Televisa	Tresalia Capital, Evercore Partners, Banco Nacional de México, Allen & Company LLC
Independent News & Media	UniCredito Italiano Bank
ITV	RSA Insurance Group plc, Hemisphere Capital LLP, Hemisphere Cap
Kinnevik	
Lagardère	Crédit Agricole, BNP Paribas, COFACE SA, Groupama SA, Crédit Suisse Société des Bourses Françaises
McClatchy	
McGraw-Hill	Evercore Partners, Protego Asesores Financieros, Citigroup, Averdale International, LLC, Strategic Investment Group, State Farm Insurance Companies
Mediaset	Mediolanum S.p.A, Quantica Sgr
Naspers	
News Corp	J. Rothschild Capital Management Ltd, Kleiner, Perkins, Caulfield & Byers, JP Morgan Chase Bank
Prisa	Libertas 7, S.A, Inversiones Mendoza Solano, Qualitas Equity Partners
ProSiebenSat1 Media	Permira Beteiligungsberatung GmbH, Kohlberg Kravis Roberts & Co. Ltd

	Allied Irish Banks, plc, National Pensions Reserve Fund
	Kontakt East Holding AB, Vostok Nafta Investment Ltd
	Principal Financial Group of Des Moines, BlackRock Closed End Funds, Alpine Partners
	N.M. Rothschild & Sons Ltd, Emerging Markets Investment Corporation, Emerging Markets Management, LLC, Barclays, Legg Mason, Inc
	Assonime, Mediobanca S.p.A., Allianz S.p.A., Centrale Finanziaria Generale, Sviluppo del Mediterraneo S.p.A, Mediolanum S.p.A, Ceresio Sim, Interbanca S.p.A, GE Corporate Financial Services Italia S.r.l, Credit Agricole Assicurazioni Italia Holding S.p.A.
	FirstRand, Momentum Life
	Apax, Banco de Valencia, Qualitas Venture Capital, Corporación Caixa Galicia

147

2009 BOARDS AND FINANCIAL INSTITUTIONS (*) *(continued)*

Company	Financial Members on the board (**)	Interlocks with financial boards (***)
RCS Mediagroup	SMEG S.p.A. and ERFIN – Eridano Finanziaria S.p.A, Banca di Roma S.p.A., Merloni Finanziaria S.p.A., Mediobanca S.p.A., Banca Popolare Soc. Coop., Merloni Invest S.p.A., Banca Popolare di Bergamo S.p.A.	Unicredito Italiano S.p.A., Unicredit Banca S.p.A., Banche Popolari Unite S.c.p.A., Venezia Assicurazioni S.p.A., Generali Servizi S.p.A., Gruppo Generali Liquidazioni S.p.A., Toro Assicurazioni S.p.A., IFI S.p.A., Pictet International Capital Management, Assicurazioni Generali S.p.A., Finadin S.p.A., Milano Assicurazioni S.p.A., Fondiaria-SAI S.p.A., Premafin Finanziaria HP S.p.A., Pirelli Servizi Finanziari S.p.A., BPU Banche Popolari Unite S.c.p.A.
Sanoma		Oy Asipex Ab, Investor AB, Ilmarinen Mutual Pension Insurance Company, Varma Mutual Pension Insurance Company
Schibsted	Formuesforvaltning ASA, Northzone Ventures, SE-Banken, Linkmed AB	Investment AB Öresund, Nordea AB
The New York Times	Commercial Worldwide LLC, S. Venture Partners, Firebrand Partners, Berger Lahnstein Middelhoff & Partners LLP, The Carlyle Group, Kohlberg & Company	Wesco Financial Corporation, J.P. Morgan Chase & Co, BHF-Bank, NRW.Bank, Fitch Ratings
Thomsonreuters	Atlantic LLC, GSC Group, Kohlberg Kravis Roberts & Co, Restoration Partners Ltd, Key Investment, Inc, The Toronto-Dominion Bank	Hudson Venture Partners, L.P., Royal Bank of Canada, ACE Ltd, BlackRock Inc.
Time Warner	Fannie Mae, Barksdale Management Corporation, Forstmann Little & Company, Kleiner Perkins Caufield & Byers, Carver Bancorp, Inc., Carver Federal Savings Bank	Rockefeller Brothers Fund, J.E. Robert Companies, Kleiner Perkins Caufield & Byers, General Catalyst Partners, US Russian Investment Fund, TIAA

148

Tribune	Equity Group Investments, LLC, Northern Trust Corporation, Secret Communications, LLC
Univision	Madison Dearborn Partners LLC, TPG Capital L.P, Saban Capital Group Inc, Providence Equity Partners
Viacom	Federal Reserve Bank of Boston, Morgan Stanley, Bear Stern Companies, Popular Inc
Vivendi	Axa Group, BNP Paribas, Bank Handlowy w Warszawie, Citigroup, Macquarie European Infrastructure Fund II, ACE Ltd, Fidelity International, Wendel Investissement Asia-Pacific
Walt Disney	The Shinsei Bank Limited, Bank of America Corporation, Visa Inc, Washington Mutual
Washington Post	The Davis Funds, First Market Bank, Citigroup Inc
Wolters Kluwer	Goedland nv, Bencis Capital Partners, Prime Financial Group, Valua Funds, Gresham Private Equity Ltd, NPM Capital nv, Veronis Suhler Stevenson

Source: Corporate webpages visited in April 2009.
 (*) On Boards of Directors, Supervisory Boards, or comparable boards.
 (**) Directors with positions in financial institutions.
 (***) Boards interconnected with the media conglomerate board through common directors.

149

From the table above we can see that the elite of financial power is well represented not only through interlocked directorates but through the direct presence of bankers and financiers (mainly top executives and chairmen of financial firms) in the boards of directors of media conglomerates. Some of the most important banking entities, private equity firms, and insurance companies sit on these boards or were linked with media conglomerates' boards in 2009 through common directors. Among the banking entities, we could find Deutsche Bank, Bank of America, BNP Paribas, Goldman Sachs, Morgan Chase Bank, Morgan Stanley, Citigroup, Banco Nacional de México, City National Bank, several U.S. reserve banks, and others.

The above information is revealing only in an early stage: that is, we are looking at the company of origin of directors in media boards (what companies they represent or hold positions in), and we are looking at other companies' boards where media directors also sit. But in those external boards, they meet other directors from financial companies. The results of this further search for three American companies in 2008 showed an amazing network of financial links for media directors.

MAIN FINANCIAL ENTITIES CONNECTED TO BOARDS
OF DIRECTORS OF GE, DISNEY, AND TIME WARNER (2008) (*)

GE (88 links in total)   *Among them*: American Express, Arvest Bank, Banco Popular de Puerto Rico, Berkshire Hathaway, Bolsa Mexicana de Valores, Citigroup, Danske Bank, JP Morgan Chase, Lazard, Lehman Brothers, Merrill Lynch, Metropolitan Life, Morgan Stanley, New York Federal Reserve Bank, Rothschild, Scotiabank, SunTrust Banks, Goldman Sachs, The Reserve Bank of Australia, UBS.

DIS (59 links in total)   *Among them:* American Express Company, Banco Santander, Berkshire Hathaway, Citigroup, Deloitte Touche Tohmatsu, Dow Jones, Ernst & Young, Federal Reserve Bank of Dallas, HomeStreet Bank, HSH Nordbank, JP Morgan Chase, KPMG, Merrill Lynch, Morgan Stanley, NIBC Bank, PricewaterhouseCoopers, Rabobank, Scotiabank, The Goldman Sachs Group, U.S. Bancorp, Visa, Wells Fargo.

TWX (86 links in total)   *Among them:* American Express Company, Banco Nacional de México, Bank of America Corporation, Bank of Israel, Carver Bancorp, China Development Bank, Citigroup, CitiStreet, Citizens Trust Bank, Deutsche Bank Group, Dow Jones, Duff & Phelps, EuroHypo, European Central Bank, Federal Reserve Bank of New York, Goldman Sachs, JP Morgan Chase, National Bank of Poland, Rabobank, Rockefeller Foundation, UMB Financial Corporation, World Bank.

Source: Annual reports and corporate websites.
(*) Boards of directors of others entities where directors serve and which belong either to financial firms or nonfinancial firms where other directors related to financial firms serve. GE: General Electric. DIS: Disney. TWX: Time Warner.

The results of this research showed a minimum of 88 different financial entities connected to GE through directorate interlockings in 2008. Those financial entities connected to the GE board of directors were mainly retail, commercial and investment banking firms, insurance companies (most of them owned by banking firms), asset managers, venture capital firms, and financial authorities. Several of them were in the U.S. Federal Reserve's 2007 List of the largest commercial banks in the United States, as is the case of JP Morgan Chase (first on the Fed List), Citigroup (third), and SunTrust Banks (eighth). Many others were among the top world financial institutions in their respective fields, such as Morgan Stanley securities, asset management and credit services firm; Lehman Brothers, Rothschild, Goldman Sachs, Lazard, and Merrill Lynch investment banks; Zurich or Metropolitan Life insurance companies; or USB Swiss banking firm. The links with Federal Reserve boards (national central banks) were also tight: GE Chairman Jeffrey R. Immelt, for example, serves as a director in the New York Federal Reserve Bank.

If we look at the Disney board of directors, we can also find significant interlocking with financial directorates, just as in the case of GE. The research showed a minimum of 59 different financial entities connected to Disney through boards of directors interlocking. Among them, we also find relevant financial entities, as shown in the table above.

As for Time Warner's Board of Directors, interlocking with financial directorates was also outstanding. We found 86 financial entities connected to Time Warner's board of directors. Again, they were mainly retail, commercial and investment banking firms, insurance companies (most of them owned by banking firms), asset managers, venture capital firms, and financial authorities.

Of course, we must stress that this information is only available through the corporate information web pages and annual reports, which vary widely on the information provided depending on companies and countries, although transparency on this issue is compulsory in most modern countries.

In any case, the previous exercise gives only an approximate idea of the real linkages of media owners with financial power because we do not consider past relations (sometimes just finished a month earlier than our analysis). Even in those cases where the past position finished before joining the media board, we must not forget that former positions can also be worthwhile assets, as is the case of GE Director Douglas A. Warner. Warner, former chairman of JP Morgan Chase & Co, The Chase Manhattan Bank, and Morgan Guaranty Trust Company between 1990 and 2001, has served as director of GE since 1992. Despite his retirement in 2001 from his last banking position, in 2009, these positions were still mentioned in his bio in all the directorship positions he held.

The same is true of Roberto Hernández Ramiro, former director of Citigroup and the Federal Reserve Bank of New York and director of Grupo Televisa in 2009. An in-depth analysis that includes past positions of members of boards of directors would provide an even clearer understanding of the extent of interlocking directorates between the financial system and media conglomerates, if clearer is possible.

SOME CONCLUSIONS

From what was asserted in the previous pages, readers can draw conclusions by themselves. However, the following summary can help in this task.

For top new media conglomerates, financialization has meant an application of the "as well be hung for a sheep as for a lamb" principle with double negative results. With few exceptions, during the beginning of the 21st century, most of the top news-media conglomerates have experienced a huge increase in their financial links and dependencies: most are publicly traded companies with a handful of institutional investors concentrating their shares; most have high or very high levels of financial debt; most are driven mainly by financial pressures in their day-to-day activities and have to share decision centers with the financial power elite; for most, entering the financial logic has meant more debt, more risk, and more external influence. The dispersion of ownership that public ownership allegedly provides has proven to be another kind of financial dependence, as a handful of institutional investors control most of the public stock in every corporation and are capable of exerting a significant amount of influence on management.

At the same time, however, financialization hasn't eliminated family or media mogul control. In fact, many U.S. corporations split their shares to reduce outsiders' influence, allowing a small number of investors (usually the former owners) to keep their dominant position. In other cases, mainly in Europe, media moguls simply have kept a control stock while the portion of ownership listed is less than 50% or, if higher, too dispersed. Finally, there are some companies where, despite being publicly traded and the founding family having turned into a minority shareholder, institutional investors support the family owners. Thus, traditional media moguls are far from being a dying species. Instead, media companies have added to this family-run public corporate governance all the pressure and dependence generated by financialization.

Corporate management and governance have been deeply modified since the financialization process began. As management handbooks insistently explain, things are different now from the old times of traditional family-run companies. However, the truth is that family/mogul-run public media companies are full of conflicts of interest (where moguls play a dual role—as heads of a family company and major investors compelled to look after the public interest of the company) and not only have to put an end to their traditional problems but have added to them the risks involved in financialization.

Institutional investors (most of them banks, insurance companies, private equity firms, pension funds, hedge funds, etc.; i.e., financial investors) have not only increased their positions (number and stakes) inside the corporate structure in media conglomerates but are increasingly emerging as control shareholders. Clear Channel Communications (U.S.), ProsiebenSat.1 Media (Germany), and Univision (U.S.) were taken over by speculative funds between 2007 and 2008, whereas Kinnevik (Sweden) is, in fact, an investment holding company, some of whose founding families' leading positions were at risk in 2009 after their companies' poor results. Obviously, corporate goals of the media conglomerates owned by private equity funds must move away from the social responsibility inherent to any news-media producer.

Furthermore, this is being experienced similarly in all modern economies with only subtle differences. Banking systems in European countries traditionally have been stronger and still are: Banking entities have had a high influence over politics in Europe. For instance, higher commissions and interests have been allowed in European countries. Actually, the financial crisis led European governments in 2008-2009 to devote larger amounts of money to help the banking system than the U.S. government did for American banks (Navarro, 2009). Again, the Anglo-Saxon countries have traditionally relied on public capital markets, thus encouraging the growth of equity markets. Nevertheless, data shown for European firms in the previous pages describe a degree of E.U. financialization comparable, as a whole, to the United States, with banking and equity markets funding being widely used in both regions.

In general terms, financialization has increased the proximity of the financial power elite to the management of media companies at the same time that it has increased the distance between management and journalistic concerns. Few boards of the world's major media conglomerates have directors with any journalism experience while there are plenty of former or current bankers, financiers, and public and private investors in governance positions. In the last decade, the results of research studies on financial pressures over newspaper ownership revealed a scenario full of dangers. The situation cannot be considered other than worse for the whole news-media industry during the current stage, as in 2009 top newspapers, television channels, radio stations, and online news were mainly in the hands of financial investors, whether through direct ownership or debt.

In 2008, annual results were bad for most top media conglomerates. Expectations were worse for 2009. Consequently, market capitalization of media firms sunk dramatically. Unfortunately, almost nobody in the industry confronted the real problem but evaded it, once more taking the "as well be hung for a sheep as for a lamb" approach. The problem was the high level of leverage of all media companies due to an irrational race for growth supported by expectations and capital markets. Therefore, the situation didn't show any sign of improvement but rather the opposite: The solution offered for indebtedness was even more debt, and the dramatic drop of quotations allowed for more concentration of the market as weaker and/or smaller firms are susceptible to be swallowed by larger ones. At the same time, major corporations everywhere were asking their governments for more flexibility—"flexibility" should be read here as "fewer restrictions to concentration"—and succeeding in most cases.

The downward trend of traditional mass media, the infinite promises of technological convergence, and the quick rise of online services have focused our attention most of the time. What the new business model will be and on what kind of support (whether paper, online, air, etc.) we will be consuming news in the future seems to be all that matters. Editorial autonomy is taken for granted due to the apparent diversity and plurality allegedly encouraged by the new possibilities on offer thanks to the ubiquitous technology. But it's time to face the true situation: These priorities and promises didn't work in the past, and there is no sign that they will work in the future. On the contrary, they prevent us from facing the real challenge, a truly alarming one from all perspectives: Finance capital has become the real owner of the world's top news-media firms.

4

Risks of Media Financialization for Journalism

The inclination of corporate media to give precedence to the economic aspects over the social aspects of journalism has been largely denounced by critical scholars in recent decades. The main concerns are twofold: advertising pressures and other business interests of media conglomerates. Conflicts of interest arise repeatedly around these two issues, and media critics claim that there is a systematic give-in from corporate media to the interests of the advertisers and an extensive self-censorship in journalists regarding their corporate businesses (Soley, 2002). In both cases, the most recurrent problem is not what is said but what is not said. We could find dozens of examples of the kinds of scenarios that should be avoided to prevent violations of journalistic ethics.

In the United States, the weekday newspaper *Philadelphia Inquirer*—winner of 18 Pulitzer prizes—launched in 2007 a new column paid for by a bank. The sponsor was Citizens Bank, the second largest bank in the Philadelphia area. The column was to run on the paper's weekday business front page. That decision was taken a few months after the newspaper was sold to a group of Philadelphia-area investors led by a former advertising executive (after the McClatchy group discarded the paper from its Knight Ridder purchase). Almost 2 years later, in early 2009, the paper had filed for bankruptcy protection to restructure its US$390 million in debt load while creditors were trying to impose their restructuring plans over the media company. The group of lenders was led by no other than Citizens Bank. The conflict of interest that arises from a banking

155

entity sponsoring a business column is quite obvious, more obvious when the banking entity is a financial creditor of the newspaper company—even leaving aside the financial troubles that Citizens Bank had to deal with at the time and that journalists had to cover, with profits turning into losses in 2008 and a parent company, the Royal Bank of Scotland, being among the most troubled of the world's large banks in the global crisis context.

Regarding conflicts with other businesses in diversified corporate media, also in 2007, the acquisition by News Corporation of Dow Jones (the owner of the *Wall Street Journal*) provides a classic example without leaving the media sector investments. The concern was, as some analysts pointed out, whether Murdoch's *Wall Street Journal* would keep its commitment to investigative reporting and, especially, to negative China coverage given Murdoch's business ambitions in China and his history of appeasing Chinese leaders (Shafer, 2007). While the *Journal* had published a series about pollution, dangerous working conditions, and income inequality in China that won the paper the 2007 Pulitzer in international reporting, Murdoch had flattered communist party leaders putting business and the thirst to conquer the Chinese market before anything else, starting with human rights. Of course, there is no conflict of interest if media are not considered a public and democratic service but rather a business product, an individual property, or a simple asset, which was the main ideological contribution brought about by the corporatization of the media. Obviously, this is the way media moguls view this issue.

Europe is also full of the classic consequences of media corporatization, starting with Mediaset owner, Silvio Berlusconi, who in 2009 was simultaneously the owner of the largest Italian media conglomerate, the owner of the largest Italian economic empire, and the holder of the largest political office in Italy. In Spain, the main media conglomerate, Promotora de Informaciones (Prisa)—owner of the most widely circulated and influential Spanish newspaper—was founded in the 1970s with the financial support of a group of individual investors among which was one of the largest Spanish advertisers, retail chain El Corte Inglés. At the time, El Corte Inglés was the largest individual funder of Prisa and still is an investor and partner of the company in lucrative businesses (e.g., in home-shopping TV). The largest Spanish advertiser, Telefónica, has in turn been the main shareholder of different relevant news media throughout its recent history, including a partnership with Prisa from 2003 to 2007 in what was then the leading Spanish pay television. In France, the Bouygues Group, the main shareholder since 1987 of the top French television channel (TF1), has been the French leader in the construction and maintenance of transport, urban, and recreational infrastructure as well as in building, civil works, and electrical contracting/maintenance. That is, the owner of the most widely watched television channel in France has been a major, if not the largest, French government contractor. The list of corporate scenarios that should be avoided in order to allow journalists to do their work without external or internal commercial/business pressures is endless. Unfortunately, nowadays we must add to these old concerns—although more vigorously than ever—the consequences of the increasing financialization of corporate media.

A FINANCIALIZED PUBLIC SPACE: FINANCE AND MEDIA CONVERGENCE

In 2005, Christian Pradié asked whether the current information-production order is evolving toward a kind of "financialized public space" model—that is, toward a space that has been globally absorbed by the rules of financial capitalism. The analysis of the world's top news-media conglomerates in 2009 certainly points in that direction. What's more, the financialization of the public communications sphere seems to be reinforcing those rules because encouraging public dissent from those rules or acceptance of them is, in large measure, in the hands of the media. This leads to the unavoidable question about compatibility, or rather incompatibility, of financial capitalism with cultural industries and, particularly, of corporate-media financialization with the watchdog role that journalism should play in a democracy.

This concern has resulted in different approaches over the years, beginning at the onset of the current financialization process. On the one hand, as Pradié pointed out, this issue has given rise to research regarding the theoretical foundations of the social and legal framework specific to information and communication activities, with the purpose of encouraging modes of ownership and economic control that will favor the development of pluralism and cultural diversity. A large part of the critical studies about the concentration of cultural industries has shown this concern for pluralism and cultural diversity. The need to find a legal framework specific to the status of publishing or broadcasting corporations was, for example, the goal of the early projects for *societés de rédacteurs* (associations of journalists) encouraged in France first by *Le Monde* starting in the 1950s and by *Libération* in the 1960s. But the efforts to devolve power to journalists were unsuccessful and were not exempt from professional dilemmas because cooperative ownership of the media by the journalists wasn't by itself a guarantee of pluralism or cultural diversity.

More recently, this concern has triggered a growing social movement that is promoting a reformation of media from the ground up. One of the strongest platforms is the one founded in 2002 by media scholar Robert W. McChesney and journalists John Nichols and Josh Silver in the United States, although some other organizations are working for media reform in other countries. McChesney, Nichols, and Silver's *Free Press* (www.freepress.org) advocates preventing large media conglomerates from influencing public legislators and promotes the participation of common citizens in government decisions. Their argument is that the communications deregulation process in the United States is a fallacy; what has been implemented is, rather, a regulation process based on top conglomerates' needs that has built a sort of government-sanctioned oligopoly. Therefore, what is needed is government policies based on common social interests.

These are examples of the difficulty of finding economic organization models that will permit the practice of professional journalism apart from economic logics, currently financial logics imposed by those who control the current system of economic organization. This also led Werner A. Meier to refer to the failure of the public communications policies fostered since the 1960s, whose deregulation, liberalization, and privatization of the communication and information sector can be viewed as a drive toward concentration on the part of the state, rather than the opposite:

> Politicians, whose preoccupation for their career makes them avid for power, influence, reputation and prestige, are always careful not to clash with dominant communication groups. [...] With the purpose of not compromising their own interests or the position of dominant national communication groups, the State and regulation authorities facilitate mergers and acquisitions rather than hinder them. (Meier, 2005: 20)

This causes some authors to talk of the deregulation paradox, in that the consequences of deregulation have been the exact opposite of the arguments used to justify the policies that prompted it.

But responsibility does not lie, according to Meier, McChesney, and others—and we agree with them—only on political power. The communication groups have their share of responsibility to the extent that in their public discourse they minimize the increase of their power, as well as the potentially negative consequences linked with concentration and with the power of the media. It is not surprising that neither of these aspects is sufficiently researched nor correctly evaluated, according to Meier. It is a fundamental contradiction in modern capitalism, an expression of the tension between, on the one hand, communications groups subject to financial logics and who can, and indeed do, exercise political action and, on the other hand, the need that democracy and society have for an independent, rigorous, and professional journalistic practice.

Thus, although the dominant discourse, amplified by the communication groups, claims that the media contribute to the democratization of society, they focus on the accumulation of profits for their owners and on legitimizing a certain social order. Therefore, the logic that drives their business—concentration, the creation of monopolies, and the oligopolization of important economic sectors—is detrimental to the practice of journalism. This is so because the economic power that accompanies concentration can logically exert influence on the messages that are transmitted, as well as on those that are omitted. If economic concentration causes a focalization on corporate interest at the expense of citizens' interests, the financial logics that are predominant in the great communication conglomerates tend to neglect even corporate interests and to give priority to the interest of a handful of shareholders, high executives who are in control, and financial investors with various divergent interests.

This is the great paradox of the cultural industries' business in the era of financial capitalism: Despite the contradiction that we have mentioned, the financial logics that are dominant in the communication and information business are not imposed logics, but rather synergic logics, because both industries (finance and information), as we have seen, need each other. All of this is sanctioned by government leaders because "negotiation and conception of public media policies are increasingly favorable to the dominant communication groups and ever less in line with public interest, or to state it better, with the expectations of a democratic society" (Meier, 2005: 38). This is so because the objective of public powers in their communication policies is first and foremost to protect economic competition. All other considerations, no matter how important, take a back seat to this.

But the consequences for communication groups of the autonomy of financial logic take the form of internal contradictions that generate important risks for journalistic practice and that exacerbate the risks of concentration and oligopolism brought about by media corporatization.

In the first place, the primacy of financial over industrial logics has no cost-free presence within news-media firms. The reason is that the increase in breadth of groups and conglomerates does not automatically increase mid-term profitability due to both industrial and financial reasons. Great corporate operations of concentration have high costs and, as we have seen, uncertain results. What's more, some of the largest financial operations have generated serious financial difficulties for the participating companies, as was the case with AOL Time Warner, whose merger was carried out on the basis of AOL's overvalued assets, which, after the slump of the U.S. technology stock exchange, lost much of their value in only 2 years. This also happened to Telefónica in its main multi-million—and failed—Internet gambles (e.g., Terra and Lycos). Thomson

Reuters recognized this in 2009 when it said plainly in its 2008 accounts: "Our acquisition of Reuters may not maximize the growth potential of, or deliver greater value for, our company beyond the level that either Thomson or Reuters could have achieved on its own."

In the second place, as pointed out by various authors, internal contradictions generated by the financialization of communication groups also bring to light a reality that has long been obscured by the digital-convergence mystique. That is, the great concentration operations don't automatically lead to an increase in productivity. In short, the famous industrial synergies are much weaker than predicted since the 1970s, when the coming convergence of telecommunications, computers, broadcasting, and publishing by virtue of digitalization was touted with enthusiasm. The convergence is real, no doubt, but its scale, pace, and goals are different from what was foretold. Consolidation of large international communication groups has shown that few communication groups carry out relevant activities in the content, networks, and electronics sectors simultaneously, as was promised by digital convergence. Furthermore, few communication groups are truly multimedia groups— that is, having relevant activity in all the main platforms (newspapers and magazines, radio, television, and online). Only a handful of companies are great conglomerates with significant income from more than one platform, and in practically every case broadcasting and/or newspapers and magazines are still the dominant business units.

Actually, it is financial and not productive logics that are at the foundation of most large corporate operations in the communication sector and have made possible the process of capital centralization, which is characteristic of cultural industries in general and the media sector in particular. At the same time, nevertheless, these financial logics come into contradiction with industrial logics that operate in these companies either because expected profitability or synergies are not attained or because, if they are, they tend to cause communication firms to forget public interest, and even corporate interest, and to prioritize financial interest. This has direct consequences on journalism.

NEWS-MEDIA FIRMS, NEWS MESSAGES, AND JOURNALISTS AT RISK

The following table is a list of the main consequences of the dominance of finance over production logics on news media firms, journalistic messages, and journalists.

RISKS OF FINANCIALIZATION

For the News Firm	For the News Message	For Journalists
• Increasing concentration and financialization	• Defense of economic -financial orthodoxy	• Censorship or self-censorship
• Greater instability and financial risk	• Financialization of the messages	• Greater pressure or capacity to influence the journalist
• Deviation from its own activity	• Omission of negative information	• Inability to develop critical capacity in financial matters
• Greater distance from social responsibility criteria		

Risks of Financialization for News Firms

(a) Increasing concentration and financialization

The first conclusion reached after analyzing dominant trends in the media sector is that financialization generates a greater tendency toward gigantism and, therefore, concentration. This in turn reduces diversity in news companies through a Darwinian selection, in which the survivors are the companies most thoroughly dominated by financial logics. The smaller the degree of financialization, the smaller the possibility of survival, so that the foremost risk of financialization is the tendency toward greater concentration and greater financialization of the industry.

During the 1980s and 1990s, all cultural industries experimented with an intense process of concentration. Nevertheless, the process did not stop, and in the 2000s the trend continued. In North America, although since 2000 the sector has maintained a certain stability in the number of major actors (to the point that there are now six great conglomerates rather than five, with the split of CBS and Viacom, although the ownership of both is still in the hands of the same businessman), on the second tier, among mid-large companies, acquisitions and mergers have by no means stopped, either among themselves or as a means of becoming part of one of the top players.

Among the best-known deals, we can mention the 2006 Knight-Ridder sale to McClatchy, Thomson's buyout of Reuters in 2007, and, the same year, Dow Jones (owner of the *Wall Street Journal*) becoming a subsidiary of News Corp. Actually, figures show that although the number of deals may vary, the total worth has been growing since 2000 as well.

According to figures from research firm Dealogic, in 2006 alone, 448 mergers (109 in the United States) took place in traditional media businesses (print, broadcast and cable TV, radio, and movies) across the globe for a total worth of US$55.5 billion. In 2007, the number of deals, also according to Dealogic, was down slightly to 372 (81 in the United States), but the world's total media mergers were worth US$93.8 billion (La Monica, 2007). In 2008, according to PricewaterhouseCoopers, media mergers and acquisitions reached a total value of US$150.8 billion (Boorstin, 2009). Therefore, even in periods of crisis, concentration goes hand in hand with financialization. Obviously, economic crises slow down this trend toward increasing worth, but at the same time crises make for more concentration as buyout costs also drop dramatically.

This logic toward concentration and gigantism is inherent to capitalism, which permanently requires steady growth rates (which, as we have seen, is technically impossible). Despite the enormous resources accumulated by some news-media groups during the 1980s and 1990s, the demand for growth has constantly pushed groups toward an increase in size. For that purpose, corporate resources have not been sufficient. The progressive going public of all the great actors, as well as the growing use of financial instruments of the capitals markets (in addition to traditional banking loans) and the accumulation of unsustainable levels of financial debt, have characterized this quest for growth during the last decade. Thus, to the extent that concentration grows, more financialization within corporate media is needed.

When the logic enters a crisis, which happens regularly and is inevitable, the results are, again, a greater concentration of the sector as the weakest are gobbled up by the larger actors. All of this reinforces, one more time, the financialization of the survivors, which are so in large measure for having managed to maintain the backing of the financial system. This Darwinian selection, therefore, is by no means natural, but rather is carried out directly or indirectly by those who control financial resources (at times pressured by political authorities to rescue emblematic national groups). Thus, it is possible to observe how bankruptcies that lead to a deep restructuring or even to the dissolution of companies are not produced in the groups with the highest debt/equity ratio, but among those that, whatever their debt ratio may be, have lost the capacity to generate confidence (among other reasons, because of the publicity of improprieties or scandals, because there are virtually no expectations to maintain a leadership position in the sector, or because the size of the groups is not critical for the creation of public opinion). In this sense, the logic works inversely to common sense: The corporate giants with the biggest financial problems have the greatest chance of prospering, although of course there are exceptions regularly (as for instance the Kirch case).

(b) Greater instability and financial risk

The financialization of the news firm also implies its incorporation into an environment of greater instability and competitiveness. The greater instability comes from the traits of stock-market capitalism, which is much more unpredictable and fluctuating than purely industrial capitalism. The greater competitiveness is due to the fact that the company no longer has to compete in its own arena—communication and information—but also in capitals markets to obtain resources because within a growingly financialized economy attaining the support of financial capital requires a considerable investment of time, money, and effort.

Therefore, the financialized news firm, when it enters a virtualized economy, multiplies its financial risks and efforts. The strategy of rapid expansion based on permanent indebtedness becomes, in turn, a permanent threat to financial/accounting equilibrium. Financialization permanently places the news firm on an accounting tightrope.

The financial crisis that started in 2007 showed the extent of this instability for many companies all over the world. In the United States and Europe, the list of groups being forced to restructure their debt included almost all top and medium players. From the list of conglomerates with more than US$2 billion from news-media revenues, we have seen that in 2008 only five companies had a debt/equity ratio of 1 or less. Paradoxically, financial risk is by no means assessable by such a ratio or other similar ones, but by future expectations of profits and consequent expectations of increasing share value in stock markets. Therefore, it doesn't matter whether your debt ratio is endangering your accounting as long as you have ambitious plans for the future.

(c) Deviation from its own activity

The financialized news firm can end up diverting a large part of its attention and operations into activities that are not proper to it, but to which it is led by its expansion or the lures of financial economy. In certain cases, the news firm even adapts its corporate purpose to its activity in financial markets—that is, it considers as an area of regular activity the speculative pursuit in capitals markets.

The radical example here is, of course, GE, a conglomerate of energy, engines manufacturing, and media that nevertheless has been obtaining its main revenues from its financial units (and its main losses as well when the economic cycle went down). Actually several media companies explicitly include in their statutes or articles of association the activity in capital markets as a firm's goal. We already mentioned

Spanish Promotora de Informaciones' bylaws that state: "[The society has as one of its aims] intervention in the capital and money market through the management of capitals, the purchase and sale of fixed or variable-yield titles or of any other kind, on its own behalf" (Article 1.f). In the same line, British ITV's Memorandum and Articles of Association considers an object of the company "to carry on business as financiers, merchants and bankers, including the borrowing, raising or taking-up of money, lending or advancing money, securities and property (...); managing property; and transacting all kinds of indemnity, guarantee, insurance agency and other agency business" (Article 4.b), as well as

> to carry on the business or businesses of acquiring, holding, selling, endorsing, discounting, issuing or otherwise dealing with or disposing of, shares, stocks, debentures, debenture stock, scrip, bonds, mortgages, bills, notes, credits, contracts, certificates, coupons, warrants and other documents, funds, obligations, securities, instruments, investments or loans, whether transferable or negotiable or not, issued or guaranteed by any company, corporation, society or trust constituted or carrying on business in any part of the world, or by any government, state or dominion, public body or authority, supreme, municipal, local or otherwise, in any part of the World. (Article 4.d)

The financialization of the news firm entails the risk not only of prioritizing corporate interest at the expense of its professional activity, but also of subordinating even corporate interest to purely financial interests, goaded by some of its stockholders, high executives, and banking or financial advisers. Great corporations' capacity to take flight rapidly in the global economy and to sink even more rapidly during crisis periods is another of the traits of financialization and, particularly, of the financialization of activity and goals.

(d) Greater distance from social responsibility criteria

All of the above throws light on a fourth risk: a renewed estrangement from the criteria of social responsibility of the financialized news firm. The corporatization of journalism had already made evident the contradiction between the corporate goals of news companies and the social responsibility of the journalist's role. Financialization not only calls forth those threats but increases the risk of separation from the social-responsibility functions of a journalistic firm. Now the contradiction is even greater, in that synergies of interests between the news firm and the actors of global financialization grow.

In addition, the financialization of the remuneration of high executives (through stock options and pension funds or through bonuses earned for achieving certain financial objectives) increases their distance from professional concerns (such as guaranteeing the staff a work environment free from internal and external pressures and avoiding scenarios that lend themselves to the violation of the professional ethical code). The proximity of these high executives to the financial power elite dramatically reinforces this tendency. This closeness is produced by the growing financialization of boards of directors, but this is not the only cause. Ever-growing financial indebtedness and the monopolization of ownership by a handful of institutional investors also increase the proximity between the financial system and the media system. Studies and interviews among executives in the media industry indicate that contacts between institutional investors (mostly financial) and the management of communication firms have done nothing but increase in recent years, as has the deviation of concerns in corporate media management.

Risks of Financialization for the News Messages

(a) Defense of economic-financial orthodoxy

Just as liberal theory has made use of its own hegemony to impose the narrative that justifies the desirability of a certain dominant system— in which the news company is presented as a supposed Fourth Estate that guarantees the health of the democratic system—financial globalization also imposes a hegemonic narrative that justifies the process of global financialization. Thus, although the financial system fails to fulfill its main function, as we pointed out in the first chapter, neoclassical economic theory doesn't address this issue because that would compromise the legitimacy of the dominant financialization processes. The financialized journalistic company, as an integral part of those processes, runs the risk of contributing to the legitimization of the orthodoxy that encourages financial capitalism. This is so in the majority of cases, as is proven by the absence of a truly vigilant economic journalism.

This legitimization of orthodoxy is carried out starting with the abdication on the part of the great communications media from all economic or financial coverage that makes a critical analysis of the organization and distribution system of the planet's resources beyond specific episodes of generalistic critique during periods of global crisis or beyond specific individual scandals. Thus, newspapers and, of course, broadcasters traditionally have been incapable of predicting, warning about, or preventing the onset of deflationary or recessionistic periods or the consequences of certain speculative or risk behaviors, or, ordinarily, of performing any watchdog functions whatsoever regarding the economy in general aside from concrete denunciations. Just like they had been taken by surprise by the burst of the Internet bubble, in recent years, they were caught unawares by the burst of the real estate bubble that was the precursor of the recession period starting in 2008.

The multiple ties and dependencies that we have described joined the news-media owners to the financial economy and turned them into agents that are too tangled up in the very scenario that they should be watching. Theirs is not, then, an ideological defense of the dominant economic status quo, but a corporate positioning consistent with the degree of financialization of the ownership and corporate governance of the great media groups, and with the large number of representatives of economic-financial orthodoxy sitting on their boards of directors.

Actually, as we have seen, there is a direct line between financial markets deregulation and media sector deregulation. The economic house of cards built by the financial system based on the culture of greed, as so many times before in history, would have had far less of a chance of progressing in modern societies if journalism hadn't failed in its role. This failure was encouraged by the progressive deregulation of media—that is, by approving rules designed to benefit the consolidation and growth of giant corporate owners rather than public service. These rules helped create the current large media conglomerates and with them (i.e., as a result of the mergers and concentration of the sector) thousands of jobs have been lost and news budgets have been slashed during the last decades. This has promoted a news scenario in which reporters and their parent news organizations cannot attend to news quality much of the time—and even much less when dealing with the democratic faults of financial and economic orthodoxy. This scenario is the perfect complement to the enormous amount of positive attention that top executives and directors of media firms lavish on the representatives of economic orthodoxy, with whom they keep close ties.

(b) Financialization of the messages

The financialization of the news firm can, and in fact does, also imply the financialization of journalistic messages. This happens on two levels: (a) in the neglect of productive economy, by both the selection criteria and the authoring of journalistic information—a neglect that translates into a thematization that disregards important aspects of the distribution of resources in society; and (b) in the prioritization of technical information exclusively destined for the financial community (investors, banking actors, financial authorities, etc.).

This trend is particularly important in non-Anglo-Saxon countries, where news-media companies are completely alien to any kind of self-criticism, thus avoiding bad news that affects them or their environs (mainly industrial or financial partners). That could explain the lack of an important financial press outside the United States and the United Kingdom. In this sense, a research study conducted in the economy sections of the leading Spanish newspapers, *El País* and *El Mundo*, in July 2006 found the following results, among others (Almiron, 2008):

1. More than 60% of the stories analyzed in both newspapers had as their main actors companies quoted in the securities market, financial intermediaries, financial institutions, financial moguls, or financial indicators. Practically no information was found concerning companies not present in the stock market.

2. By sectors, the stories dedicated specifically to the financial sector—banks, savings institutions, insurance companies, agencies, and authorities—were the most numerous. In both newspapers, the financial sector received the greatest coverage: 24.13% of the stories in *El País* and 30.21% in *El Mundo*. They were followed, at a considerable distance, by the electricity and gas sectors, air transport, technology and telecommunications, and the air space, real estate, and building sectors.

3. The information—whether financial or not—eminently targeted investors and entrepreneurs. Specifically, most financial information covered four technical or growth-related aspects: markets, expansion, results, and public offerings (54% of stories in the financial section of *El Mundo* and 48.8% in *El País*).

4. The lack of independent journalistic investigation in most of the information was almost absolute. The majority of the information items were generated using press releases, declarations, or reports issued by the main actors in the economic and financial sectors.

5. The public sector, the labor market, pertinent legislation, and key sectors in the economy such as agriculture, automotive industry, and commerce received less attention than the topics mentioned in the first point. Even less present in the economy sections studied, or completely absent from them, were subjects related to labor rights, the environment, speculation, and financial corruption. Even stories that directly affect aspects of citizens' everyday lives (prices, interest rates, and taxes) were dealt with in ways that emphasized, if not prioritized, the effects that they could have on corporate results and, ultimately, on financial results or stock-exchange quotations.

Information related to financial economy—markets, expansion, results, and public offerings—has thus become the main kind of economic information. In the same way that the economy has become financialized, economy pages and newscasts have also become financialized. When the news firm is financialized, the sensibility and capacity for counteracting this tendency are drastically reduced.

(c) Omission of negative information

The legitimization of dominant economic orthodoxy and the financialization of content logically become, in turn, a significant curb when making critical assessments regarding the present state of affairs. Because a large part of information on productive economy may contain connotations that are clearly negative for the financial system, the financialized news firm also runs the risk of having the tendency to omit messages that are most likely to generate tension for its financialized structure, such as those that may affect its owners, investors, or financial creditors concerning banking crises, financial corruption, judicial probes, or presence in tax havens. This, in turn, reinforces the tendency toward the financialization of messages and the defense of dominant orthodoxy.

This omission can sometimes become ridiculous, as happened with the censorship of an ad and an opinion column in Spain's leading newspaper, El País (Prisa group), in 2009. The first case was an advertisement for the French monthly paper Le Monde Diplomâtique that included the heading of one of its stories: "Prisa Group Quakes." In the second case, an opinion column by journalist Enric González that was censored stated: "Any day now, in some company, workers' salaries are going to be cut in order to finance the owners' compulsive-gambling behavior in the stock-market."

Unfortunately, omissions tend to be much more serious. They may touch on the media owners' tax avoidance, irregularities in the stockholders' companies, or any kind of important negative incident that involves the media group's partners, stockholders, owners, creditors, or advertisers. There still are considerable differences among countries in this respect. The Anglo-Saxon countries are the least prone to this kind of self-censorship, whereas the media in southern Europe or Latin America are the most prone. In the study on the economy section of Spanish newspapers El País and El Mundo mentioned previously (Almiron, 2008), the results in this sense were clear: Only 4.44% of the news in El País dealt with plainly negative economic or financial issues, such as judicial probes, crises, or corruption. This percentage was significantly higher in El Mundo (20%), but only one subject concentrated most of the coverage (i.e., a financial scam by a philatelic society that had affected 400,000 small investors).

Risks of Financialization for Journalists

(a) Censorship or self-censorship

The internal contradictions caused by financial logics within a news firm can generate tensions between the company and the journalists that tend to be resolved through prior or subsequent censorship or by self-censorship on the part of journalists. These tensions can even be non-existent when the synergies between communication groups and financial actors are so great that the media firm generates or controls information about the latter from the highest corporate levels, precisely where there is the most contact with partners, investors, creditors, and financial intermediaries.

In 2005, and for 5 months, the *Chicago Tribune* held a story that criticized the pay package of Tribune Company's CEO, but eventually editors decided to kill it (Fairness and Accuracy in Reporting, 2007). In 2008, the Fairness and Accuracy in Reporting organization cited the *Wall Street Journal*'s failure to break the story about its own parent company's imminent purchase by Rupert Murdoch as a "perfect example of corporate media outlets' inability to report on themselves" (Fairness and Accuracy in Reporting, 2008). The truth is that many journalists recognize in surveys that they avoid whatever would hurt the financial interests of their employers (Tsai, 2007).

Those situations arise in all journalistic activity, but, as Arrese (2005) points out, economic and financial media and economic and financial news in general are the scenario where "the tensions between the interests of shareholders, professionals, readers, news protagonists and society in general are hair-splitting (...)" (Arrese, 2005: 90). Thus, states this expert in corporate governance, if there is always a possibility of falling into a certain procorporation prejudice, "the inclination is even bigger" in these scenarios (Arrese, 2005: 92). According to this author, there are many domains in which conflicts can arise in general terms. We have adapted this for our purpose here to offer a summary of the conflicts of interest generated by financialization that can affect journalistic independence and, therefore, encourage censorship:

- The first domain of conflict of interest is topics of public consequence (politics, law, etc.), which could affect the corporate activity of financial investors, partners, owners, or creditors of the media firm or, of course, the media firm's activity.
- The second domain of conflict is any kind of news concerning financial investors, partners, owners, or creditors of the media firm (news on their corporate activity, financial situation, investments, troubles, etc.).

- The third domain of conflict is the financial situation of the media firm.
- The fourth domain of conflict includes relationships, agreements, joint ventures, and all kinds of corporate activities of the media firm with the financial actors in general, as well as any nonjournalistic business held by the media conglomerate.
- The fifth domain of conflict is news on traded companies in which the media firm or its corporate allies—financial investors, partners, owners, or creditors—have invested.

But there is another type of nondeclared censorship that consists of gradually reducing the resources allocated to media for news gathering. Generalized work force cuts that have affected the industry during recent decades have left newsrooms with a chronic resources deficit that generates impossible-to-meet agendas, impossible-to-confirm information, and the inability to go beyond press-release journalism (i.e., news stories that are mere rewritten passages from a press release). Investigative reporting is simply not possible when the journalist is permanently rushed. Obviously, time for gathering, contrasting, and learning about a subject (something especially critical in finance or economic issues) is always missing. That is what usually happens with banking organizations' press releases. Many news items about the U.S. Fed, the European Central Bank, or numerous private commercial banks are merely an exercise of press release regurgitation, as can be confirmed any time by visiting the corporate websites where the original press releases can be found, almost identical to the news published or broadcast. That has led some people to call for the printing or broadcasting of press releases directly as they come and honestly letting the audience know it. In general, this lack of resources leads to a scarcity of true investigative journalism, poor and noncontrasted sources, increasing coverage of superficial issues, and, as Kovach and Rosenstiel (2001) stated, an increasing false polarization of ideas (what is in fact the essence of superficiality).

(b) Greater pressure or capacity to influence the journalist

Financialization of the news firm can also increase the capacity of financial logics to influence or exert pressure on the journalist. Stock options are in fact a financialization of salaries that incorporates a nonjournalistic dimension into the goals of the professional's work. By the same token, agreements with privileged conditions that banks can establish with a news firm or with journalists' professional associations constitute elements of pressure over the journalist, and they are becoming ever more widespread with the advance of global financialization and particularly of the financialization of news firms.

To the factors that make it impossible for journalists to discharge their duties correctly, time pressures and lack of resources imposed by financialization, and to the various spheres where conflicts of interest can be generated between the news firm and journalists, is added the financialization of their work environment.

In some cases, executives high up in the corporation as well as salaried workers are economically compensated with company stock. In others, local, regional, or national journalists' federations and associations procure advantageous conditions for their members from certain financial societies. Thus, thousands of federated journalists can have access to means of payment, accident insurance policies, credit lines, mortgages, collateral, leasing contracts, and other services with special conditions.

These personal links, along with the salaries of journalists or their superiors and the proximity of the latter with the financial elites, can have an enormous impact on the professional's day-to-day work, which compounds the pressure exerted directly on the newsroom by financial firms' public relations teams. In periods of corporate crisis, when companies are forced by their creditors to restructure their debts (which generally means refinancing them through the access of new borrowers, which results in greater interest to be paid by the indebted firms), the autonomy of journalists to inform critically about any event unfavorable to the financial actors involved is reduced to the minimum.

However, the transference of journalists into the communications and public relations departments of financial firms is a common occurrence. For financial societies, incorporating former journalists into their staff has a threefold benefit: (a) the firms acquire the professionals' experience in communications; (b) with the new employees, they take in and assimilate the media's communicative logic, which allows them to optimize their capacity of influence over the media; and (c) they establish direct ties with the professional collective because the former journalists who have been hired maintain their contacts and personal and professional links with their old companies, in addition to having a third-party address book that they bring to their new job.

If traditionally it is said that political journalism is practiced from positions that are too close to power, economic journalism has the same, if not a worse, problem as practitioners are regularly invited to personal meetings with the purpose of simulating a closeness and preferential relation that completely eradicates their perspective and undermines their critical capacity (i.e., their capacity for detachment). If the journalist's salary is complemented with stock options and a pension plan in a financial society, and he is personally preoccupied with a mortgage and various loans, as is commonly the case, the conditions are ripe for a complete interiorization of the logics of financialization in both outlook and analysis.

(c) Inability to develop critical capacity in financial matters

Last, derived from all of the above, financialization of communication in general, and of the news firm in particular, implies dynamics inimical to critical education in those aspects that can be most useful to a journalist in order to assess a specific financial circumstance. Economic-financial orthodoxy, for instance, is doing a good job of turning economic journalism in most communications schools into a mere technical specialty, in which the priority is the mastery of economic-financial techniques and jargon, rather than the development of an ability for independent analysis of the inherent contradictions of the system. In that sense, the dominant economic-financial orthodoxy has a history of years of hard work transforming elite universities into factories that produce perfectly trained individuals ready to understand, if not satisfy, the current laundry list of media companies (performance, cash flow, operating income, revenue, pretax income, net income, and total shareholder return), as well as their laundry list of abbreviations (EBIT, EBITDA, OI, OBDA, FCF, OFCF, etc.). But at the same time, they are left tremendously defenseless in the face of the ethical challenges of their chosen profession.

The financialized news firm increases the lack of critical training in the journalist, who runs the risk of ending up immersed in the perverse logic that was so well expressed by U.S. journalist Upton Sinclair: "It is difficult to get a man to understand something when his salary depends upon his not understanding it." In this line, some experts blame journalists and ask for a greater activism on their part. But embedded in the financialized logic of their media companies, many conscientious and aware journalists see it otherwise: The choices aren't more activism or less activism but rather to resign themselves or resign. That is why the scarce investigative journalism that is still extant is usually done by freelance journalists or professionals with weak ties to corporate media. This is true of all areas to be covered, but it is especially true of economic issues. Financialized corporate media are becoming a sort of forbidden ground for critical thought.

What's more, the process of assimilation of financialization logics is produced gradually and often unconsciously. Lack of time and resources, hurry, pressures derived from the professional's personal situation (often unstable in the news firm or precarious and generally entailing domestic indebtedness), and subtle but permanent pressure from the corporate structure and the newsroom environment (where most colleagues suffer from the same scarcity of time and resources, workload, instability, and personal indebtedness) all act as a kind of anesthetic that acts slowly but firmly on the critical capacity of the journalist.

To summarize, we can conclude that financialization exacerbates or creates the conditions for eroding the journalist's independence and his or her critical capacity in financial matters. It does that mainly through four mechanisms that Danny Schechter (2009) illustrated greatly with his own and third example.

First, financialization increases the proximity of journalists to the economic power. Many top journalists are embedded in the business elite—and thus, in the financialized business corporate culture—through selective invitations to participate in special programs for top editors. These invitations are a means by which to join business leaders in all sorts of activities (often including leisure activities resulting in increasingly close friendships among them). Let's think, for instance, of the World Economic Forum scenario where several journalists of top news media are being given full credentials to mingle with top business elite. This proximity is what explains the common jumping of journalists from pure reporting to hedge funds, banking entities, and so on, and which explains their lack of detachment and perspective. Hendrik Hertzberg, a senior editor at *The New Yorker*, gave this answer to Danny Schechter when asked why the media missed the 2007 credit crisis: "You could say that business journalism was in bed with, or embedded, in the institutions the way that war correspondents were embedded in the units in Iraq" (Schechter, 2009: 24).

It looks as if this embedding took place more deeply in the United States than in Europe, but it is also hard to find a top newspaper or TV channel that didn't buy into the culture of money-making in Europe. The evidence shows that no big media conveyed a real sense of true alarm until institutions began to collapse, despite the situation pushing to collapse was largely erected in public view with the help of news media. On the blame of journalists, Schecter obtained this blatant answer from former British *Observer* Editor Will Hutton:

> General journalists, as well as business journalists, are really guilty in this. They have indulged madness in the last five years [...]. Journalists for the most part missed the build-up to the crisis and did not warn the public. We all kind of believed that we had fallen upon some kind of alchemy, that capitalism had changed [...]. We suspended our judgment and we are paying a big, big price. (Schechter, 2009: 25)

Two other mechanisms have been increasingly hampering the critical capacity of journalism in financial issues, both of them deeply related to financialization logics as we have seen: (a) the critical slashing of investigative resources, and (b) the growing presence of junior journalists without experience or financial memories in their background—and, worse, without senior professional role models to look up to as they increasingly are hired to replace older and more experienced journalists. All of them lack proper education in financial logics. Financial illiteracy (i.e., the lack of understanding of how financial logics really work) makes a fatal combination with the endless cut of investigative resources that newsrooms have been subjected to in the last decades.

Finally, financialization produces the kind of personal pressures we mentioned before, with journalists troubled with a large list of concerns involving their own professional situation as well as their bosses' business issues. With business firms armed with powerful public relations and law departments ready to spot and suppress the least sign of bad press, it is hard for courage to become a rising asset in newsrooms. Meanwhile superficial and uncritical coverage is the main consequence of what Schechter (2009) calls "the unfortunate dialectic between financial failures and media failures" (Schechter, 2009: 26).

Although it is a great truth that all changes must start with oneself (we must be the change we wish to see in the world, stated Gandhi), it is no less true that media corporatization first and later their financialization have constituted a scenario that turns journalistic autonomy into an illusion.

WHEN EDITORIAL AUTONOMY IS AN ILLUSION

Today, the primary force shaping the behavior of news media firms is finance. Journalism has become managed from the perspective of the value of the shares of the parent companies that own newspapers, magazines, radio and television channels, and online news venues.

The vested interests of news firms in the corporate system denounced recurrently by scholars such as McChesney (see, for instance, 2008) have become a vested interest of corporate news media in the finance system. The censorship scenario presented by the corporatization of media to the advertisers' business is far more complex today because it involves a lengthy list of financial links with financial investors, creditors, and financial partners who can also be advertisers, owners, and directors of media firms. The conflicts of interest generated are not only commercial but financial, sometimes involving other traded companies of the news-media conglomerate. Salary is financialized, as are aims and goals of financialized corporate media, where management can be so closely attuned to Wall Street (or to the City or whatever financial center is heeded) that journalism is not simply considered a product but a key asset to obtain profits by direct and indirect means, and of course a key asset to exert influence on hypersensitive capital markets (through analysts).

This is especially true now, when top media companies are also key actors for the financial system (huge debtors, lucrative banking customers, interest investments, and big players in the capital markets). Above all, this is especially true in economic information, which is part of a communication paradigm distinguished by the relation between elites (information from the elites to the elites) (Arrese, 2005). Despite the apparent independence of some legendary newspapers, according to some analysts, not one (of the analysts or of the newspapers) has ever been able to predict a major financial downturn even though they have been documenting the incredible crescendo of speculation and irrational behavior of the financial system year after year.

At the current time, the financial system is increasingly dependent on the flow of information in which information travels swiftly from end to end of the planet and can alter in a few hours the value of a financial or commercial transaction based on titles quoted in the stock market. Therefore, for financial actors, major conglomerates are, in addition to great banking business, precious allies in their corporate course. This interrelationship between the banking and media systems is not expressed, nevertheless, as down-up control, as claimed by liberal and populist theories, nor as up-down control, as described by critical theory. In other words, the bidirectionality in power relations between the financial and media systems does not have as a purpose a domination of the former over the latter in order to subvert the freedom of action of the media. Nor is it a democratic exercise in vigilance by the media system over the financial system that implies publicity and denunciation of irregularities and excess. Rather, the bidirectionality in power relations between these two great sectors means, first and foremost and for both, the maximization of their respective financial objectives.

Convergence of economic, financial, and strategic interests between news-media owners and finance has but increased with globalization, thus generating an enormous degree of symbiosis, affinity, and association among major communication groups, major banks, public and private investors, funds, equity firms, and so on. Financialization doesn't disintegrate power in communication groups, but rather it maintains an ownership hard core increasingly linked to financial spheres; it expands the power of creditors and stockholders; it increases corporate instability; and it reverses goals, more linked to virtual expectations that may raise quotations than to tangible expectations related to quality and social responsibility in the activities carried out. Thus, financialized multimedia communication groups are today more a market power—with multimedia influences and convergent interests with financial groups—than guardians of liberty, creators of consensus, egalitarian democratizers, or subverters of the structures of authority. Faced with such a scenario, it is not difficult to conclude that believing in the possibilities of the editorial autonomy of media is nothing but an illusion.

THE MAIN RISK: FROM CRISIS TO COLLAPSE

The instability of the world financial system and the increasing dominance of finance over the real economy, what we have called here *financialization*, experienced one of its major collapses between 2007 and 2009. It was nothing new whatsoever. The consequences of periods of overcapacity are always the same: crisis and a bigger concentration of the sectors affected, in which competitors absorb the bankrupt companies' assets and clients. Meanwhile, the doctrine that maximizing shareholder value must be the main aim of a firm deteriorates it a little more, particularly if we look at the exacerbation of inequalities that financial capitalism encourages. But the truth is that in crisis capitalism doesn't learn from its own mistakes, and the main logics of financialization keep moving forward: Politicians keep talking of permanent growth, securing shareholders' investments, growth through leverage, restoring the trust of capital markets, and so on.

In the media sector, the 2007–2009 crisis had a strong impact. Thousands of jobs were lost around the globe, many foreign news bureaus closed, hundreds of companies went bankrupt, many subsidiaries were sold, and pluralism suffered another defeat at the hands of the consequences of the period as concentration increased. Nevertheless, the financial and economic turbulence starting in 2007 was by no means what made corporate journalism enter a crisis. Nor was it the Internet or TICs and digital convergence and their new business models waiting to burst. Nor was it the advertising slump or changing consumer patterns. Rather, financialized corporate logics have been demolishing the democratic foundations of journalism throughout the last decades.

As we asserted in the introduction, we consider journalism to be in a permanent crisis: a historical crisis as it had to confront a set of ideal values with the historical construction of a profession and an industry ever subject to the instrumentalization of dominant classes, whether religious, political, or economic. Today, nevertheless, the leap forward is unprecedented as financialization drives what was left of historical democratic values in journalism into a sort of collapse.

It may seem paradoxical, but that is how it has always worked: The criterion that pushed the giantism and oligopolism of the media sector to its 2007–2008 situation (i.e., that pushed it to a critical juncture) is the same criterion that is applied to come out of the crisis. We could state the same for the whole economy as a matter of fact. That criterion is that if revenues and profits stop coming in at the desired rate (although impossible at the expected scale and pattern), then costs must be reduced. Because corporations have been acting as if the revenues and profits growth ratio could escalate permanently, crises have always caught them unawares. Hence, most of them need a drastic restructuring at the onset of a crisis. That is, costs are drastically reduced, sometimes completely (by going bankrupt).

In general terms, reducing costs has always had the same consequences in media companies: Fewer journalists (and a higher proportion of inexperienced journalists) with fewer resources. Apparently they are expected to do the same job as before the layoffs and budget reductions took place, but of course this isn't what really happens: Content quality is the first victim. After commercial television and radio, with few exceptions, almost abdicated from practicing true journalism, newspapers were apparently left as the only place where some depth in news gathering and reporting could still be found. As the 2007–2009 crisis produced a cascade of bankruptcies and/or restructurings of newspaper publishing companies, some started talking about the definitive dismantling of journalism, that is, about its definitive collapse as a tool to scrutinize private and public affairs in democracies (Nichols & McChesney, 2009). They may be right.

It is interesting to note that newspapers haven't been bad businesses by any means, even after the arrival of the Internet. On the contrary, some of the largest conglomerates have grown (and still are growing) based on the profits generated by newspapers, and most of the largest newspapers are still profitable. The problem is that media giants' strategies have contaminated their profitable assets with risky and capital-demanding initiatives to fulfill the holy maxim: growth. Nevertheless, when restructurings take place, blame is first laid on journalism for being expensive and not profitable. Actually this isn't true: It just isn't profitable enough to sustain irrational gigantic growth strategies. But should journalism's aim be to sustain irrational gigantic growth strategies? The answer is obviously no if we consider journalism as a democratic value that must be protected as a public good.

Nowadays journalism is missing from most commercial radio and television stations, online media, and even many newspapers. Unfortunately, it is also missing from several public radio and television channels in democratic countries. Of course there are still journalists doing a wonderful task with a public service aim: scrutinizing public and private affairs. But the general trend is to substitute journalism with a sort of superficial, pointless, and irrelevant flow of show business provided by communicators. That is, the trend of substituting entertainment and spectacle for content has been a total success. Media are still a good source of power but not on behalf of public interest but rather at the service of private interests.

Financialization has exacerbated this trend dramatically as private interests and priorities become more urgent when financialized aims are adopted. Thus, financialization has pushed for an even further reduction of the watchdog role of the media. The industry has become fully embedded in the ethos of greed and money. At the same time, it has been spinning a thick web of links with the financial system that prevented journalism from spotting and denouncing the predatoriness and immorality of financial practices. Instead, the news-media industry became an accomplice to what was going on as the critical coverage scrutinizing and questioning these practices was missing. Nevertheless, everything was taking place in the public view, as the ads in newspapers, television channels, and radio stations consistently showed (cheap credit ads filling up thousands of pages and minutes).

Unfortunately, periods of global crisis throughout the 20th and early 21st centuries, rather than being opportunities for change, accelerated the process of dismantling journalism as governments have permitted an increase in concentration and a decrease of professional guarantees to attend to corporate demands. At the end, what it is left is an even more diminished version of democracy.

Notes

1. This and the following section was more extensively described in the following article: Almiron, Núria. (2007, February). ICTs and financial crime: An innocent fraud? *International Communication Gazette, 69*(1), 51–68.
2. Hamelink included under the term of *information industry* not only media and production for mass media but basic computer services, hardware manufacturers and software companies, all those enterprises that buy and sell information, and those that operate data processing and transmission systems.
3. EUREX (European Electronic Exchange at www.eurexchange.com) and SWIFT (Society for Worldwide Interbank Financial Telecommunication at www.swift.com), for instance, are financial-transaction networks created in the late 1960s. The computerization of transaction networks made it possible not only to increase safety safeguards but also to accelerate operations, which nowadays are carried out in real time.
4. Clearing houses, or clearing societies as we saw previously, are organizations whose function is to clear transactions carried out among financial entities throughout the world.
5. The importance of stock swaps in mergers, acquisitions, takeovers, and so on becomes evident when we look at the definitions specified by European Community legislation that regulates the common tax system applicable to all these operations when they occur across national borders (article 2 of Council Directive 90/434/CEE, July 23, 1990, regarding a common system of taxation applicable to mergers, divisions, transfers of assets, and exchanges of shares concerning companies of different Member States).
6. It is also a recurrent subject of debate in light of the conviction with which institutions such as the World Bank expound that all economic growth and progress in general are due to and depend on ICTs—"The increase in the use

and production of ICTs has significantly contributed to economic growth [...]. Increase of production of ICTs has improved manufacture, employment and exports, while the use of ICTs has increased productivity, competitiveness and growth" (World Bank, 2004: 1–2)—as opposed to what has been termed *the productivity paradox* (Bosworth & Triplett, 2001; Sardoni, 2003).

7. Of special interest is Philip Bouquillion's (2008) analysis of some of the most clamorous failures in mergers between large media conglomerates, whose lack of real synergies did not prevent the merger from taking place. This led Bouquillion to state that a good part of these processes of concentration are propelled by financial logics that have nothing to do with the corporate logics related with the actual productive activities of the merged companies. Mergers such as Time Warner with AOL and Viacom with CBS, among others, were analyzed by the French academic from this viewpoint (Bouquillion, 2008: 55–94).

8. Figures are provided here in U.S. dollars for comparative purposes. U.S. dollars were chosen simply because they were the most widely used currency among corporations on the list.

9. Vivendi owned 65% of Canal+ France through Groupe Canal+, the other shareholders being Lagardère (20%), TF1 (9.9%), and M6 (5.1%) in May 2009.

References

Ackrill, M., & Hannah, L. (2001). *Barclays. The Business of Banking 1690-1996*. Cambridge, MA: Cambridge University Press.

Adam, G. S., & Clark, R. P. (2006). *Journalism. The Democratic Craft*. New York: Oxford University Press.

Almiron, N. (2006). *Poder financiero y poder mediático: banca y grupos de comunicación. Los casos del SCH y PRISA (1976-2004)*. Doctoral dissertation, Autonomous University of Barcelona, Barcelona. Available at http://www.tesisenxarxa.net/TDX-1220106-102823/.

Almiron, N. (2007, February). ICTs and Financial Crime: An Innocent Fraud? *International Communication Gazette, 69*(1), 51–68.

Almiron, N. (2008). La información financiera en la prensa diaria: análisis de contenido en *El País* y *El Mundo*. In J. Benavides, E. Fernández, D. Alameda, & N. Villagra (Eds.), *Nuevas tendencias de la comunicación* [CD-ROM]. Madrid: Universidad Complutense de Madrid.

Almiron, N., & Jarque, J. M. (2008). *El mito digital. Discursos hegemónicos sobre Internet y periodismo*. Barcelona: Anthropos.

An, S., & Jin, H. (2004). Interlocking of Newspaper Companies with Financial Institutions and Leading Advertisers. *Journalism and Mass Communication Quarterly, 81*, 578–600.

An, S., & Jin, H. (2005). The Effects of Interlocking Directorates on the Financial Performance of Publicly Traded Newspaper Companies: A Longitudinal Approach. In R. Picard (Ed.), *Corporate Governance of Media Companies* (pp. 11–28). Jönköping, Sweden: Jönkoping International Business School.

Arendt, H. (1951). *Origins of Totalitarianism*. New York: Harcourt.

Arrese, A. (2003). Dow Jones y Financial Times Group: el desarrollo de empresas especializadas en información económica. In A. Arrese (Ed.), *Empresa informativa y mercados de la comunicación. Estudios en honor del prof. Alfonso Nieto* (pp. 193–223). Navarra: Eunsa.

Arrese, A. (2005). Corporate Governance and News Governance in Economic and Financial Media. In R. Picard (Ed.), *Corporate Governance of Media Companies* (pp. 77–126). Jönköping, Sweden: Jönkoping International Business School.

Arrighi, G. (1994). *The Long Twentieth Century: Money, Power, and the Origins of Our Times*. London: Verso.

Bagdikian, B. H. (1983). *The Media Monopoly*. Boston: Beacon Press.

Bianco, M., & Pagnoni, E. (1997). Interlocking Directorates Across Listed Companies in Italy: The Case of Banks. *Banca Nazionale del Lavoro Quarterly Review, 50*, 203–224.

Blankenburg, W., & Ozanich, G. (1993, Spring). The Effects of Public Ownership on the Financial Performance of Newspaper Corporations. *Journalism Quarterly, 70*, 68–75.

Blecker, R. A. (2005). Financial Globalization, Exchange Rates and International Trade. In G. A. Epstein (Ed.), *Financialization and the World Economy* (pp. 183–209). Northampton, MA: Edward Elgar.

Bosworth, B. P., & Triplett, J. E. (2001, Spring). What's New About the New Economy? IT, Economic Growth and Productivity. *International Productivity Monitor*, pp. 19–30.

Bouquillion, P. (2005). La constitution des pôles des industries de la culture et de la communication. Entre "coups" financiers et intégration de filiares industrielles. *Réseaux, 23*(131), 111–114.

Bouquillion, P. (2008). *Les industries de la culture et de la communication. Les stratégies du capitalisme*. Paris: Presses Universitaires de Grenoble.

Bouquillion, P., & Combès, Y. (Ed.). (2007). *Les industries de la culture et de la communication en mutation*. Paris: L'Harmattan.

Bouquillion, P., Miège, B., & Pradié, C. (2003). Financisarisation des industries de la communication et mutations corrélatives. In *Panam, industries culturelles et dialogues des civilisations dans les Amériques* (pp. 416–433). Paris: Presses de l'Université de Laval.

Boorstin, J. (2009, March 1). *2008 Media Mergers and Acquisitions Likely to Drop*. Retrieved May 2009, from http://seekingalpha.com/article/123323-2008-media-mergers-acquisitions-likely-to-drop/.

Bouvier, J. (1992). *Les Rothschild*. Paris: Éditions Complexe.

Brenner, R. (2002). *The Boom and the Bubble: The US in the World Economy*. London: Verso.

Brenner, R. (2003). *La expansión económica y la burbuja bursátil. Estados Unidos y la economía mundial*. Madrid: Akal. (Original work published 2002)

Burstin, H. (2005). *L'invention du sans-culotte. Regard sur le Paris révolutionnaire*. Paris: Odile Jacob.

Bustamante, E. (Ed.). (2003). *Hacia un nuevo sistema mundial de comunicación*. Barcelona: Gedisa.

Bustamante, E., & Zallo, R. (1988). *Las industrias culturales en España*. Madrid: Akal.

Carcanholo, R. A., & Nakatani, P. (2000). Capital especulativo parasitario versus capital financiero. In J. Arriola & D. Guerrero (Eds.), *La nueva economía política de la globalización* (pp. 151–170). Bilbao: Universidad del País Vasco.

Chesnais, F. (2001, October 11–12). *La théorie du régime d'accumulation financiarisé: contenu, portée et interrogations*. Paper presented at Forum de la régulation, Université de Paris-Nord, Villetaneuse.

Chesnais, F. (Ed.). (2004). *La finance mondialisée. Racines sociales et politiques, configuration, conséquences*. Paris: La Découverte.

Chesnais, F., & Plihon, D. (Eds.). (2000). *Les pièges de la finance mondiale. Diagnostics et remèdes*. Paris: La Découverte-Syros.

Chesnais, F., & Plihon, D. (Eds.). (2003). *Las trampas de las finanzas mundiales*. Madrid: Akal.

Collins, J. C., & Porras, J. I. (1994). *Built to Last: Successful Habits of Visionary Companies*. New York: HarperBusiness.

Compaine, B., & Gomery, D. (2000). *Who Owns the Media? Competition and Concentration in the Mass Media Industry* (3rd ed.). Mahwah, NJ: Lawrence Erlbaum Associates.

Cranberg, G., Bezanson, R., & Soloski, J. (2001). *Taking Stock: Journalism and the Publicly Traded Newspaper Company*. Ames: Iowa State University Press.

Croteau, D., & Hoynes, W. (2001). *The Business of Media: Corporate Media and the Public Interest*. Thousand Oaks, CA: Pine Forge Press.

Crotty, J. (2005). The Neoliberal Paradox: The Impact of Destructive Product Market Competition and "Modern" Financial Markets on Nonfinancial Corporation Performance in the Neoliberal Era. In G. A. Epstein (Ed.), *Financialization and the World Economy* (pp. 77–110). Northampton, MA: Edward Elgar.

Curran, J. (2002). *Media and Power*. London: Routledge.

Dawson, M., & Foster, J. B. (1998). Virtual Capitalism. In R. W. McChesney, E. M. Wood, & J. B. Foster (Eds.), *Capitalism and the Information Age. The Political Economy of the Global Communication Revolution* (pp. 51–68). New York: Monthly Review Press.

Dickens, E. (2005). The Eurodollar Market and the New Era of Global Financialization. In G. A. Epstein (Ed.), *Financialization and the World Economy* (pp. 210–219). Northampton, MA: Edward Elgar.

Dodd, R. (2005). Derivatives Markets: Sources of Vulnerability in US Financial. In G. A. Epstein (Ed.), *Financialization and the World Economy* (pp. 149–182). Northampton, MA: Edward Elgar.

Dooley, P. (1969, June). The Interlocking Directorate. *American Economic Review, 59*, 314–323.

Dore, R. (2002). Stock market capitalism and its diffusion. *New Political Economy, 7*(1), 15–27.

Dreier, P., & Weinberg, S. (1979). Interlocking Directorates. *Columbia Journalism Review, 18*(53), 51–68.

Duménil, G., & Lévy, D. (2001). *Crise et sortie de crise: ordre et désordres néolibéraux*. Paris: Press Universitaires de France.

Duménil, G., & Lévy, D. (2005). Costs and Benefits of Neoliberalism: A Class Analysis. In G. A. Epstein (Ed.), *Financialization and the World Economy* (pp. 17–45). Northampton, MA: Edward Elgar.

Epstein, G. A. (Ed.). (2005). *Financialization and the World Economy*. Northampton, MA: Edward Elgar.

Epstein, G. A., & Jayadev, A. (2005). The Rise of Rentier Incomes in OECD Countries: Financialization, Central Bank Policy and Labor Solidarity. In G. A. Epstein (Ed.), *Financialization and the World Economy* (pp. 46–76). Northampton, MA: Edward Elgar.

Fairness and Accuracy in Reporting. (2007). *Fear & Favor 2006*. Retrieved May 2009, from http://www.fair.org/index.php?page=3132.

Fairness and Accuracy in Reporting. (2008). *Fear & Favor 2007*. Retrieved May 2009, from http://www.fair.org/index.php?page=3323.

Fitch, R., & Oppenheimer, M. (1970). Who Rules the Corporations (Parts 1, 2, and 3)? *Socialist Revolution, 1*(4), 73–107; *1*(5), 61–114; *1*(6), 33–94.

Flichy, P. (1997). *Une histoire de la communication moderne. Espace public et vie privée*. Paris: La Découverte.

Fligstein, N., & Brantley, P. (1992). Bank Control, Owner Control, or Organizational Dynamics: Who Controls the Large Modern Corporation? *American Journal of Sociology, 98*, 280–307.

Fohlin, C. (1999). The Rise of Interlocking Directorates in Imperial Germany. *Economic History Review, 52*(2), 307–333.

Fowler, T., & Curwen, P. (2002). Can European Media Empires Survive? The Rise and Fall of the House of Kirch. *Info, 4*, 17–24.

Fuentes, I., & Sastre, T. (1998). Mergers and Acquisitions in the Spanish Banking Industry: Some Empirical Evidence (working paper no. 9924). Banco de España, Servicio de Estudios.

Galbraith, J. K. (1993). *A Short History of Financial Euphoria*. New York: Viking Penguin.

Galbraith, J. K. (2004). *The Economics of Innocent Fraud: Truth for Our Time*. Boston: Houghton Mifflin.

Garnham, N. (2000). *Emancipation, the Media and Modernity: Arguments About the Media and Social Theory*. London: Oxford University Press.

Hall, M. (1992). On the Creation of Money and the Accumulation of Bank-Capital. *Capital & Class, 48*, 89–112.

Hallary, I. (2003). Las promesas incumplidas de la globalización financiera. In F. Chesnais & D. Plihon (Eds.), *Las trampas de las finanzas mundiales. Diagnósticos y remedios* (pp. 73–92). Madrid: Akal. (Original work published 2000)

Hamelink, C. J. (1984). *Finanzas e información Un estudio de intereses convergentes*. México: Instituto Latinoamericano de Estudios transnacionales. (Original work published 1983)

Harvey, D. (1982). *Los límites del capitalismo y la teoría marxista*. México: Fondo de Cultura Económica.

Hernández-Vigueras, J. (2005). *Los paraísos fiscales*. Madrid: Akal.

Hernández-Vigueras, J. (2008). *La Europa opaca de las finanzas y sus paraísos fiscales offshore*. Barcelona: Icaria.

Hilferding, R. (1985). *El capital financiero*. Madrid: Tecnos. (Original work published 1910)

Hobson, J. A. (1902). *Imperialism: A study*. New York: J. Pott & Company.

Iwanami, F. (2006). The Structure of Interlocking Directorates and Corporate Power in the U.S. and Japan through Social Network Analysis. *Ritsumeikan Business Review, 154*, 4.

Kotz, D. (1978). *Bank Control of Large Corporations in the United States.* Berkeley: University of California Press.

Kovach, B., & Rosenstiel, T. (2001). *The Elements of Journalism.* New York: Crown Publishers.

Krippner, G. (2005). The Financialization of the American Economy. *Socio-Economic Review, 3*, 173–208.

La Monica, P. R. (2007, May 14). *The Return of Media Merger Madness.* Retrieved May 2009, from http://money.cnn.com/2007/05/14/news/companies/media_mergers/.

Lacroix, J. G., & Tremably, G. (1997). *The "Information Society" and Cultural Industries Theory.* Toronto: Sage.

Lacy, S., Shaver, M. A., & Cyr, C. (1996, Summer). Effects of Public Ownership and Newspaper Competition on the Financial Performance of Newspaper Corporations. A Replication and Extension. *Journalism Quarterly, 73*, 332–341.

Llorens, C. (2001). *Concentración de empresas de comunicación y el pluralismo. La acción de la UE.* Doctoral dissertation, Autonomous University of Barcelona, Barcelona. Available at http://www.tesisenxarxa.net/TDX-0111102-124855.

Maguire, M. (2003). Wall Street Made Me Do It: A Preliminary Analysis of Major Institutional Investors in U.S. Newspaper Companies. *Journal of Media Economics, 16*(4), 253–264.

Maguire, M. (2005). Hidden Costs and Hidden Dangers: Stock Options at U.S. Newspaper Companies. In R. Picard (Ed.), *Corporate Governance of Media Companies* (pp. 29–46). Jönköping, Sweden: Jönkoping International Business School.

Mariolis, P. (1975). Interlocking Directorates and Control of Corporations. The Theory of Bank Control. *Social Science Quarterly, 56*, 425–439.

McChesney, R. W. (2007). *Communication Revolution: Critical Junctures and the Future of Media.* New York: The New Press.

McChesney, R. W. (2008). *The Political Economy of Media: Enduring Issues, Emerging Dilemmas.* New York: Monthly Review Press.

McChesney, R. W., & Scott, B. (Eds.). (2004). *Our Unfree Press: 100 Years of Radical Media Criticism.* New York: The New Press.

McChesney, R. W., Wood, E. M., & Foster, J. B. (Eds.). (1998). *Capitalism and the Information Age. The Political Economy of the Global Communication Revolution.* New York: Monthly Review Press.

Meier, W. A. (2005). Media Concentration Governance: une nouvelle plate-forme pour débattre des risques? *Réseaux, 23*(131), 17–52.

Merrill Lynch/Cap Gemini Ernst & Young. (2001). *World Wealth Report 2001.* Available at http://www.ml.com and http://www.us.capgemini.com.

Meyer, P., & Wearden, S. T. (1984). The Effects of Public Ownership on Newspaper Companies: A Preliminary Inquiry. *Public Opinion Quarterly, 48*, 566–577.

Miguel de Bustos, J. C. (2003). Los grupos de comunicación: la hora de la convergencia. In E. Bustamante (Ed.), *Hacia un nuevo sistema mundial de comunicación* (pp. 227–256). Barcelona: Gedisa.

Mosco, V. (1996). *The Political Economy of Communication: Rethinking and Renewal.* London: Sage.

Mosco, V. (2005). *The Digital Sublime: Myth, Power, and Cyberspace.* Cambridge, MA: The MIT Press.

Naredo, J. M. (2004). Prólogo a la segunda edición. Evolución reciente del pensamiento económico: entre la reconstrucción intelectual y la congelación conceptual. In M. Etxezarreta (Ed.), *Crítica a la economía ortodoxa* (pp. 49–66). Barcelona: Autonomous University of Barcelona.

Navarro, V. (2009, April 16). La respuesta insuficiente de la UE. *Público*, p. 5.

Nichols, J., & McChesney, R. W. (2009, March 18). *The Death and Life of Great American Newspapers.* Available at http://www.thenation.com/doc/200904 06/nichols_mcchesney

Norich, S. (1980). Interlocking Directorates, the Control of Large Corporations and Patterns of Accumulation in the Capitalistic Class. In M. Zeitlen (Ed.), *Classes, Class Conflict and the State.* Cambridge: Winthrop Publishers.

Organization for Economic Co-operation and Development. (1993). *Les conglomérats financiers.* Paris: Author.

Organization for Economic Co-operation and Development (1998). *Harmful Tax Competition: An Emerging Global Issue.* Paris: Author.

Organization for Economic Co-operation and Development. (2000). *Towards Global Tax Co-operation.* Paris: Author.

Orléan, A. (1999). *Le pouvoir de la finance.* Paris: Odile Jacob.

Palazuelos, E. (1998). *La globalización financiera. La internacionalización del capital financiero a finales del siglo XX.* Madrid: Síntesis.

Parejo, J. A., Cuervo, A., Calvo, A., & Rodríguez, L. (2004). *Manual de sistema financiero español.* Barcelona: Ariel.

Picard, R. (1994). Institutional Ownership of Publicly Traded U.S. Newspaper Companies. *Journal of Media Economics*, 7(4), 49–64.

Picard, R. (Ed.). (2002). *The Economics and Financing of Media Companies.* New York: Fordham University Press.

Picard, R. (Ed.). (2005). *Corporate Governance of Media Companies.* Jönköping, Sweden: Jönkoping International Business School.

Pollin, R. (2000). El actual estancamiento en su perspectiva histórico-mundial. *New Left Review, 5*, 127–143. Madrid: Akal. (Original work published 1996)

Pollin, R. (2001). Estructuras financieras y política económica igualitaria. *New Left Review, 8*, 48–91. Madrid: Ediciones Akal. (Original work published 1995)

Pradié, C. (2002a, October 7–9). Industrie culturelle et marchés financiers. Les mutations de l'entreprise de presse au XIXème siècle. *Inforcom 2002, 13ème Congrès national des sciences de l'information et de la communication.* Marseille.

Pradié, C. (2002b). La financialisation des industries culturelles—L'emergence de la presse à la bourse de Paris au XIXème siècle. In ADHE (Ed.), *Histoire des industries culturelles en France–XIXème–XXème siècles.* París: Association pour le développement de l'histoire économique.

Pradié, C. (2005). Capitalisme et financialisation des industries culturelles. *Réseaux*, *23*(131), 83–110.

Progressive Living: The Mass Media and Politics. An Analysis of Influence. Retrieved May 2009, from http://www.progressiveliving.org/mass_media_and_politics.htm.

Prisa. (1989). *Estatutos sociales*. Madrid: Promotora de Informaciones.

Quirós, F. (2002). La prensa del siglo XXI El final del perro guardián. *Telos*, *51*. Available at http://www.campusred.net/telos/cuadernoGrabar.asp?idarticulo=5&rev=51.

Read, D. (1992). *The Power of News. The History of Reuters 1849-1989*. New York: Oxford University Press.

Robert, D. (2002). *La boîte noire*. Paris: Arènes.

Robert, D., & Backes, E. (2001). *Révélations*. Paris: Arènes.

Sardoni, C. (2003, March). Money, the "ICT Revolution" and Economics. *Development*, *46*(1), 61–65.

Schechter, D. (2008). *Plunder: Investigating our Economic Calamity and the Subprime Scandal*. New York: Cossmo Books.

Schechter, D. (2009, March). Credit Crisis: How Did We Miss It? *British Journalism Review*, *20*(1), 19–32.

Schiller, D. (2007). *How to Think About Information*. Urbana, Chicago: University of Illinois Press.

Schiller, H. (1989). *Culture Inc. The Corporate Takeover of Public Expression*. New York: Oxford University Press.

Seabrooke, L. (2001). *US Power in International Finance: The Victory of Dividends*. New York: Palgrave.

Segovia, A. I., & Quirós, F. (2006). Plutocracia y corporaciones de medios en los Estados Unidos. *Cuadernos de Información y comunicación*, *11*, 179–205.

Selznik, P. (1949). *TVA and the Grass Roots: A Study in the Sociology of Formal Organization*. Berkeley: University of California Press.

Serfati, C. (2003). La dominación del capital financiero: ¿qué consecuencias? In F. Chesnais & D. Plihon (Eds.), *Las trampas de las finanzas mundiales. Diagnósticos y remedios* (pp. 59–72). Madrid: Akal. (Original work published 2000)

Shafer, J. (2007, May 8). Eight More Reasons to Distrust Murdoch. *Slate*. Available at http://www.slate.com/id/2165839.

Soley, L. (2002). *Censorship, Inc: The Corporate Threat to Free Speech in the United States*. New York: Monthly Review Press.

Soloski, J. (2005). Taking Stock Redux: Corporate Ownership and Journalism of Publicly Traded Newspaper Companies. In R. Picard (Ed.), *Corporate Governance of Media Companies* (pp. 59–76). Jönköping, Sweden: Jönkoping International Business School.

Soloski, J., & Picard, R. (1996, September 11–12). Money; The New Media Lords; Why Institutional investors Call the Shots. *Columbia Journalism Review*.

Starr, P. (2004). *The Creation of the Media. Political Origins of Modern Communications*. New York: Basic Books.

Suárez Suárez, A. S. (2001). *Nueva economía y nueva sociedad. Los grandes retos del siglo XXI*. Madrid: Prentice Hall.

188   References

Sweezy, P. (1939). Interest Groups in the American Economy. In *National Resources Committee: The Structure of the American Economy, Part I*. Washington, DC: U.S. Government Printing Office.

Sweezy, P. M. (1994, June). The Triumph of Financial Capital. *Monthly Review*, 46(2), 1–11.

Tabb, W. K. (1999, October). Labor and the Imperialism of Finance. *Monthly Review*, 51(5), 1–13.

Tax Justice Network. (2005). *Briefing Paper: The Price of Offshore*. London: Tax Justice Network.

Tsai, M. (2007, July 10). *Reporting on Yourself*. Retrieved May 2009, from http://www.slate.com/id/2170041/.

Vázquez Montalbán, M. (2000). *Historia y comunicación social*. Barcelona: Mondadori.

World Bank. (2004). *Contribution of Information and Communication Technologies to Growth* (World Bank working paper no. 24). Washington, DC: Author.

About the Author

Núria Almiron is a lecturer and researcher in the Department of Communications at the Pompeu Fabra University (UPF), Barcelona, Spain. Her research focuses on the political economy of media, stressing the role of corporate and market structures from a nonmanagerial point of view. Rather, she has developed a media criticism based on the harmful consequences of financial capitalism logics when embedded into mass media corporations in democracies.

Almiron has also taught journalism and communication at the University of Girona (UdG) and the Autonomous University of Barcelona (UAB) and has participated in and conducted government-commissioned research studies as a member of the Institute of Communication (Incom-UAB). She is also a member of the Unity of Research of Broadcasting Media at UPF, as well as of the Observatory of Communication of Conflict at UAB, and she participates in competitive national research projects. She has been a visiting fellow at the University of Manchester (UK), University of Amsterdam (The Netherlands), Université Paris 8 (France), and University of Westminster (UK). Prior to starting her academic career, she worked as an ICT journalist from 1994 to 2004.

Almiron received a PhD in communications from the Autonomous University of Barcelona and also holds a degree in Political Sciences from the same university. She has written, edited, or participated in 30 books, and she has published more than 100 journal articles and more than 20 academic papers. In addition to her regular writing and teaching, she contributes to nongovernmental organizations in the fields of media criticism and financial capitalism.

Books authored by Almiron include *Cibermillonarios* (2002), *De Vannevar Bush a la WWW* (2001), *Los amos de la globalización* (2002), *Juicio al poder* (2003), and *El mito digital* (2008, with J.M. Jarque). She can be contacted through www.almiron.org (nuria@almiron.org or nuria.almiron@upf.edu).

Author Index

Subject Index

122(t), 126(t), 129, 135, 138(t), 143, 145, 148(t), 150(t), 159, 180(n7)
Tribune, 92(t), 95(t), 98(t), 99(t), 100(t), 120, 121, 126(t), 128, 138(t), 142, 149(t), 169
Turbulences, *See also* Financial turmoil, 13, 130

Univision, 93(t), 96(t), 97, 100(t), 120, 126(t), 128, 136, 137, 138(t), 149(t), 153

Vested interests, 174
Viacom, 56(t), 92(t), 94, 95(t), 97, 100(t), 111(t), 112, 113, 117(t), 122(t), 126(t), 128, 129, 136, 138(t), 149(t), 161, 180(n7)

Vivendi, 13, 57(t), 64, 92(t), 101, 102(t), 106(t), 110, 118, 122(t), 126(t), 139(t), 140, 149(t), 180(n9)
Vivendi Universal, 13

Wall Street Journal, 48, 97, 99(t), 135, 156, 161
Walt Disney, 57(t), 92(t), 94, 95(t), 97, 100(t), 111(t), 112, 122(t), 126(t), 138(t), 149(t),
Washington Post, 92(t), 95(t), 97, 100(t), 107, 114, 122(t), 126(t), 127(t), 138(t), 145, 149(t)
Wolters Kluwer, 92(t), 102(t), 106(t), 118, 126(t), 139(t)
World Bank, 22, 30, 41, 71, 150, 179(n6)

Breinigsville, PA USA
03 September 2010
244776BV00001B/5/P